How I Met Your Father

AMINAH HART

ALLEN&UNWIN

SYDNEY•M

D1646533

First published in Australia and New Zealand by Allen & Unwin in 2016

Copyright © Aminah Hart 2016

Arena Books, an imprint of
Allen & Unwin
83 Alexander Street
Crows Nest NSW 2065
Australia
Phone:(61 2) 8425 0100
Email: info@allenandunwin.com
Web: www.allenandunwin.com

Cataloguing-in-Publication details are available
from the National Library of Australia
www.trove.nla.gov.au

ISBN 978 1 92526 6900

Internal and cover design by Deb Parry

Set in 12/16 pt Bembo by Midland Typesetters, Australia
Printed and bound in Australia by Griffin Press

10 9 8 7 6 5 4 3 2 1

For my daughter Leila. For my mum Helen.
In ever loving memory of my sons Marlon and Louis.

ACKNOWLEDGEMENTS

Thank you is never enough to express my appreciation for my mother, Helen, for all that she has done for me and continues to do as my mum, my mentor and my hero. She gave me life and since then has saved my life many times over.

There are no words to describe my love for my children, Marlon, Louis and Leila. I thank each of them for choosing me for their mum. They are the three shining lights that guide me.

Each and every one of my family and friends has my utmost gratitude for carrying me through the toughest of times with unyielding love, loyalty and support. You are all the family I choose.

My deepest love and thanks goes to my husband, Scott, for our family and for your courage and selflessness in becoming a sperm donor. By doing so you gave me the precious gift of Leila, our daughter.

Love and special thanks to Luke, Jye, Bailey and Belle for embracing Leila and I into your family. There is nobody I'd rather be 'steppie' to than each of you.

I'm incredibly grateful for the opportunity to share my story as a lasting legacy to my sons and I thank my publisher Louise Thurtell as well as Belinda Lee and Tom Gilliatt from Allen and Unwin for believing I could find my voice to tell it in my own words.

Finally, I wish to thank all of the men and women, the world over, who choose to donate their gametes to help bring the joy of children to those who otherwise might not realise their dreams of creating a family.

PART I

I. A Victorian Girl

My grandfather, Louis Buvelot Marshall, was born in 1890, the youngest of ten surviving children of a Presbyterian minister; two of his other siblings had died in infancy. The Marshall family emigrated from Scotland to Australia when Louis' father was invited to head up the Scots Church in Melbourne.

In 1915 Louis enlisted in the Australian Army and was deployed to the frontline in France during World War One, where he fought the Germans. In the years after returning to Australia from the war, Louis began his own shipping business.

Born in 1902 in Melbourne, my grandmother Blanche Lindsay Scharp was a highly independent woman for her time. On completing school she became a pharmacist. After she and Louis married in 1928, Blanche put her career ahead of starting a family, continuing to work at a chemist shop. By the time she and Louis had their first daughter, Alison Jane (known as Jane), Blanche was 36 and Louis 48. My mother Helen followed two years later.

Despite his conservative background and experiencing the Great War and the Great Depression, Louis was remarkably progressive for his era. He and Blanche took a relatively open-minded approach to raising their daughters, although in line with family tradition they sent Jane and Helen to the Presbyterian Ladies College in East Melbourne. Though PLC placed great emphasis on academic pursuits and achievement, Blanche and Louis encouraged their daughters to pursue their own interests. It turned out that Jane preferred the creative arts while Helen developed a love of theatre and dance that inspired her to leave school at 15. She did a secretarial course and got a respectable day job to assuage her parents' concern while she pursued her true passion for dance at night, teaming up with a black Brazilian dance partner by the name of Antonio Rodrigues to dance in Melbourne's theatres and clubs. During this time she met another aspiring dancer, Johanne, and, realising there were few opportunities to make a career of dancing in Melbourne, Helen and Jo set their sights on the bright lights of London's West End.

Blanche encouraged Helen's plans to go to England, worrying that her headstrong daughter might fall for Antonio, who was not only black but also married. Such was Blanche's enthusiasm, in fact, that she expedited Helen's departure by lending her the fare to sail on the *Arcadia* to England.

Helen's excitement overshadowed any trepidation she felt as she farewelled the party of family and friends who gathered at the Port of Melbourne to wish her bon voyage. In her diary, she described how she stayed up on deck as the ship pulled away from the dock, watching the faces of her loved ones slowly recede into the nothingness of the night. She also marvelled at the wonderful people she was leaving behind as she sailed into the unknown.

The four-week journey to England via the Suez Canal took the two wide-eyed twenty-year-olds, chaperoned by Jo's mum, through the exotic lands of Ceylon, Yemen and Egypt. When they arrived in England it was a year into the sixties, London was in full swing, and Helen and Jo found the city's sense of liberation intoxicating. They quickly embraced London's nightlife, which was awash with a diversity of culture, arts, music and dance they'd never experienced

HOW I MET YOUR FATHER

before. They'd soon made friends from all over the world and their social diaries were filled with parties.

There was never a shortage of potential suitors and Helen enjoyed dates with several men but none of them really took her fancy until the night she met Tony Hart.

A tall, dark, handsome West Indian with an intense demeanour and a short, nappy Afro, Tony Hart's charm offensive began as soon as he was introduced to Helen at a nightclub. He dominated her attention for the duration of the evening, clearly intent on winning her over. However, when he later offered Helen a lift home, she politely declined saying she'd be leaving with the friends she'd arrived with. Not to be dissuaded, Tony offered them all a lift and saw Helen safely to her door in a suitably gentlemanly manner.

After that first meeting Tony pursued Helen intently, asking her to go out with him until she finally agreed. Taken by Tony's enigmatic manner, Helen became more and more intrigued by this West Indian. He'd recently returned from filming *Lawrence of Arabia* in Jordan, where he'd played the part of Omar Sharif's bodyguard, which seemed very glamorous to the young Australian. He told Helen he was trying to make a career in film rather than continuing a short-lived apprenticeship he'd begun at the Ford factory in Dagenham.

As Helen saw more of Tony she became increasingly fascinated by the culture of his Trinidadian homeland, with its exotic blend of African, Indian, Asian and European inspired food, music and dance. Tony introduced her to his mother Bernice, half-sister Sybil, and infant nephew Peter, who were living in London temporarily while Bernice learnt hairdressing. Their lives, so different to Helen's, captivated her and she soon fell in love with Tony.

As a couple, Helen and Tony enjoyed London's progressive lifestyle, with other mixed-race relationships not uncommon in their social circles. Still, Helen was aware of undercurrents of racial tension in some quarters of English society, which, unbeknownst to her, also simmered in Tony, who had encountered a wall of racial hatred at the Ford factory.

Mindful of her mother's earlier apprehension about Antonio, Helen was concerned that her family would disapprove of her falling in love with a black man. While her parents had generally accepted her lifestyle choices, she wondered if an interracial relationship might push the limits of their tolerance. When Blanche visited Helen in London during her first year there, Helen's fears were allayed by Blanche's lack of criticism, taking it as tacit acceptance of her choice of partner. This helped cement Helen's commitment to Tony and meant she felt free to move to Rome with him to pursue work opportunities in the thriving Cinecitta film industry.

Despite her deepening love for Tony, Helen found him an elusive, restless character who avoided any conversations that scratched deeper than the surface. He shared only glimpses of his upbringing in Trinidad and said very little about the males in his life. He never discussed his father, although he claimed to know who he was. And though he'd spoken of his stepfather, 'Smithy', Helen couldn't make our whether Smithy lived with the family in Trinidad or came and went with his job as a sailor. Tony never gave a straight answer about whether Smithy and Bernice were married, but from the little Helen could gather Smithy wasn't Sybil's biological father either.

Tony did speak fondly of his pipe-smoking grandmother 'MaMa' but didn't say whether a grandfather had ever been in the picture. From what Helen could gather, men were in short supply in the Hart family and marriage didn't appear to be as important a custom to them as it was to her family. Instead it seemed to be a very matriarchal society where women didn't need to have a husband in order to have children.

When it became clear that Tony's big break in the film industry wasn't going to happen in Rome, Helen returned to London with him. When she'd left Australia with dreams of success in the West End Helen hadn't thought about how long she would stay in England or where else life might take her. Neither had she planned to fall in love or stay away from Australia forever. But back in London, as the expense of living became a reality, her fantasy of West End stardom fell by the wayside, replaced by the need to earn a living. This made her even more uncertain about her future and much more aware of what a comfortable life and supportive family she'd left behind.

By this time Blanche's seemingly benign reaction to Helen's relationship with Tony had been replaced by nuances of displeasure in her letters. Though she never said so directly, it was clear to Helen her mother was disconcerted that she'd 'taken up' with a black man. Blanche let her know she hadn't told Louis about Tony, hinting that the news wouldn't go down well.

Helen, who adored her father and didn't want to let him down, was confused about what to do next. So when Blanche began to put pressure on her to come home Helen felt torn. Eventually Tony helped make the decision for her by returning to Rome for work. Rather than risk alienating her family and pursuing a life with a man she didn't fully understand, Helen decided to head home to Australia.

2. Camden Town

As soon as Helen got back to Australia she realised she'd under-estimated the power of her love for Tony. She hadn't accounted for the strength of his hold over her or how impossible it would be to keep him from her thoughts. Regardless of his perplexing change-ability she missed him terribly, a feeling intensified by the letters she received from Tony trying to entice her back.

Helen had also changed and grown in the four years she'd been away. Melbourne felt much smaller and less cosmopolitan than London, with its vigour and vibrancy. And despite enjoying the warmth of her family and the company of good friends she found it hard to settle back into her old life. As soon as she landed a secre-tarial job her feet started feeling itchy again.

Blanche quickly saw she wouldn't be able to stop her determined daughter returning to London. And so, having paid off her debts working two jobs, and saving for her own fare, Helen returned to the high seas.

The six-week journey to England took Helen through Tahiti, Panama and the Caribbean. And though she'd left Melbourne on her own this time, her gregarious nature meant she'd soon made friends on a ship that was brimming with other adventurous people.

With regular parties on-board she was having a ball, leaving little time for her to think ahead to what would happen when she got back to London.

Helen hadn't told Tony she was returning to England so when she disembarked there was nobody to greet her. She organised to move in with friends in Chelsea and then went about getting herself a job. She still hadn't contacted Tony when she began work as a secretary in the London bureau of CBS Television but eventually bumped into a friend who said he'd tell Tony she was back.

When Helen finally caught up with Tony the spark between them was instantly reignited and not long after they decided to move in together. On discovering Mary, the wife of Tony's good friend and fellow Trinidadian, Horace Ové, was renting out two levels above her clothes shop Dudu in a building she owned at 95 Parkway in Camden Town they took up residence on the top floor.

For a while Tony and Helen were very happy in their new home and Helen felt like she'd made the right decision in returning to London and giving their relationship another chance. But Tony was still very changeable and much moodier and more secretive than Helen remembered. He also seemed to expect her to pay for all their household bills out of her earnings and to be there for him at all times while he chased rainbows in the British film industry.

Even more ominously, Tony was becoming increasingly involved with the Black Power Movement. He spent a lot of time with his West Indian friends including Michael de Freitas, the self-styled leader of the Movement. Also known as 'Michael X', de Freitas was a passionate promoter of West Indian culture and instrumental in the establishment of the Notting Hill Carnival. But he was also a bitterly angry man with a militant approach to civil rights and a violently divisive stance against the 'white man'.

As Tony's affinity to the Black Power Movement grew, his talk often turned angrily to his resentment of the white men whose racial discrimination he blamed for making life such a struggle for him and his black 'brothers'. He also became more aloof, and managed to alienate Helen's friends. Before long Helen's social life had narrowed to the point where she felt her only social contacts were with Tony's friends and through her demanding job at CBS News.

Helen wondered whether she could sustain her love for Tony if he continued to be so angry, elusive and mysterious. But when Tony talked to her about the two of them going into business with Mary, opening another shop, Helen was reassured she was part of Tony's plans for the future. She hoped that, with the possibility of some more money coming in, Tony's hard-done-by outlook would decrease and their relationship could flourish again.

In order to help start the business with Tony and Mary, Helen wrote to Blanche, who was the money manager of her family, to ask for a loan of one thousand pounds. After Blanche agreed, Helen offered to help Tony apply to the London School of Film Technique so he could simultaneously try to kick-start his film career. She also convinced him they should go on holidays together, hoping to distract him from the influences of the Movement for a while and see if they could improve their relationship.

Having originally left Australia when she was just 20, Helen was now approaching 30 and wanted to start a family. Horace and Mary had a baby, Zak, and her good friend Jo had married Howard, a talented South African jazz pianist, and given birth to a son called Zvi. Other Australian friends she was close to had married, had children and returned home to Australia.

During their three-week holiday in Spain, Helen was reassured to see Tony relax into his old skin, and felt positive enough about their future together to try to get pregnant. She didn't have to 'try' hard, with a doctor confirming her pregnancy seven weeks after their holiday, calculating a due date of June third, which Helen thought serendipitous because it was Tony's birthday.

In the afterglow of their Spanish sojourn and with a baby on the way, Helen hoped Tony would 'settle down' and focus on family life. But no sooner had she worked up the courage to write to her mother saying she was living with Tony than their relationship took a turn for the worse. Instead of being supportive and loving, Tony seemed to deride Helen's every word and treated her more like a domestic servant than the mother of his child. His moods became so erratic that Helen felt like she was living with a 'Jekyll and Hyde' character, and was never sure which version she'd wake up to on any given day.

When Helen received Blanche's thousand pound loan, instead of using it to kick-start their business, Tony found innumerable reasons to dip into it. He also began to come home less, and disappeared to Sweden with his friends from the Movement along with Sammy Davis Junior and his entourage. When Tony returned from Sweden the bulk of Blanche's loan was gone and their proposed new business never came to fruition. Yet despite his use of her family's money, Tony was more confrontational than ever, eventually insisting Helen get with the 'think black' thing or leave.

By the time of Tony's ultimatum, Helen was fed up with his belittling mistreatment, prolonged absences and neglect. She was also worried that the oppressive atmosphere of their domestic situation would only worsen once the baby arrived and give Tony greater leverage over her so she chose the latter, packing her bags and moving in with Jo, Howard and Zvi in Paddington.

Tony didn't object or put up any resistance when Helen left but neither did he want to relinquish her completely, visiting her at Jo's and sometimes inviting her back to 95 Parkway. Helen still preferred her new living arrangement because she felt like she'd regained her independence. Sometimes when she saw Tony she even felt as if he'd reverted to the early days of their courtship when he'd been so charming and fun. But Helen also realised Tony only saw her when it suited him, often failing to show up when he promised and frequently behaving in a way that left Helen uncertain about the precise status of their relationship.

Eventually, exasperated with Tony's fixation on his 'blackness' and irritated by many of the disparaging things he said, Helen resolved to cut him out of her life. But her feelings about Tony continued to fluctuate and she developed a pattern of vowing not to see him and then feeling guilty and lonely and scared about being on her own. She felt powerless to close the door on Tony completely because it would mean her baby not having a father around, so he was often able to sway her.

The insecurity of her situation became more unsettling for Helen as her pregnancy progressed. She was worried by the fact she hadn't heard from Blanche since writing to her to confess she was living with Tony and she started to fear what would become of her when the baby arrived. The Government's maternity allowance wouldn't be enough for her to rent a flat by herself while she took maternity leave from CBS and she couldn't keep staying with Jo and Howard indefinitely.

Things got even worse when Tony became feverish and unwell with an apparent case of bronchitis. Despite being heavily pregnant and feeling exhausted, Helen visited him after work most days to cook dinner and take care of him.

Then, to Helen's immense relief, a scan confirmed she wasn't having twins as she'd feared, and she finally received a letter from Blanche reassuring her she hadn't been disowned and that no harm had been done to their relationship. This was followed by a gift of money for Christmas accompanied by an invitation to return home, though Helen worried Blanche wouldn't have been so welcoming if she knew Helen was pregnant with Tony's child.

No sooner had Helen taken comfort from her mother's letter than she got a call from Tony saying he'd been diagnosed with tuberculosis. He asked her if she could take him to Colindale Sanatorium where he could be medically supervised and nursed back to health.

In the blink of an eye Helen's life had changed completely.

3. Truth and Honesty

Tony ended up having to stay in Colindale for three months, throwing Helen's life into further disarray. Despite their relationship problems she felt sorry for Tony's malaise and continued to visit him daily after work, taking him 'soul food' and keeping him company.

After leaving Colindale Tony defied doctor's orders to rest and returned to his association with Michael X and the Black Power Movement. He also reverted to his itinerant ways despite Helen's natural desire to have a settled, secure environment to bring the baby home to.

Eventually Helen decided to write to her sister Jane to tell her about her pregnancy and ascertain the lie of the land should she need to return home. Jane wrote back cautioning Helen against telling their parents, which didn't bode well that they'd accept an illegitimate, mixed-race grandchild. Around this time Tony received a letter from his sister Sybil, who was living back in Trinidad, wishing him a happy birthday and enquiring about Helen and the pregnancy.

In case the baby arrived on its due date on Tony's birthday, Helen baked a cake for him the day before. She also presented him with a copy of *The Koran* and a *Rubaiyat* in recognition of his conversion from the Catholic faith he'd been born into to the principles of the

Nation of Islam, which was the leading black power movement in America. Afterwards they went to sleep with the tantalising promise that the next day might deliver them both the gift of a child.

As it turned out, June the third came and went without the baby appearing so Helen decided to return to the security of Jo's home in Paddington, where she'd be closer to the hospital and could relax more easily. When there was still no sign of any action three days later an amnioscopy at St Mary's suggested Helen might still have a while to wait, so she knitted frenetically to distract herself from the discomfort of being so heavily pregnant and her uncertainty about Tony.

A week later, Helen had readied everything for the baby's arrival a dozen times over and was growing frustrated that nothing was happening when telling pains finally began. Jo took her back to St Mary's for another amnioscopy which suggested things were finally moving so they kept her in hospital, 'parking' her in the labour ward to wait for nature to take its course. The day dragged by interminably, and, without progress, Helen began to fear another false alarm would send her home again. But just after midnight her waters broke and her contractions kicked in with a vengeance.

After a night of painful labour I was born at 6.35 the next morning, an 8lb 12oz (4kg), 23-inch (58-cm) bouncing baby girl with a mop of curly black hair.

Much to Mum's delight, Tony showed up at the hospital unexpectedly that afternoon carrying flowers for her and appearing pleased as punch with me. His pride and obvious pleasure in this 'beautiful and angelic' new daughter who was the image of him restored some of Mum's hope for the future. Over the coming days she wrote in her diary that I was relaxed, easy-going and a good eater and sleeper who didn't give her any trouble. She also commented on my resemblance to my father as remarkable, particularly when I frowned with annoyance, and expressed her hope my temperament wouldn't be too similar to his.

While she was still in hospital with me, my dad asked Mum to return to live with him and she decided to give it another try, though with his track record of broken promises and flexibility with the truth she didn't let her hopes get too high this time. After leaving hospital, she joined Tony in preparing a new home in Highgate for us with a spring clean and a fresh coat of paint.

Mum variously referred to me as 'cherub', 'angel', 'junior' and 'little one' before secretly deciding that Yolanda might make a nice name for me. But she wasn't too surprised when my dad expressed a preference for giving me an Arabic name in line with his Black Power philosophies, saying names of such origin were more meaningful. He suggested Aminah, Ayesha and Leila as possibilities, with Aminah his preference of the three.

Having never heard of any of Tony's suggested names, and with no idea of what Aminah meant or how to spell it, Helen contacted the London Mosque and learnt Aminah was the name of the prophet Mohammed's mother and meant 'truthful', which appealed to her as a value to live up to.

Despite Mum's ongoing concerns about Tony, who refused to continue his TB treatment because it made him feel so sick, she relaxed into motherhood like a natural, cherishing every moment with me. For a brief time she enjoyed a happy household with a regular stream of visitors and the occasional social outing to see friends. However, within a month of moving into the Highgate flat they were broke again and dark clouds had gathered.

Mum was distressed at the thought of having to leave me to return to work at CBS News, wanting to put it off for as long as possible. But finding herself stuck in oppressive domestic drudgery and with poverty setting in, she decided that going back to work would at least restore her connection to friends and the outside world.

Mum's employers at CBS were keen for her to return, so she made preliminary enquiries about child care. But the authorities were aware of Tony's tuberculosis as well as his failure to complete the full course of treatment. They refused to risk exposing other children in child care and their families to TB so Mum remained caught at the mercy of Tony's erratic comings and goings.

During this time Tony refused to say where he was spending his time when he was away from home and when he did return, although he doted on me, he was often distant, leading Mum to suspect there might be another woman on the scene. Besides me, she could only telephone friends for company, so she kept herself busy writing letters to family and friends and eagerly awaiting news from home.

She had written to her sister to inform her of my birth, but Jane insisted my grandparents still shouldn't be told. So though Helen dearly wanted to share the joy of motherhood with her own mother, she continued to heed Jane's advice.

Each time Tony did come home he seemed more hung up and critical about the 'white race', continually blaming 'them' for all his misfortunes in life. With a young baby to care for, Mum wondered how much longer she could put up with him. Her formerly gregarious and sociable nature was slowly being eroded by the precarious situation she was in and she felt increasingly depressed and lonely. Her only pleasure was looking after me as I reached new milestones. To all intents and purposes she felt like a single mother and regretted moving back in with Tony.

The idea of going home to Australia was taking hold with Helen and she'd just registered my birth with Canberra House, when Tony received a letter from Trinidad with the shocking news that his sister Sybil had died suddenly from a thyroid condition, leaving behind two young children. Naturally Tony was devastated by his sister's death and wanted to return to Trinidad immediately but by then they barely had two shillings to rub together so the cost of a flight was out of the question.

Unhappy at not being able to go home to Trinidad, Dad took his grief out on Mum, refusing to speak to her and even actively discouraging her from the knitting and sewing she did to clothe me.

A small consolation came in the nick of time for Mum when her maternal uncle, Lou, visited London and she was able to share her unhappiness about her situation in a teary phone call with him. Unfortunately a planned meeting between Mum and Lou never eventuated because Dad was still reeling from the loss of his sister and persuaded Mum not to go. Uncle Lou did, however, promise Mum he would break the news about me to Blanche and Louis on his return to Australia.

Poverty took a harsh hold that winter and Dad, having not made it home to Trinidad since Sybil's death, withdrew completely. As Christmas loomed Mum scraped together what money she could to send some gifts home to her family and to rustle up a Christmas meal. She hoped a belly full of goodness might prompt some festive cheer in the house for my first Christmas and she busied herself with cooking on Christmas Eve.

On Christmas Day Tony disappeared until lunchtime, and Mum described lunch as a very 'un-Christmassy' affair lacking in any merriment between them. She spent the rest of the afternoon washing nappies before friends arrived for the evening meal, which was also very low key.

After such a lifeless Christmas Mum was tired of her life in London. Her feelings for my dad had dissipated further and she thought she'd be happier living apart from him with just me to care for.

On New Year's Eve she stayed in with Tony but they had little to say to each other and she thought back to the dawning of 1969 when her happiness at being pregnant was mixed with unhappiness about the state of her relationship. Now, a year later, she was ecstatically happy to be my mum but realised her relationship with my dad was irretrievable. She made a resolution to take charge of her life and change it for the better, hoping to be in Australia by the same time next year.

As the New Year got underway with weeks of unpaid rent, Mum had to resort to cracking open the gas meter to retrieve coins to feed us. It seemed that without financial assistance, we would never be able to escape poverty. Having received no news from Australia, despite Uncle Lou being long since returned, Mum worried that perhaps the news of my birth had gone down badly.

Then, finally, a letter from her father arrived in mid-January, though it made no mention of me. A couple of days later she received a letter from Blanche which was full of news from home but suggested Blanche was still unaware of my existence.

It took another month of alienation from Tony, and her discovery that he was seeing a woman called Diane, before Mum reached the end of her tether. And despite her inner conflict about taking me away from a dad I adored, she began to secretly plot our departure for Australia. Mum's plans were bolstered when, to her great relief, she got a letter from Blanche in mid-February to say she knew about me. Though Blanche was conciliatory she made it clear she was hurt that Mum had gone against her upbringing and said she'd decided not to tell Louis for fear he might turn his back on his daughter.

After receiving Blanche's letter Mum applied for a new passport for the two of us. She was relieved to discover that because she'd never married Tony she wasn't required to get his authority for my passport application form. However, the embassy told her she might have to wait two months for our passports to come through.

Mum's great love affair with Tony and London was over and she could hardly wait to get back to Australia, though she worried whether a single white mother with a mixed-race daughter would be welcome.

With the day of our passport's arrival drawing near Mum finally wrote a letter to her mother saying she wanted to bring me back to Australia to live and asking if Blanche could help with the fare. Despite her reservations and disappointment, Blanche agreed to buy us plane tickets home on the condition they couldn't be converted to cash.

Tony took us to the airport on the day we left, though Mum suspected he didn't think we'd be away for very long. Meanwhile, back in Australia, Blanche had decided not to tell Louis he was about to meet his 11-month-old first grandchild until she was sure we were definitely on our way home.

4. The Name of the Father

On our flight back to Australia Mum felt a mixture of relief at having escaped an impossible situation, and trepidation at the reception we would receive. She needn't have worried. We were welcomed home with open arms by both her sister Jane and her parents, who took us back to the family home in Eaglemont. In stark contrast to the poverty and isolation Mum had left behind, we now had a secure and loving family environment to settle into.

Blanche and Louis stepped enthusiastically into their new roles as grandparents without a word of complaint or criticism for the choices Mum had made, loving us both unconditionally. In spite of their advancing years, they embraced the unfamiliar energy of a toddler I brought into their house, and I embraced them equally. Unable to pronounce their names when I was learning to talk, Blanche and Louis became my 'Banchie' and 'Louda'. And once I grew steady on my feet I became the little shadow who followed them around adoringly, my grandmother's love of flora and fauna resulting in my first words including 'raphiolepis' and 'ornithorhynchus paradoxus'.

Unfortunately Australian laws were not quite so accommodating and didn't allow me to be recognised as a legitimate citizen of

Australia while I still carried my father's surname Hart. Refusing to jump through bureaucratic hoops just to conform, Mum decided to fight for me to keep my surname. With the help of a barrister in the family Mum launched an appeal and was ultimately successful in changing the law. I became the first 'illegitimate' child to be granted Australian citizenship with a different name from my mother.

For Mum, the Australian life she'd left for greater excitement was now a comfort to fall back into, though she continued to write letters to my dad to keep him updated. Tony replied sporadically though he said more than once he would join us in Australia as soon as he had enough money.

I enjoyed a cocooned existence at the centre of my family and regularly spent time with Mum's lifelong friends and their children. I was never told I was different by the people who filled our lives and I was too young to notice the undercurrent of disapproval from our nearest neighbours.

After concluding that secretarial work wouldn't sit well with her responsibilities as a single mother, Mum decided to become a teacher in order to share the same working hours and holidays as me once I started school. My grandparents were happy to look after me while Mum went to night school to finish her HSC, and when Mum was ready to move onto teachers' college she enrolled me in a tiny day care centre called 'Pixieland'. I loved playing with the other kids my age at Pixieland, though I always looked forward to the afternoons with Louda when he picked me up and invariably surprised me with a sweet treat.

My idyllic childhood, enveloped in love in the protective bubble of home and family, changed dramatically after I began at Ivanhoe East Primary School. To my dismay, within a year of starting there the playground had turned into a battleground for me, with a group of boys making my life miserable with racial taunts. In contrast to my home life where I was so secure, I felt singled out as a lone target for being the only one of 'my kind' in my class apart from an Indian girl who never appeared to encounter similar torment.

The first time one of the boys said, "You're black," I was surprised. Having never really thought about it, my initial thought was, *Am I?* I knew my skin was brown but I'd only ever been given compliments about it before I'd arrived at school, so it was news to me that being 'black' was unacceptable and something to be ashamed of.

After the same boy called me an 'Abo' I asked Mum what it meant. She told me it was an abbreviation of Aboriginal, and explained I wasn't Aboriginal, that my dad was from the West Indies, which was how I'd got my 'lovely' skin.

On another day at school, when one of the boys called me a 'bloody Abo', I realised he meant it was a bad thing. The germ of hatred caught on quickly, and I was subjected to a wildfire of harassment from that group of particularly mean boys. The insults they poured on me escalated, with daily taunts of 'Ab-or-ig-in-e'. They took to cornering me in the playground and dancing around me, performing a crass corroboree in which they imitated the sound of didgeridoos and pretended to throw spears at me. I stood trapped, alone and mystified by their cruelty, trying with all my might not to cry. I'd look around the playground desperately hoping somebody might come to my rescue but nobody offered me any help and somehow the boys always managed to catch me when there wasn't a teacher around.

I felt angry and indignant as well as deeply hurt by their mistreatment. I hadn't ever been in an argument or fought with anybody before I started school so it was a very rude awakening to suddenly find myself trying to avoid bullies every day.

When I asked Mum why the boys picked on me because of the colour of my skin, she said they were jealous because I had such a nice tan and suggested I tell the teachers if the boys continued to hassle me. But when I did tell, the teachers just said to ignore them and eventually they'd go away. Sadly, the more I tried to avoid the boys and pretend their words didn't hurt, the more pleasure they seemed to take in teasing me, increasing their repertoire of abuse to calling me a 'dirty boong' and a 'nigger' and spitting belittling taunts at me like, "Can't you get the dirt off in the shower?" and "Did you forget to wash the mud off in the river, you dirty Abo?" and "Betcha ate witchetty grubs for dinner last night, ya dirty boong."

I couldn't understand why they would target me so viciously and then my tormenters somehow found out that my dad wasn't around and started inferring my family wasn't my real family and my mum could not possibly be my 'real' mum because she was white. They claimed I must have been adopted because my 'real' parents were 'Abos who'd died from sniffing petrol'.

Even more than the colour of my skin, these barbs about my origins cut deeply because my awareness of conventional families had grown and I was sensitive about not having my dad in my life, especially because I was aware enough to realise he was my 'black half'.

In the past I'd never let my tormenters see my tears and had done my best to shrug them off or rebuke them verbally, but once they brought my family into it I decided I'd had enough and I wasn't going to take any more. Equally frustrated by the inaction of the school around the same time Mum suggested I try sticking up for myself.

I was always one of the tallest amongst my peers, so I took Mum's advice and changed tack with a physical response. After delivering a few decisive well-placed kicks and some slaps across the face in response to the boys' ongoing aggravation, it took them by such surprise that they beat a hasty retreat. Afterwards I felt more confident of a level playing field and continued to mete out my own brand of punishment whenever the school authorities let me down. And not only did I dish it out to those who bullied me but also in defence of other victims I saw being mistreated.

I soon developed a reputation for being volatile because if there were enough witnesses around to any conflict I'd walk away and choose a more appropriate time and place to deliver my retribution. Sometimes it was in the bike shed after the school bell had gone or walking home from school or if I came across one of them on the school oval and thought nobody was looking.

For a while I enjoyed my revenge for all the hurt these boys had caused me, but as my reputation for fighting grew my few friends started to distance themselves from me and my teachers were compelled to take action against my physical response to the boys. My sense of injustice peaked when I was sent to the principal's office to explain my actions after a fight and was told that racial abuse from bullies was no excuse for violence. When I refused to apologise for my behaviour the school called my mother.

Much to the principal's chagrin, Mum was equally unrepentant about my physical retaliation to bullies when she arrived, telling her she found it unacceptable that the school had failed to protect me from bullying. However, she agreed to deal with my 'problem behaviour', sitting me down later and advising me to start using words rather than my fists now that everybody knew I was capable of defending myself. She also explained that bullies usually lacked intelligence and self-esteem, causing them to try to deflect attention away from themselves onto others they perceived as vulnerable. She told me that because I was smart I could beat them just as well in a verbal stoush as a physical one.

After that I stopped resorting to violence as my primary form of defence and started to use words as my weapons against their attacks, while being ready for a physical fight if necessary. I never silenced the bullies completely but I always stood my ground.

Despite the capacity I developed to defend myself, the effects of the bigotry I was subjected to remained with me because I came to believe the colour of my skin was ugly and unacceptable. I filled an antique miniature notebook Banchie had given me with 'my wishes', which included wishing I had white skin, straight blonde hair, a narrower nose and thinner lips so I could fit in and so the boys would let me join in when they played 'kiss chasey' with the other girls. I hated my name too and wanted to change it to 'Samantha' after the character in *Bewitched* who could make people she didn't like disappear with a wiggle of her nose.

At home I'd let my true feelings out to my mum, saying, "How can they hate me just because I have brown skin? Why do they have to be so mean?"

"You'll always be beautiful to me," Mum would say hugging me tightly. "Why do you think they like to get a suntan?" she'd add, trying to comfort and reassure me.

"I don't know. Why Mum?"

"Because they're jealous, they all want to be as beautiful as you. I wish I had your skin," she'd say and kiss me on the cheek.

I never showed Mum my book of wishes and while she always said everything to reinforce my worth, I did begin to wonder about my dad. Louda was my idol so I didn't miss having a male role model, but sometimes I wished my dad were around to back me up or put the bullies in their place. I also wished I could see him for myself because I was told so often how much I looked like him.

I dreamt of the time I would go back to London and find him, and when he opened the door to my knock he'd recognise me instantly, saying, "My Aminah!" and embrace me in a big bear hug.

My dad had fuelled my fantasies by sending me presents for my early birthdays. One year he sent me a silver bracelet, another year he sent a silver locket on a chain and another I received a black-skinned doll from him who I named Zoe. Dad also continued to tell Mum he was coming to Australia, though he always failed to materialise and generally gave an excuse relating to money.

Eventually Tony started to fade into the past for my mum along with her memories of the life she'd had with him in London.

Away from the schoolyard, my childhood continued to be full and blissful with my mum at the centre of my world. We spent most of our leisure time with our family or mum's friends and their children, going on weekends away to their beach houses and regular camping holidays, often to the soundtrack of acoustic guitars and sing-alongs as we segued into hippiedom and the carefree seventies.

Mum finished her teacher training when I was seven years old and found a job as an art and ceramics teacher at a local high school. She also started going out with Rick, a long-haired and bearded graphic artist ten years her junior. Although my grandparents never said so, Rick's bohemian style probably wasn't entirely to their liking, so Mum decided it was time for us to fly the supportive nest they'd so lovingly provided.

Just before my eighth birthday we moved all of three doors up Carlsberg Road where I immediately spotted a girl in the house across the road who looked around my age. One day I picked a plum off the tree at the front of our new house and threw it across the road to get her attention. She retaliated in kind and Emma and I quickly became the tightest of friends, spending the long summer days frolicking in her swimming pool, playing hopscotch on the footpath or roaming the neighbourhood in dress-ups complete with mum's platform heels or roller skates. As well as Emma, I also befriended a boy called David, who lived up the road and went to the same school as me.

Rick moved in with us and though he never attempted to be my parent, Mum rarely mentioned my dad, effectively relegating him to the past for both of us. Dad's contact with us had gradually diminished by then anyway and Mum realised it was unlikely he'd ever come to Australia. But she received a nasty reminder of their relationship when a medical assessment for her teaching job turned up a dubious x-ray and she was diagnosed with tuberculosis.

Thankfully Mum never reached the infectious stage of TB and was able to keep her teaching job while she underwent 18 months of treatment. During her recovery she and Rick went on a holiday to Bali, leaving me with my grandparents. After falling in love with Bali during that first trip abroad since returning from London, Mum took me back with her the following year during the mid-year holidays of Grade 5 to escape the winter cold.

In Bali I immediately enjoyed the feeling of blending in with the darker skin of the Indonesians who mistook me for one of their own. I was only ten years old at the time but being tall, several men mistook me for being much older and approached Mum to ask for my hand in marriage. Naturally Mum told them in no uncertain terms that I was far too young. Though I was shocked that they wanted to marry me I also took it as a compliment that they saw a beauty where some of my peers observed only ugliness.

That same year I discovered basketball and formed a team with Emma and some girls from my school. Through basketball I established firm friendships and for the first time I felt like part of a group. My growing ability on the basketball court and my trip to Bali altered my outlook positively and improved my self-confidence. I began to think differently as I learnt more about Indigenous Australians and I reasoned that had I been Aboriginal it would be a point of pride and make me more Australian than the bullies themselves. I told them as much and my evolving point of view removed much of the power from their words so that eventually they backed off.

One of my most vivid memories of sixth grade was of walking to school one morning and spotting one of my basketball teammates across the road. In my haste to greet her I ran onto the street, oblivious to an approaching car. There was a sudden screech of brakes before the car hit the back of my legs and threw me up in the air. I smashed my head against the windscreen and somersaulted off the bonnet onto the road.

Later as I was being loaded into the ambulance feeling dazed and sorry to have caused such a fuss, I saw Mum leap from her car and run to my side before we both burst into tears. When I arrived at the Austin Hospital I was assessed by doctors and thankfully given the all-clear from any serious head injury. They said the cushion provided by my thick mop of wild West Indian curls had possibly helped save my life.

I was grateful to be alive and delighted to miss the sixth grade camp to Canberra. A few months later as my primary school days drew to a close, I walked out through the gates of Ivanhoe East Primary School hoping never again to lay eyes on the bullies who'd made much of my time there so unhappy. I also resolved that from day one at secondary school I would make it clear to everyone that I was not to be messed with.

5. Rich Dad, No Dad

Meanwhile a new battle had begun on the home front, with Mum and me at odds over which secondary school I would go to. Mum was insisting I attend the private girls' school she'd gone to, but I dreaded the thought of going into the strict and religious confines of Presbyterian Ladies' College. It wasn't fear of racism that concerned me about PLC so much as the conflicts that might arise from my lack of desire to become a 'lady' or to conform to any particular religious doctrine or disciplinary code.

My preference was to go to the local Banyule High, where I would at least be with some of my basketball mates. And though I realised some of the bullies from primary school would probably go there too I figured that at least they'd be the devils I knew.

I was already a rebel in training by then with a strong anti-racist agenda born of my own experience and a lot of anger that my schooling so far had been a big disappointment.

Despite my rebelliousness Mum said going to PLC wasn't up for discussion. I remained defiant, worried that if Mum forced me to go there I'd have to spend another six years feeling excluded and lonely, not necessarily because of my skin colour but because I suspected PLC would be full of bitchy girls. While boys could be bullies I'd learnt how to deal with them, but I fully expected to run into trouble if I got into fights with girls, especially if they happened to be 'ladies'.

Despite my intransigence, Mum insisted on taking me to do the entrance exam. When she pulled up in the school's car park to deliver me, her 1964 VW station wagon contrasted sharply with the rows of prestige cars parked there.

As I reluctantly followed Mum into the entrance hall, she pointed out an imposing life-sized portrait hanging in a gilt frame outside the grandly named Wyslaskie Hall and told me it was a portrait of her grandfather, The Reverend Dr Alexander Marshall.

"Great," I muttered as she left me to enter the hall on my own. "Bloody ancestors to watch my every move. There's absolutely no way I'm going to this school."

After I wrote my name at the top of the exam paper I proceeded to sit in silent protest for the next two hours, hoping my failure to do the exam would guarantee I went to Banyule High School.

I knew my hopes had been dashed, however, when we returned to PLC to dress and equip me with second-hand uniforms and books for Year 7. Clearly Mum had beaten me at my own game. I learnt later that after my exam protest she had leveraged family connections to ensure my place at her alma mater.

Passing old Alec's portrait again in the hallway that day I was convinced I could see a smirk in his eyes that I'd been outsmarted and would get a 'proper' education whether I liked it or not. My humiliation was complete, my fate was sealed and I was forced to concede to Mum's wishes, though I remained defiant and promised myself the Presbyterians would never make me a lady.

On my first day of secondary school I arrived with my crested school bag bearing the PLC motto *lex dei vitae lampas* – 'the law of God is the lamp of life', along with a bad attitude and an intention to break the rules.

After realising the Latin we were forced to learn in Year 7 was no

HOW I MET YOUR FATHER

longer spoken I locked the Latin teacher, Mrs Pilling, in the store-room while she was getting some textbooks, and defied anybody from attempting to free her without any consideration for the disruption I was causing. Later, an inevitable announcement came over the public address system calling me to what would be the first of many visits to the vice-principal's office for misbehaviour.

Much to my pleasant surprise I made friends at PLC more easily than I had imagined and heard not a single racist comment directed at me. After a while I realised the school, which prided itself on equality and respect, would never tolerate the sort of discrimina-tory behaviour I'd experienced previously which partially curbed my desire to ensure my peers were scared of me. However my tough façade was ingrained by then, protecting the vulnerable and wounded girl that still lived inside me.

The student body at PLC was far more racially diverse than the 'waspish' Ivanhoe East, with girls from Asia, India and Sri Lanka providing a more balanced blend of colour. I still managed to feel like the odd one out though because, as far as I could tell, most of the other girls came from conventional families with two parents and siblings. And, for the first time, I became aware of snobbery, which was a new phenomenon for me.

The social stratification at PLC resulted in the formation of different cliques and many of those who didn't fit into them were consigned to a life without party invitations or plans for the weekends. There was a large group of pretty girls whose non-academic interests mainly lay in the latest fashion trends and the boys at our 'brother' school, Scotch College.

I joined a group of girls with edge and attitude who were more interested in rebelling, smoking cigarettes and hanging out with 'bogans', who appeared to have more freedom and to generally live more interesting lives than those at my conservative school.

Eventually the school tempered my rebellion, refusing to satisfy my desire to be expelled. I managed to avert suspension in getting away with the offence of smoking. And on admitting that a Bacardi bottle discovered under a portable classroom by teachers had been left there by my group of friends after we'd spent a compulsory Saturday sports day drinking there, my hope for an early exit was thwarted by an appointment with the school counsellor.

Gradually I grudgingly accepted that the school had some good points and I'd made some good friends there.

As well as my PLC friends, I remained close mates with my childhood friends Emma and David, who had also gone on to private schools. Em and I spent more time with David during secondary school and our friendship flourished, though sometimes the spectre of my skin colour arose when I was introduced to David's friends.

By the time we were in Year 9, my friends and his would occasionally go to the MCG together to watch the cricket and we'd sit in Bay 13 with all the 'yobbos'. Back then spectators were still allowed to drink beer from cans, and when the Aussies came up against the then-dominant West Indies side racial heckling was rife amongst the yobbos.

David's friends would sometimes tease me playfully by saying I looked like Joel Garner, which they meant as an insult. In retaliation I'd cheer triumphantly at the superior skills of the West Indies' team and lay claim to them being my father's compatriots, only to be met with abuse and a flurry of 'VB' beer cans being hurled my way by others in the crowd.

I'd turn and raise my finger in rude defiance and respond to racist taunts with loud comments about poor sportsmanship and sore losers, though underneath my bravado I still felt very hurt by such insults. I secretly wished Viv Richards would turn out to be my long lost father to shut all of their mouths permanently.

6. Like a Needle in a Haystack

Unlike many of my peers who knew where they were headed, by Year 10 I still had no idea what sort of career I wanted to pursue. I wasn't particularly good at any subject other than English and I had no intention of studying hard enough to become a luminary in any field. Like most 15-year-olds I was also starting to explore a sense of identity, which led to me feeling much more curious about my father and 'being black'.

We hadn't heard anything from my dad for a few years by then. Though Mum had occasionally wondered aloud what had become of him, despite my earlier dreams of a perfect reunion between us, I was inclined to believe that he'd simply forgotten about both Mum and me.

One day during the devastating Ash Wednesday bushfires on Melbourne's outskirts, Mum had received a call from a telephone operator asking if she'd accept a 'reverse charge' call from Tony. It turned out that he'd seen headlines in the British tabloids proclaiming Melbourne was 'burning' and had been worried enough to call and check we were okay. Once Mum had reassured him that we were both well and happy, he'd gone off the radar again.

Now she knew Tony was still in England and thinking it was time I met him, Mum decided to take long service leave from her teaching job the following year, and take me back to London and introduce me to my father.

Despite my eagerness to get to London to meet my dad, Mum insisted on a cultural education tour of Greece and Italy to impart her passion for art history and ancient civilisations in which I showed little interest. But I did make some new friends and loved the European style and sophistication.

When we eventually reached England we went to stay with a teaching friend of Mum's in Tunbridge Wells, a village about 60 kilometres from London. I was disappointed that I might be doomed to boredom in such a tiny town but as soon as we visited London I felt the pulse of the city's buzzing energy and was enthralled at the mixture of people of different nationalities and skin colour walking its streets. I felt instantly like I fitted in and wanted to soak in as much of it as I possibly could.

We caught the tube to Camden Town and Mum started recalling her days there with Horace, Mary and my dad. Arriving at the underground station we walked up Parkway to number 95 where Mum was relieved to find that the Dudu boutique was still there. Stepping inside she recognised Mary immediately. They had a short conversation revealing that Mary and Horace were no longer together and Mary had remarried. Then over coffee at a nearby café Mum brought up the subject of my dad but Mary became vague and reluctant to say much. She suggested we speak to Horace and said we'd probably be able to find him at the upcoming Notting Hill Carnival.

Mum and I left Mary and returned to Tunbridge Wells feeling deflated that she hadn't been able to tell us anything concrete about my dad. A phone number and old address Mum had for him also led nowhere, but Mum was hopeful we'd find out more at the Carnival where she told me my dad used to play steelpans.

If London had captivated me with its chaotic liveliness, the Carnival opened my eyes to an even more intoxicating new world.

The exotic attractions of the Caribbean captured my imagination and gave me a tantalising taste of where my father came from.

Mum looked for familiar faces while I soaked in the unfamiliar sights, sounds and smells, imprinting them to hold on to until I returned, which by then I'd decided I surely would. As Mary had predicted, Mum eventually spotted Horace in the heaving crowd and introduced herself when his memory seemed to have escaped him. In turn he introduced his wife Annabelle and their small children Ezana and Kaz. However, when Mum asked Horace about Tony he assumed the same vague demeanour as Mary, saying he hadn't seen him in a long time and didn't know where he was. And just like that our hopes of finding my dad vanished into the crowd of West Indian faces.

Before we'd left Australia I'd been convinced I'd finally meet him and that he'd be overjoyed to see me, but our search had amounted to nothing. But I couldn't allow my disillusionment to take hold because I believed there had to be a simple explanation. Perhaps he'd gone back to Trinidad to live. Maybe he was living in Europe. Meanwhile, I'd fallen in love with London's vitality and vowed to return and find Dad by myself as soon as I could get school out of the way.

Having left home six weeks earlier for the holiday of a lifetime, I returned embarrassed to have to tell my friends I hadn't found my dad, though the sense of humiliation was nothing compared to the disappointment I felt in my heart. I needn't have worried because my school friends were unanimously sorry and supportive that I hadn't achieved my dream and before long we'd moved onto discussing the gorgeous guys I'd seen during my travels. The opposite sex and music were the hottest topics of conversation amongst my group of friends at the time and we thought little about the bigger picture of our lives beyond plans for the next weekend.

The following year it was time to think about the subjects that would lead me towards university, the expected path for PLC girls. I still felt unsuited to the academia of the school and was tempted to leave but again Mum had other plans, despite having short-circuited her own education. She found an unlikely ally in her bid to keep me at school when my economics and legal studies teacher, Mr Edwards, sat me down and urged me to give the HSC a go.

"Aminah, you have plenty of ability to pass HSC," he said, "you're just too distracted to realise your own potential. When did you last study properly for an exam?"

I looked him in the eye and couldn't lie. I'd become expert at time wasting and avoidance when it came to study, and could usually be found hiding somewhere smoking a cigarette or skiving off to friends' houses to avoid homework.

Mr Edwards had a point. I had no idea what I could achieve if I actually made an effort. So for the first and only time I let the reason of any teacher pierce my resistance and, much to my mum's satisfaction, I agreed to stay at PLC until the end of Year 12.

Despite committing to doing the HSC I saw other things as much more important than my studies, especially my friends, boys, smoking, music and good times in pretty much that order. My life as a teenage schoolgirl was busy and full of melodrama, so thoughts of my dad faded into the background for a while though I still intended to return to London as soon as I could.

On the home front Mum had split with Rick before we'd gone to Europe. She bought her first house a whole seven blocks away from Banchie and Louda which we'd moved into on our return. Well into his nineties by then, Louda had begun to ail and though he'd never been one to complain he'd started to lament outliving all his siblings and friends as well as a few of his friends' children who had died too. When he broke his hip it triggered a downward spiral. His doctors said his strong heart could keep him going but he stopped eating, having lost the will to live. It took a few weeks but finally he got his way and just before I was due to do my practice exams in Year 12, my beloved Louda died.

My world felt shattered when I was told that the loving lynchpin of my happy family was gone. Louda had already turned 80 when we'd moved in with my grandparents and he'd been more energetic and full of life than much younger men, and somehow I'd always imagined he'd go on and on.

The Queen's chaplain happened to be in Melbourne when Louda died and he agreed to preside over the funeral but I didn't hear a word he said because of my overwhelming grief. I'd never witnessed anything as sad as watching his coffin being lowered into his final resting place with his father and mother and baby brother John who had died shortly after birth.

It was probably fortunate I didn't have time to dwell too much on my grief with the amount of schoolwork I had to do – or perhaps it was my tendency to be easily distracted that helped me through the pain of losing my grandfather. A part of me wanted to make him proud of me so I studied harder than I ever had before and, as Mr Edwards had predicted, I passed my HSC respectably and secured a place at university.

I had honoured my mum's wishes to finish school and now she was starting a relationship with a new partner, David, I finally felt able to spread my wings and start making my own decisions.

I left PLC with grudging gratitude, especially towards Mr Edwards, realising that if he hadn't told me I could succeed in my final exams I probably wouldn't have tried, but now opportunity lay ahead and I was set on doing a degree that would lead me into advertising.

7. Breaking the Chain

As soon as I started university I was free to reinvent myself as an individual rather than trying to be like everyone else at school or getting into fights because I wasn't. My anger at the world abated once I felt like the shackles of formal education had been removed. I relished the sense of independence and the ability to be self-determining – choosing when and how often to study, work and play. But I did hold onto my strong sense of justice and anti-prejudice and I remained quick to react to any bigoted comments directed my way or jump to the defence of others I saw being bullied or victimised. Occasionally the angry beast reared its ugly head and I felt it necessary to use my physical size to advantage, including one night at a party when a guy started having a go at me, calling me a 'black bitch'. The ensuing scuffle ended up with him landing heavily on the ground on his backside and a cautionary suggestion from me that he stay down there if he knew what was good for him.

I hoped nobody could see me shaking with a mixture of adrenaline and abject fury. Mum had warned me I was now old enough to be arrested if I hit people and as a general rule I kept my temper reined in but I felt he had deserved it.

Other times my male friends would defend me, indignant at similar mistreatment. Many a night we were thrown out of a club for fighting but sometimes I just put up with racial slights such as my best friend's boyfriend calling me 'chocolate drop'. Though he thought this was harmless and hilarious, I found it rude and offensive, but I let it go because I'd had more conflict in my life because of my colour than I cared to remember. The thought of falling out with him and, potentially, my closest friend over it wasn't worth the effort.

Such incidents lessened over time and as I got older and grew more comfortable in my skin I began to take less violent umbrage at being picked out for my colour. I'd still bristle each time I heard myself described as the 'black girl over there' or 'the big black girl' but gradually my skin had thickened enough for me to shake it off and I felt much happier in the many friendships I had without the social partitions of a private girls' school.

A casual job as a checkout chick in a supermarket that allowed for flexible hours around my university commitments provided the funding for the all-important social life that dominated my time and attention. I wasn't the best at budgeting but I always made sure I had enough to enjoy the revolving door of late nights at the latest nightclubs.

It was during one of these nights out with my girlfriend Sue, who was single and had her eye out for a new boyfriend, that a loveable rogue with the gift of the gab charmed his way into my life. As we stood at the bar to order drinks, Sue noticed a guy with messy blonde hair standing nearby. "What do you think of him?" she said, gesturing in his direction.

I glanced around only for him to catch me looking. When he smiled devilishly in our direction Sue quickly changed her mind. "He's not my type," she said. "He looks like trouble."

But it was too late; he'd already interrupted his conversation with the guy next to him and was headed in our direction. "Shit," said Sue, "now he's coming over."

"You never know, Suze," I said. "He might be a nice guy."

"G'day, I'm Davo," he said reaching out his hand to me.

"Hi, I'm Jude," I replied randomly, "and this is Sue," I added, moving aside so he could talk to her. "We were just getting drinks, do you want one?" I added.

Handing Sue her drink and leaving mine on the bar I then excused myself to go to the toilet. When I returned, Sue shot me a wide-eyed look with a slight shake of her head.

"Not my type at all," she whispered just before Davo turned his attention my way.

"So, Jude," he said, "what do you do?"

At first glance Davo wasn't my type either with his unkempt blonde haired, blue-eyed surfie looks despite being well dressed. But Davo immediately set out to prove me wrong. He introduced us to some of his mates in an obvious ploy to distract Sue so he could chat me up in earnest. Within minutes he had me laughing hysterically at his jokes and more and more taken with his witty banter. By the time the bouncers did their rounds at closing time, Davo and I had spent the entire night talking and laughing.

Before leaving, when Davo asked for my number, I felt conflicted because I'd been seeing another guy on and off for a couple of years though I wasn't exactly sure whether we were currently off or on.

"I'm really sorry," I said to Davo, "I'm sort of seeing someone."

"Go on."

"I really can't," I said again. "If we're meant to see each other again, we will."

"Okay, Jude," he said with a wink before grabbing me around the waist and kissing me passionately on the lips while his friends yelled and whistled from a car across the street.

We parted ways without me giving him my number or even telling him my real name but I quietly hoped I'd see him again.

We went back to the Cadillac Bar the following Saturday night and sure enough Davo appeared with the same enthusiastic pursuit as the week before. I came clean about my name and apologised for lying but he just laughed. He said I owed him my phone number now and, having confirmed my single status during the week, I gladly gave it to him before we parted with another kiss.

The next day Davo called to invite me to a gathering with his mates, a hard-partying group of guys, where the drinks, conversation and laughs flowed freely. And he called me every day after that until I finally agreed to be his girlfriend.

With Davo as my boyfriend an already busy social life was taken to a whole new level. I'd always enjoyed good times at pubs and clubs around town but Davo and his tight group of about a dozen close mates were heavily into the Melbourne club scene. There was a different club for every night of the week except Monday, we always got priority entry, free-flowing drinks and I was never allowed to put my hand in my pocket. If we'd partied for most of the week we'd sometimes decamp to Davo's family's beach house at Phillip Island so he could surf and when we were alone I felt like the most important person in his world. I was still playing basketball once a week and regularly catching up with friends when I met Davo but it wasn't long before I submerged myself in his fast-paced life to the detriment of my university education. I still didn't prioritise study and having barely established new friendships at university I needed little excuse to miss lectures altogether. It was hardly surprising when I failed two of my economics subjects but I didn't really care as long as I could spend every spare moment with Davo, who I'd completely fallen for.

Every day with him felt new and exciting. Each time I tried to contribute some of my limited supermarket earnings to our lifestyle, Davo refused to take my money and I started to wonder how his job in retail could afford us such an extravagant lifestyle. But he shrugged off any questions I asked and my infatuation with him erased any niggling doubts. He pulled me into the fast lane and kept his foot firmly on the accelerator. His enthusiasm was contagious and I was exhilarated by his wild zest for life. We hung out with singers and actors and models and sportspeople in the latest bars and clubs and if I wasn't sure where Davo was after work I'd be sure to find him at the Saloon Bar in South Yarra.

We ate at the best restaurants in town as he introduced me to a lifestyle I couldn't otherwise have afforded and I enjoyed being spoilt. Davo's generosity was profligate as long as it guaranteed him someone to drink with. One night an African-American basketballer playing in the local National Basketball League was blatantly chatting me up in the Saloon. Rather than getting angry or jealous like some men would, Davo offered to buy him a drink and invited him to come with us to a club afterwards.

For me receiving that sort of attention became more commonplace and I enjoyed it being positive for a change. Being different had suddenly become cooler. I accepted compliments and quickly learnt the art of elusive flirtation. I even started to like being me but I couldn't completely ignore the fact that I was still regularly defined as 'the black girl'.

Many of the flatterers and charmers and sleazebags who approached me were from other corners of the globe and they triggered my desire to go back to London and explore the wider world. Karen, my best friend from school, had married as soon as she finished university but with Davo I felt as though my life had just begun.

Davo eventually got a job with a computer company, and our friendship group widened to include his successful bosses. They also offered me a part-time job to rescue me from the checkout and Davo's commissions brought his earnings into line with our lifestyle. I still occasionally wondered how he paid for it all but now he was buying flash cars and boats and we both became accustomed to the high life we were living

After an extra year of study to make up for the economics subjects I'd failed due to my pleasure-seeking lifestyle, I finally graduated.

8. Ready to Fly

My first job in a small advertising agency told me I'd made the right career choice and also put the brakes on my partying so I could focus on getting ahead. Being a small agency of only a handful of people, it wasn't glamorous or even particularly social but I got in-depth exposure to the process of advertising from a sketched concept on butcher's paper through production and into the media and I relished every part of it. Eighteen months later I felt like I'd learnt all I could there and with nowhere to progress I moved on. A recruiter put me forward for a job at a new agency called Republic that was founded by a notorious advertising creative director, Ted Horton, who was known as much for tempestuousness as for his brilliant ideas, along with his business partner, Mark Pearson.

In an awkward interview with Ted's assistant, who was also babysitting his three-year-old son, it was impossible for us to talk properly because the little guy refused to do as he was told. When I spotted a plate of grapes on a desk I picked the child up and sat him on my knee then fed the grapes to him one by one to keep him quiet while we adults talked. Susie could finally explain that the account manager's job I'd come to be interviewed for had just been given to somebody else.

We got chatting anyway, getting on like a house on fire, so she convinced Ted to meet me in case they needed another account manager down the track. An hour later I'd met Mark as well, they'd created another position for me and I walked out of their office with a new job.

Mark and Ted were both seasoned 'admen' who sped up my learning curve by throwing me into new situations at the deep end and further inspiring my love for the creative process of advertising with their own unique approach to the business.

Davo was going great guns at computer sales too but he didn't see his work as a career so much as a way to bankroll his excess. I was keen to keep a clearer head so I could keep learning and progress but Davo wanted to keep partying ever harder because he'd proven he could still sell ice to an Eskimo on just twenty minutes' sleep.

As our ambitions diverged cracks began to show in our relationship, which quickly became gaping holes as we found ourselves fighting all the time. Davo's propensity to write himself off so completely he barely knew what day it was not only worried me but began to embarrass me as well as I found myself making excuses for his wayward behaviour.

Just as I'd started to feel my love might be getting in the way of my life, Mark and Ted decided to close Republic and I found myself redundant. But as chance would have it Ted was judging some creative awards and he brought a fellow guest judge from the UK into the agency to see our work. Steve Henry was the co-creative director of his own advertising agency in London that was doing very well and told us to look him up if any of us ever found ourselves in England.

This was exactly the nudge I'd needed to revive my desire to return to London, which had been waylaid by love. It was time to cut my ties to Davo once and for all for a change of scene and go to London to continue my career and, more importantly, find my dad.

★

Around this time it became obvious Banchie was ready to die. During her 92 years she'd been an independent young woman, a successful pharmacist and a wonderful wife, mother and grandmother.

Before her father's death Mum had always joked that Banchie wouldn't know what to do without Louda to nag, but after he died Banchie showed no signs of giving up, stubbornly rebuffing talk of nursing homes and staying alone in her house in Carlsberg Road for two more years. Mum and I had taken turns to bathe her daily, style her hair and pluck her rogue white whiskers. I loved and laughed at the vestiges of her vanity, which had her demanding a stool under the light in front of the mirror so she could ensure I didn't miss a single hair.

Inevitably old age had brought unsteadiness to her feet and she'd had falls when nobody was there to pick her up, so eventually, reluctantly, she'd agreed to move into nursing care at a home called Lumeah. Unlike Louda, she wasn't the most social or outgoing of people, but during her early years there she surprised and delighted us by joining a choir and taking up other social activities to occupy her time.

Since I could recall she had fought a valiant battle against the ravages of crippling osteoarthritis, which hunched her spine into a u-bend. Her eyes were permanently cast to the ground unless she elevated herself above 45 degrees using her walking stick. But her physical frailty belied a strong and determined woman who had previously been unbowed by the ravages of time. Now she probably realised she was living longer than she'd anticipated and began to withdraw.

Her retreat was gradual with her interest in conversation waning and her desire to know what was going on in our lives diminishing. She'd always slept upright in her bed against the stack of pillows she needed to support her curved spine, but once she decided she'd had enough of living the pillow stack came down, she refused to get up in the morning and lay in bed curled up in a foetal position keeping her eyes closed even when awake.

Mum, Jane and I, along with my Uncle Gianni and cousin Kate, visited her on alternate days, sitting devotedly at her bedside talking to her and gently holding her hand. But we could all see that she was a tired old lady with nothing left to do and no good reasons left to keep waking up each day. When Louda had chosen his time to die I'd wanted him to keep on going forever, but with Banchie I was able to look at it less selfishly and accept her desire to leave this world.

Two days before Mum's 54th birthday, she received a call saying Banchie had died in her sleep. Afterwards Mum told me how she'd woken that night with an indiscernible sensation and I hoped it was my grandmother's spirit passing through to say her final goodbye.

My grandparents had been ancient since I could remember so worries about them dying had been a permanent fixture of my youth but when Banchie died my grief was tempered by an over-whelming feeling of pride that each of them had lived long and meaningful lives and gratitude to have had them in my life for so long. I was 25 and hoped I was living guided by the values and lessons my grandparents had taught me.

I'd been wanting to travel and find my dad since I was 19, but as well as falling for Davo, I'd worried Banchie might die while I was away. And I wanted to be there when her time came, the way she'd always been there for me. I wanted to thank her and say goodbye.

The relationship between Davo and I had reached its final act not long after Banchie's death. We'd been on again and off again more times than I could remember. We'd break up in a fit of anger and for a short time I'd be resolute in staying away from him and even dated other people in between, but inevitably I'd drift back to him like an addict. Ours had become a destructive love, bringing out the absolute worst in each other. I'd come to believe it was up to me to break the habit once and for all before we did anything that couldn't be changed. Many of our friends had started getting married and having babies and I knew if I didn't make the break with Davo we could easily slip into a similar fate.

I called on Mandy, who'd been a friend for more than a decade by then, for advice. The concentric circles of our lives meant Mandy and I were always destined to meet. One of her closest friends lived next door to one of mine and I had been at PLC with her next-door neighbour Julie. But it was her sister Jodie, who was also best friends with Sue, who first introduced me to Mandy, and her megawatt smile and magnetism impressed me immediately. I had become close with Sue and Jodie when we'd dated guys from the same friendship group and spent a lot of time at Jodie's house where we'd met her younger sister Mandy. Eventually Jodie drifted off with a new boyfriend from a different scene while I grew closer to Mandy as our own social lives merged. From the moment I'd met Mandy we shared a sense of humour and a similar wanderlust and desire for adventure.

Since then she'd witnessed the travails of my relationship with Davo from close quarters and I had watched hers with her boyfriend Mickey. Davo and Mickey hit it off immediately when we introduced them and we'd quickly become an inseparable foursome with a mission to party. For a year or two Mandy and Mickey gave Davo a run for his money in being the last to go home from our debauched nights but eventually, at least for three of us, Melbourne had grown tiresome. We hankered after a different kind of excitement to Davo. We all had the travel bug but wanting to travel in opposite directions had driven Mandy and Mickey's relationship onto the rocks as well.

I wanted to find my dad and see the world in that order, while Davo had little desire to travel further than his beach house at Phillip Island or – at a stretch – go on a surfing trip to Bali with the hope of better breaks.

Despite Davo's dad abandoning him to return to England when Davo was still a toddler he showed little interest in seeking out his father and confronting him for answers. As far as Davo was concerned he didn't have a 'real father', his stepdad John having stepped into the breach as a loving substitute. Beneath his protestations I believed that, far from being indifferent, Davo had simply buried his feelings of abandonment by his father, impeding his ability to communicate about anything emotional, including our relationship. Instead he sought refuge in late nights and alcohol, excusing himself from speaking sense or taking things seriously on the few occasions I'd tried to broach his father with him. Only once did I crack his surface detachment and he almost let me in but just as quickly he shut down again. Since then I'd given up trying.

Mandy and Mickey were more similar to each other than Davo and me. They each had great business brains and entrepreneurial flair. And they were both shiny, happy party people, irrepressible ravers with a love of techno music and the underground dance party scene. On a trip to Thailand they'd gone to a full-moon party where Mickey had immediately spotted the potential to make money from organising raves wherever backpackers gathered.

Mickey wanted his next stop to be Manali in India, where he hoped to cash in on its growing reputation for trance parties. While Mandy shared Mickey's nocturnal passions, she didn't want to be hemmed into one place. Her intrepid nature made her more inclined to want to climb the world's mountains and dive in the depths of its oceans as well as dancing to famous DJs at every infamous rave around the globe.

When I called her one morning to say I needed to get away from Davo before we destroyed each other it was a rare solemn moment between Mandy and me — previously my morning calls to her were for moral support to deal with a hangover. With her eternally positive outlook she would find an upside or make a joke that would send me into peals of laughter. We were each other's hangover cure administered via telephone on a regular basis.

Our weeks went something like this: Monday, when I'd call her complaining that Davo had disappeared for the entire weekend and I was worried for his safety, Mandy would provide similarly hilarious counsel. On Tuesdays we would call each other every half-hour to help pass the day at work as the last weekend's escapades really took their toll. By Wednesday we'd be planning the next night of fun and those plans would play out over the following four nights.

Undoubtedly we were all living a little too hard but while Mandy and Mickey shared my aspirations to broaden our horizons, I worried Dave's outlook would always lie at the bottom of a glass. His hard living reflected his need to escape from the pain in his soul but his inexhaustible need to 'have fun' and act the clown eventually wore me out.

In a last-ditch attempt to keep the wheels on Davo asked me to move in with him, but weeks later the final death knell sounded and I told him we were done.

I called Mandy and told her Davo had run off with a flight attendant.

The following day we booked one-way tickets to London via Bangkok for three weeks later. The plan was to go to London and work for a few months before we travelled on to South America for The Big Adventure.

Finally I was ready to make my dream of meeting my dad a reality. But that meant saying goodbye to my mum and leaving her for an indefinite period of time. Mum had always been the beacon that guided me safely home when my life went off course and I wasn't aware of my dependence until I was preparing to leave Australia.

At the airport a small posse of Mandy's friends and mine came to see us off along with my mum. Both Mandy and I were brimming with the thrill and anticipation of adventure but when I hugged my mum in a final farewell I cried and struggled to relinquish our embrace.

Eventually Mum pushed me towards Mandy having whispered in my ear the parting words that she hoped I'd find my dad. With tears still streaming down my face I ignored her suggestion not to look back one last time for a final glimpse of her face before the doors slid closed behind us.

PART II

9. Princes of Darkness

We arrived in London after a month in Thailand where we'd stopped to get ourselves into travel mode. We'd celebrated my twenty-sixth birthday on Koh Phangan at a full-moon party which had shaken off the sadness of our broken relationships.

In London I immediately got the same sense of belonging I'd felt in 1984 from being amongst such a diversity of races and I loved feeling like just another black person amongst many. Wherever I went I was intrigued by the multitude of accents and languages being spoken whether I was on the underground or walking in the streets. And I found London's intense energy even more exhilarating and filled with promise than I had as a teenager.

Wanting to find my father as soon as possible, I went to the Registry of Births, Deaths and Marriages to see if any information about him was recorded there. More than a decade had passed since he'd last called us to make sure we had survived the Ash Wednesday bushfires so Mum and I had wondered whether something untoward might have happened to him since then.

My heart sank when I came across an entry in the death register for an Anthony Hart who had died 15 months earlier, but I was heartened when I saw that the date of birth listed for the dead man was incomplete and even then didn't match my dad's. My next step was to try and find Mary, Horace Ové's ex-wife, to see if she could point me in Horace's direction, in the hope he'd be able to shed some light on Dad's whereabouts. But when I arrived at the building where Mary's shop, Dudu, had been it was no longer there and my hopes felt dashed. I went into the shop anyway to ask if anybody knew where Mary was.

I introduced myself and briefly explained my situation to a friendly, dreadlocked man named Hassan, who told me he was a good friend of the family and that unfortunately Mary had passed away. He also told me that Horace had returned to Trinidad to live, though he still visited London regularly, then added that Mary's son Zak lived in a flat upstairs but was away in New York. He said my best hope would be to visit Mary's daughter Indra in another branch of Dudu on the Finchley Road in Swiss Cottage.

"Thanks, Hassan. I'm really grateful," I said.

I crossed the road to look up at the building that had been my parents' home. The phallic symbol Mum had described as part of its façade was gone and the exterior had been painted a smart navy blue, toning down the brightness of its colours in the sixties. I hadn't taken much notice of the building the last time I'd visited with Mum but it now represented a door to my history and I couldn't wait to find out what was behind it.

Dudu was easy enough to find on the Finchley Road but I hesitated at the door, suddenly feeling inexplicably nervous. Hovering outside for a moment to gather my thoughts and emotions I ventured inside.

"Hello, are you Indra?" I asked the first woman I saw inside.

"Yes, I am," she said in surprise.

"Hi Indra, my name's Aminah Hart. I've just been talking to Hassan at 95 Parkway. I was looking for your mum, well your dad, actually I'm looking for my dad," I said before taking a breath and starting again. "Sorry, it's a bit of a long story, but Horace is a friend of my dad. My parents lived above Dudu in Parkway in the sixties.

Mum took me back to Australia when I was a baby and I haven't seen my dad since. I was hoping Horace could help me find him."

"Oh Aminah," she said, with a broad smile that dispelled the earlier unfamiliarity. "I'm sure Horace will help you. He's in Trinidad at the moment. I'll give you his number, and I'll give you Zak's too."

After our brief exchange I left Dudu with the promised phone numbers that replaced my worry about the incomplete details for the Anthony Hart I'd seen on the death register with new hope and I headed home content I would be speaking to Horace soon. In the meantime I could focus on enjoying London.

Mandy and I spent our first few days doing the tourist thing, sightseeing alongside the hordes of other visitors to the city. As we pounded the pavements we were surprised at how often we were accosted by random men.

Initially when a guy stopped us in the street and asked for our phone number we thought it was a one-off thing, but by halfway through the first day's exploration we'd been stopped in the street by countless others, asking us out on dates or wanting our phone numbers. When we tried to make our excuses and walk on, several of them scribbled phone numbers on scraps of paper and shoved them into our hands. One guy wound down his window as we strolled down Charing Cross Road minding our own business and shouted, "If I book the church will you marry me?" pointing his finger at us.

"Wasn't quite what I'd envisaged for a marriage proposal," I said to Mandy, laughing. "What the hell is going on?"

"I have no idea," Mandy replied, laughing too. "Do these guys have no shame?"

"It's almost like we have 'new in town and single' tattooed across our foreheads," I said. "I mean, you've always been a man magnet, mate, but this is ridiculous."

"Bullshit. It's because we look hot after a month in the sun living on rice and vegies."

"And whisky and vodka. And having the runs for two weeks," I added, laughing.

"Anyway, in case you hadn't noticed, they're all black guys and it's you they're after," said Mandy with a wicked grin.

"Makes a nice change," I said.

On the off-chance I'd find my dad's number listed in a phone book, I parted company with Mandy to go to the Westminster Reference Library. Even though I knew it was a long shot, I thought it best to leave no stone unturned. On the way to the library yet another black guy approached me and asked for my number. I apologised, saying I was just visiting but he insisted on getting my number. Without Mandy there for moral support I mumbled apologetically that I didn't have a pen or paper and was in a hurry to meet a friend before heading in the opposite direction from my destination. No sooner had I rounded the corner than he appeared again with his name and number written on a scrap of paper which he pressed into my hand and I could only laugh at his bold persistence and offer a maybe in reply to his insistence that I call him.

When I got to the library, as expected, I didn't find any listing for my dad in the phone directories so I went back to meet up with Mandy again. As we rode the tube to Tower Hill where we were staying nearby I recounted the tale of Conrad's dogged determination.

"Look at this," I said pulling multiple pieces of paper from my pockets. "We should make a collage from all the numbers."

"Yeah, a collage of sleaze," she said pulling more pieces of paper from her own pockets and giving me a mischievous look.

Mandy's observation had been right, all the men who'd approached me had been black men, but not all of them had been sleazy. Some had simply offered a friendly greeting as they went by and, perhaps naively, I enjoyed the acknowledgement of kinship, which gave me a sense of camaraderie I'd never really felt from my community.

On the third day of familiarising ourselves with London, Mandy and I ventured across London to Portobello Road. Once again we were enjoying the novelty of new places when we were stopped by a very tall and imposing black man who was riding a bike that looked way too small for his impressive stature. He was wearing dungarees that showed off his physique and had a head full of thick dreadlocks.

"Do you know where The Grove is?" he asked in a polished accent that sounded incongruous with his ragamuffin style.

"Do we look like we know where The Grove is?" I replied. "What is The Grove anyway?"

"The Grove café," he said, smiling, "and what is that accent anyway?"

"Australian," I replied defensively.

"Gidday," he said in a dreadful impression of an Australian accent, laughing as he pedalled away on the tiny bike.

"Another one," said Mandy, grinning at me.

"Yeah but he's gorgeous," I said widening my eyes back at her.

"Those dreadies are cute," she said. "He looks like a golliwog."

"You can't say that," I exclaimed.

"But golliwogs are cute," she objected.

"Mands, you really can't say that, or at least not out loud," I said though I knew Mandy didn't have a racist bone in her body and was innocently sincere in her fondness for the soft toy of our childhoods.

A while later, as we ambled along carefree, we came upon the same guy further down Portobello Road. He was staring down at his bike looking perplexed.

"Got a flat?" I asked as we came up behind him.

"I think it's broken," he replied.

"Well you're clearly too big for it," I said.

"It's my younger brother's, he'll be pissed," he replied with a nonchalant laugh. "Anyway, my friend is having a party tonight in South Ken, you girls should come. Here, take my number and call me later for details," he added, handing me yet another scrap of paper with his name and number on it.

"Bloody hell, he's arrogant," I said to Mandy once he'd wheeled the pushbike out of earshot. "Do you think he faked the broken bike as an excuse to talk to us again?"

"Yep," said Mandy, "but we might as well go to the party."

That afternoon, I called the number he'd given us and asked the woman who answered for 'Obard'.

"Who is it?" she replied impatiently in an accent I couldn't place.

"It's Aminah speaking," I said

"Ah-mi-nah? Who do you want to speak to?"

"Obard," I said again, wondering if he'd given me a dud number.

"Please wait," she said putting down the phone with a thud.

After what seemed like minutes a deep male voice spoke down the line. "Obard? Only an Aussie would call me Obard. It's Obaro."

"Oh Obaro, sorry, it looked like a 'd' not an 'o' the way you wrote it," I replied, laughing. "What sort of name is that anyway?"

"Nigerian," he said, as if I should have known, "and you're cheeky, Aminah. The party tonight is at D'Karma in South Kensington. I'll see you there around 9," he said in a bemused voice before hanging up.

When Mandy and I arrived at the door of D'Karma that night, another very good-looking black man was greeting guests at the door. He welcomed us and introduced himself as Shola. The bar we entered was full of mainly black people drinking cocktails and vodka from an ice statue on top of the bar.

A man standing by the barman introduced himself to me as Ade and when I told him my name was Aminah he said, "That's a Nigerian name, where are you from?"

"It's actually an Arabic name and we're from Australia. You're Nigerian, are you?"

"I am," he said proudly.

"What do you do, Ade?" I asked.

"I'm a prince," he said, with not a trace of irony on his face.

"Oh right," I said glancing over my shoulder to see if Mandy had heard what he'd said. "Will you excuse me a moment while I go to the bathroom?"

I grabbed Mandy by the arm and dragged her towards the toilets giggling and saying, "Did you hear that guy say he was a prince? And I'm the Queen of bloody Sheba."

Mandy laughed too but her expression turned serious as she said, "Let's just stick together and make sure we go home together, okay?" with a note of caution in her voice.

It turned out Ade was only the first of several Nigerian 'princes' Mandy and I met during that night of extravagant excess. We had a great time and Obaro was charming and elusive enough in equal measure to keep me in his thrall. However, when he invited me back to his place at the end of the evening I heeded Mandy's advice and refused.

Awakening with a thick head the next day we received an invitation from Obaro to go out to lunch with him and his friends. I was eager to find out more about them.

Over the coming days it became clear Obaro and his clique of Nigerian friends were supremely self-confident. In fact they had an air of entitlement and self-assurance that wouldn't have been out of place in royal circles. I found their confidence intriguing because it was so at odds with the angry black men – like my father – who Mum had described to me from her time in London in the sixties. The West Indian men she'd known had been bitter young malcontents aggressively indignant about the oppression of their people and intent, sometimes to the point of violence, on gaining equal rights.

Obaro and his circle of friends were neither angry nor downtrodden, they were proudly Nigerian, proudly African and proudly black with no need to justify their blackness. And though they sometimes appeared arrogant, as I got to know them better I realised they simply shared a strong sense of identity and national pride. Having been raised in a predominantly white society, where negative stereotypes of Indigenous Australians prevailed and where being black had resulted in me being ostracised as a child and often singled out as an adult, I found myself drawn to my new Nigerian friends' pride in their racial and cultural identity. The fact they were fun-loving, good-looking and generous made them even more appealing.

Nevertheless, Mandy's ongoing caution about the Nigerian men we were hanging out with proved to be justified because it became apparent they were intent on having their way with as many women as possible. I was less concerned by this and happy to spend time with Obaro and his posse because I had an agenda of my own.

London turned on the charm that summer with unusual hot days and long balmy nights. Mandy and I enjoyed a whirlwind introduction to its entertainments in a constant round of nightclubs and parties at the palatial London homes of our Nigerian friends.

Obaro and I were never officially an item – I realised there was no point falling for him given his voracious appetite for women and wandering eye. So I just had fun while it lasted before he returned to university in America at the end of the summer. When Obaro did eventually leave for the States, Shola and I became very close mates as he invited me into his life and introduced me to his family and wider circle of friends.

During this time Mandy and I found ourselves a tiny flat in Pimlico and were lucky enough to land great jobs – mine as a project manager at Steve Henry's advertising agency HHCL & Partners, which had developed a reputation as a 'creative hot shop', Mandy managing Elton John's financial affairs working at John Reid Enterprises. Each of us quickly broadened our own networks in our respective industries which were both renowned for their work hard and play even harder ethos and it wasn't long before we felt completely at home in our new London lives.

Eventually, after being distracted by a season of decadence and late nights, I settled into a daily work routine and finally managed to make contact with Horace. However, much to my dismay, he had no idea where Tony was and hadn't seen or heard from him in many years.

When I asked him if my dad might have gone back to Trinidad, he replied apologetically in his deep melodious Trinidadian accent. "No, no, I'd know if he was back home."

"Oh," I said deflated with disappointment.

"I'll ask around down the Grove," Horace said.

"Is that the café on Portobello Road?" I asked hopefully.

"No, Aminah, Ladbroke Grove," he said amused. "If anyone knows where Tony is I'll find out there. I'll call you, I'll call you," he promised before hanging up.

I felt crushed with disappointment, knowing it wasn't a good sign that Tony had faded so far from view. The incomplete and mismatching birth date on the death register came back into my mind, though I tried to push any dark thoughts away by telling myself it could be that Horace was out of touch with his old circles, having moved back to Trinidad himself.

10. In the Ghetto

As the Notting Hill Carnival approached at the end of August I felt really excited by the prospect of going again. When I'd gone to the Carnival with Mum as a teenager it had been my first real exposure to West Indian culture. It had remained vivid in my mind with its kaleidoscope of colours, the spectacular, larger-than-life costumes of 'masqueraders' dancing through the streets, the unforgettable sound of the steelpans and the delectable smells and tastes of jerk chicken, ackee and saltfish, curry goat and 'rice n peas'.

When Mum had spotted Horace at the Carnival eleven years earlier and asked him if he knew where Tony was he'd been evasive and non-committal. I knew the chance of finding my dad at the Carnival this time was remote, but not having heard back from Horace in the weeks since our first contact I had nothing to lose and I wanted to believe I would recognise my father if I spotted him, particularly if we looked as alike as I'd been told.

Falling in with the crowds alongside the trucks with their booming sound systems I soon realised that finding a familiar face amongst the masses would be almost futile let alone someone who had aged by 30 years from the photos I'd seen. Eventually I gave up looking for his face and lost myself in the atmosphere of the sights and sounds and smells of my father's homeland and listening to the deep thundering bass beats of the soundtracks of Black Britain.

As the weeks passed after Carnival without word from Horace I started to lose hope and wondered whether I'd ever hear from him again. He'd hinted that perhaps Tony didn't want to be found but, having come so far to fulfil a lifelong wish, I wasn't about to give up just yet. Eventually realising that Horace wouldn't know my new home or mobile numbers I called him, hoping he'd have some news.

When Horace's singsong voice came down the line sounding sombre and hesitant I braced myself for bad news. "Aminah. I've been trying to contact you," he said. "I'm sorry, but Tony passed away. A couple of years ago is all I know. I'm trying to find a cousin of his for you."

I tried to keep my voice from cracking, saying, "Oh right. I thought that might be the case. It makes sense, given it's been so long since we last heard from him."

"Aminah, I'm sorry. I know you wanted to find him," Horace replied, his voice thick with sympathy.

Hot tears escaped down my cheeks. "I did. But at least I know now. Thanks, Horace."

As soon as I hung up I rushed to the office bathroom before I was overcome and started sobbing in a cubicle. My dream of finding my father was finally shattered.

No sooner had I composed myself than my boss's concern when he noticed I'd been crying made me cry again. When I told him what had happened he said I should go home. After thanking him, I donned dark glasses and sat in lonely sorrow on the tube ride home.

Until that day I'd often looked at older black men just in case they could be my dad, but now I knew his face would never be among them. And though I'd known there was a chance he was the man in the death register with the incomplete birth date, I'd preferred to remain in denial because I so wanted to see my father in person. With the news he was dead came an aching sense of loss.

I tried to reason with myself that I couldn't miss something I'd never had. But while I'd never felt deprived of a father figure with Louda in my life, I'd still desperately wanted to get to know my dad, to tell him that although we'd been apart for so long he'd never been replaced in my heart and I'd always loved him in my own way. Despite never having known him, I'd missed the idea of him. Now that he was gone I feared I'd always be missing a part of myself.

I walked through the door at home, collapsed into an armchair and cried solidly for hours as I said goodbye to a lifetime of the hopes and dreams I'd attached to the day I would meet my father. When the phone rang I did my best to put on an unaffected voice as I answered.

"Aminah, are you okay?" came Horace's voice. "Don't be alone. Come over here to Zak's place."

I gathered myself enough to get to Camden Town without falling apart but my stomach flipped as I walked through the door of 95 Parkway. Upstairs the door to Zak's flat was open and as I peered in I was struck by how much the cluttered room, with its artefacts from around the world, reminded me of Mum's house.

"Come in, Aminah," said Horace, standing to welcome me. "This is Zak," he added.

Once I'd entered the flat, Horace embraced me warmly and then stood back and looked into my face. "You're very like Tony," he said, motioning for me to follow him up the stairs to the second floor.

"Yeah, I have been told I look like him before," I said as I climbed the stairs. "I'll never know now."

"This was your parents' place," Horace said, gesturing around the bedroom and bathroom that had formed their entire flat. He gestured for me to sit down and told me how he'd found out the news of Tony's death from mutual friends at the Carnival.

Then Horace began to reminisce about his and my dad's lives in the sixties. He recalled how, when they'd arrived in London from Trinidad, Horace had been an aspiring young filmmaker, and my father also had ambitions to work in film. Together they had gone to Rome in 1963 to work as extras on the set of *Cleopatra*, earning good money and enjoying an unfamiliarly rich lifestyle, though all their scenes in *Cleopatra* had ended up on the cutting room floor. He recounted what Mum had already told me about Dad playing Omar Sharif's bodyguard in *Lawrence of Arabia*. After getting this first big break, Horace told me how Tony returned to London full of hope he could make it in the movies.

However back in England it was a different story for immigrants from the Caribbean, with the white establishment making it clear that black people were neither wanted nor welcome – other than as servants. They found London's racism oppressive, and were infuriated when they saw signs on doors of public buildings saying 'No blacks allowed'. Both Horace and my father had encountered prejudice personally with doors slammed in their faces.

Horace told me how their mistreatment and marginalisation had resulted in West Indians banding together in enclaves like Brixton, Ladbroke Grove, and the Holloway Road, where Michael X had founded the 'Black House', to plot their ongoing revolt. They stuck together and held closely to their culture of music and creativity and chose to make their own way in the arts where their talents were better appreciated rather than be beholden to the 'white men' who continued to repress them.

Though I sobbed through much of Horace's storytelling, learning more about my father was fascinating and I felt a great pride in the way he and others had struggled against a bigoted society to build a life for themselves. The tales of racism did make me wonder why both my father and Horace had ended up with white women, though I was too shy to ask him.

A couple of hours later I had a much better insight into my dad from the perspective of another black man who'd had similar experiences and Horace felt like less of a stranger and more like an old friend.

"We're family, Aminah," Horace said as he led me back downstairs where we continued our conversation, with Zak interjecting to tell anecdotes from his childhood growing up in London and Trinidad.

It was two in the morning when I finally succumbed to exhaustion and Zak offered to drive me home.

"Aminah, Horace was right with what he said earlier," said Zak as he drove. "We are family now. You're welcome at my place anytime."

I hugged and thanked him when he delivered me to my door.

"Family," he repeated, hugging me back.

As Zak drove away I remembered Mum telling me how she'd babysat and made clothes for him while Mary was busy with the shop. Now he and Horace had welcomed me into their family and given me a new link to my West Indian heritage I'd thought would be lost now my father was gone.

The flat was in darkness when I entered, but the light on the answering machine was flashing. The messages were all from Mum and her voice sounded increasingly concerned with each message as she realised I still wasn't home in the wee hours.

I felt wide awake, my mind in overdrive despite feeling emotionally spent, so I rang to reassure her I was okay and that I'd been out visiting Horace and Zak. When I told her Zak lived in the two storeys above the shop at 95 Parkway and that Horace had shown me the floor where she and Dad had once lived, she fell silent before softly saying, "My goodness, Aminah, you realise you've gone full circle, don't you? That's also where you were conceived."

I burst into tears again at her words, which reminded me how the circle had closed.

As always, she reassured me with love and promised we'd talk again after I'd had some sleep. I so wished I could be with her as I hung up the phone. I'd never needed her arms around me more as I was once again overcome by a sorrow which had been echoed in my mother's voice. Although I'd never shared my fantasy father–daughter reunion scenario that I'd held so dear, Mum knew I'd always intended to find him and she was truly saddened I would never get to meet him.

I sobbed into my pillow until I eventually fell into a fitful sleep full of disturbing dreams, waking with a start several times with an alarming sensation that I was falling. When I finally awoke the next morning I was overcome by the need to call Mum again for comfort and counsel.

After talking for a while Mum suggested I go back to the Registry of Births, Deaths and Marriages to see if I could get Tony's death certificate. I took her advice and was disappointed to learn I'd have to wait five days to receive the full certificate of death.

For the first time in my life I dreamt about my dad, as grief infiltrated my sleep. Tony also started appearing in Mum's dreams, beckoning her ominously from the pulpit of a church.

I managed to keep my emotions in check at work but fell in a heap when I got home, overcome by grief and conflicting emotions.

Mandy and our flatmate Susie weren't sure how to help when they'd arrive home from work to find me crying inconsolably, because neither had seen me so emotional or down before.

"What can I do to help, darls?" Mandy asked one day. "I feel so useless seeing you upset all the time."

When I told her I could use a hug she put her arms around me stiffly and admitted she wasn't much of a hugger. I could feel that it didn't come naturally to her and I appreciated her effort. I'd previously assumed everybody grew up with parents like my mum who'd got me through the ups and downs of childhood with comforting hugs affirming that I was valuable regardless of how the bullies taunted me about being black.

From then on Mandy gave me daily hugs having seen the healing effect they had on me. She even learnt to relax a little into a warm embrace and would later laughingly tell others that I taught her how to hug.

As soon as the five-day wait was over I collected my father's death certificate from the Registry, though I resisted tearing it open until I was safely at home. It turned out he'd died from a pulmonary embolism just over a year before I'd arrived in London. After more than two decades apart I'd missed him by such a short time. Scanning the certificate for more information I saw that a woman called Petronella Pryce was listed as the 'informant of death' and a cousin of my dad. Her address indicated she lived in Ladbroke Grove and I wondered whether she was the person Horace had been trying to locate.

Thinking it was probably another long shot I called directory assistance and asked if they had a phone number for Petronella at the Ladbroke Grove address. Much to my surprise they did.

After ordering my thoughts for a while I dialled the number directory assistance had given me, expecting to hear a recorded voice telling me the number had been disconnected. Instead it rang and my heart started pounding with anticipation.

"Hello," a voice with the now familiar Trinidadian accent answered.

"Hello," I replied nervously. "Is this Petronella?"

"It is, who is this speaking?" she asked politely

"My name is Aminah Hart, I am…" I began.

"I know who you are," interrupted Petronella, sounding unsurprised. "We heard you were here looking for Tony but thought you'd gone back to Australia after you'd found out he died."

"Oh right. No, I'm still here. Would it be possible to meet you some time?" I asked.

"Of course, child," she said, "Come round with Ayesha. She knows where I live. Have you met her yet?"

"Who's Ayesha?" I asked recognising the name Ayesha as one of the three my father had suggested for me. Aminah, Ayesha and Leila he'd said to my mum.

"Ayesha? She's your sister," Petronella said.

"I don't have a sister," I replied. "I'm an only child."

"She's your sister alright. Your father had another daughter. And Ayesha has a son too."

"Does she know about me?" I asked feeling a mixture of shock and confusion that Dad had neglected to mention having another daughter.

"She knows," Petronella replied.

Eager to get off the phone and absorb this extraordinary new information, I gave Petronella my number and said Ayesha was welcome to call me.

After saying goodbye I hung up, bewildered, and immediately called my mum to tell her that apparently I had a sister named Ayesha.

Mum replied after a pause, saying she wasn't entirely surprised given how secretive Tony had been. When I told her I felt upset that he hadn't told us about his other daughter, Mum said, "Maybe he thought we'd never come back if he told me he'd had another child. Who's her mother?"

"I don't know, Mum, but I wonder if there are others?" I replied. "Maybe I've got a brother somewhere too. All this time I could have had an ally. Somebody else like me, a sister. But he never bothered to mention her."

"Darling, you still would have grown up in different countries, in different lives. The good thing about finding Petronella and learning you have a sister now is that you might be able to get another perspective about your dad than the one-sided view I'm able to give you. I'll dig out the letters he wrote to us and send you copies to give you a little more insight."

Mum always found the positives and she was right in highlighting the opportunity I had to find out more about my father, even if it didn't turn out to be what I wanted to hear.

Less than a week later I walked in the door of our flat to the phone ringing and when I answered it was my newly discovered sister on the other end of the line.

"Hi, Aminah, this is Ayesha speaking, your sister," came an East London accented voice.

"Hi, Ayesha. I always wanted a sister," I said and laughed nervously.

II. Sisterhood

Those first words I exchanged with a sister I'd never known were some of the most surreal moments of my life. I'd thought about what I would say to my father and how our reunion would play out countless times but I'd never imagined doing so with an unknown sibling.

Afterwards I reached out to Zak who'd become a close friend by then and whose counsel I'd sought after an incident with a Nigerian guy who'd become quite aggressive with me after I'd refused to go out with him. He ended up calling me a coconut and it was clear he meant it as an insult but I hadn't heard the phrase before and disarmed him when I laughed and replied that everybody loved coconuts.

When I'd recounted the story to Zak and asked for his opinion he'd suggested that the Nigerian man had probably been offended by my rebuttal and coconut was a derogatory term for a black person who is white on the inside and bereft of any black identity.

"Well, I suppose I am a coconut then," I said to Zak. "I can't really win, can I? In Australia I'm a 'bloody Abo' and here I'm a bloody coconut. Why does it even matter?"

"Don't worry," Zak had said, "I've put up with that sort of shit my whole life. You're a Trini, Aminah, and that's something to be proud of."

When I asked Zak for advice about how to approach a sister I'd never known about he suggested I embrace her as family in the same way the Ovés had with me.

A week later I was sitting on a bus thinking about the recent twists in my life that were leading me towards my first meeting with my sister. The fact that Dad had never told Mum or me that I had a sister had pushed him off his pedestal, leaving me with mixed emotions. Fairly or not I felt like he'd replaced me with another child, despite his letters to Mum, which I'd read by then, having articulated his love for us and conveyed his hope we'd be together again.

It felt like minutes passed while I stood at Ayesha's door working up the courage to knock. I'd never been the nervous type about meeting new people but I was daunted by the prospect of meeting my sister for the first time. I'd nagged Mum relentlessly for play-mates as a child and now I desperately wanted the woman behind the door to like me and to like her in return.

I wondered if I would have had a similar crisis of courage if I'd had the opportunity to stand at my father's door.

I finally sucked in a deep breath and tapped lightly on the door. As soon as Ayesha opened it, I recognised her as my sister because her pointed chin mirrored my own.

"I knew I was supposed to be tall," she exclaimed as she looked me up and down.

"Well, you seem to have stolen my chin," I replied, laughing.

After that we both looked to the little boy in Ayesha's arms and she said, "Kaynahn, say hello to your Aunty Aminah."

"Hello, little one," I said, thankful to have him as a focus for conversation and thinking he was the most gorgeous-looking child I'd ever seen.

"Please come in, would you like something to drink?" Ayesha asked politely.

"Thanks," I replied and then felt uncharacteristically uncertain of what to say next. "How old is Kaynahn?"

Ayesha picked up the thread, telling me how her beautiful son had recently turned one. She also told me about his Moroccan father, Najim, who also had a sister called Aminah, making me Kaynahn's second aunt of the same name.

"What are the chances?" I said. "In Australia I know of only one other girl called Amenah."

I went on to tell Ayesha how my heart had skipped a beat when Petronella had mentioned her name because it was one of the three our father had suggested to my mother as names for me. In turn, Ayesha told me she'd always known about me and how her mother, Diane, had recalled meeting me as a baby. Ayesha had thought she'd never meet me given Australia was so far away and so big, and the only clues she'd had were mine and my mother's first names. She hadn't known whether I'd kept our surname Hart or what Mum's surname was.

"I often asked Dad about you but he didn't ever tell me much," she said.

"Were you very close to him?" I asked.

Ayesha looked at me intently for a moment before saying, "Not exactly." There was a pause as she looked like she was trying to gauge what to tell me, then she added, "Aminah, I loved Dad but he wasn't always there for me. My feelings about him have been quite mixed up since he died. I still have nightmares about him sometimes."

As Ayesha spoke the likeness of her hands to mine and the way she used them to communicate really struck me. I'd always assumed I used my hands to express myself in the same way as my mother but now I wondered whether Ayesha's similar communication style had been pre-programmed in our DNA.

"Oh, I'm sorry to hear that," I said. "Mum never really told me huge amounts about Tony other than answering my questions. She certainly never said anything negative about him – I think because she wanted me to make up my own mind when I met him. So I guess I've idealised him a bit."

"I'm sorry you didn't get to meet him," Ayesha replied, "but to be honest, you might not have got the dad you were hoping for."

I heard a more brutal truth about my father that night than I'd been prepared for, but I found the way Ayesha was so willing to be honest with me disarming and endearing. We told each other the stories of our respective childhoods and I realised it hadn't only been the distance between us that had kept Tony from being my father in the true sense of the word. He often hadn't been a father to Ayesha in much but name despite them living in the same city.

I also got an insight into what my childhood might have resembled if Mum had chosen to stay in London and it was very different from my romanticised image.

Ayesha had grown up in a large and loving family that included her Trinidadian mother and four siblings. Though her older brother and sister and two younger sisters weren't Tony's children, his erratic behaviour had fractured their lives at times.

Ayesha wove tales of a father who was absent much of the time or caused trouble when he did make an appearance.

The more I heard the more grateful I felt that Mum had left England when she did and that Banchie and Louda had been so supportive of us, giving me so many opportunities in such a relatively comfortable upbringing. Regardless of any hard times I'd had at primary school it was far better than what the London alternative would have been as Mum and Dad had so little money.

By the evening's end I had warmed to Ayesha and appreciated her sincerity and candour with me because it made me more able to accept my father was gone while still holding onto the idealistic notion he'd been a less troubled person in his younger days when he and Mum had fallen in love.

I hugged Ayesha as we said our goodbyes that night and thanked her for her honesty and openness. She promised to arrange to introduce me to Petronella, Tony's only other relative in London, having assured me Tony had no other children she was aware of.

I left Ayesha's flat wishing I'd known of her existence earlier and thinking that, being so close in age with just under three years separating us, we could have given each other support through difficult times in our childhoods, even if just through letters. And I felt even more dumbfounded that our father could have omitted a development in his life as significant as another daughter from a letter he'd written to Mum just months after her birth.

A couple of weeks later, we visited Petronella, who was able to tell me about Tony's childhood in San Fernando. She also told me more about our grandmother Bernice, who had died many years before.

Petronella went on to describe Tony's funeral, before handing me a photo of him lying dead in his coffin. I reeled at the sight of a dead person that I'd never seen before, let alone taking in that the dead person was my father. Feeling overwhelmed by the image I felt the need to get away. As Ayesha and I stood to take our leave a short time later, Petronella handed me a plastic bag and said, "I cremated your father and took his ashes back to Trinidad but we never got a chance to scatter them so I've got them back again to give you."

"You mean this is our dad's ashes?" I asked in alarm as I looked into the bag to see a plain cardboard box.

"Yes, they're his ashes. They were lying in a cupboard in Trinidad so I thought you might as well have them."

A rush of tears threatened but I managed to hold them back before saying my thanks and begging my pardon to leave.

"Did that really just happen?" I asked Ayesha once we were outside in the cold November night air.

"Mmm, I didn't expect that," she replied.

"Do you want the ashes?" I asked Ayesha.

"No thanks, I deal with enough ghosts of him without having his ashes in my house as well."

Ayesha hugged me as we went our separate ways, telling me that the rest of her family were keen to meet me too.

I put the plastic bag at my feet in the car and then felt bad for doing so and placed it on my lap instead, wondering whether my life could possibly feel any more bizarre than it did at that moment.

As soon as I got home I rang Mum and described the evening to her. As usual she took the drama out of the situation with her soothing voice of reason, saying, "At least you found out some more information about Tony that I couldn't have told you. Petronella is another connection to your family and that's the main thing."

In the end I figured that having Dad's ashes back from Trinidad might give Ayesha and me the chance to scatter them together.

Knowing I would be away from my family for Christmas for the first time in my life, Ayesha welcomed me to spend Christmas Day with her family. I felt nervous about meeting the others knowing how they felt about the upheaval they felt Tony had caused in their family and their lives. But far from tarring me with the same brush as our father, Ayesha's family embraced me with incredible warmth, as Ayesha's sister and one of their own. The gathering of extended family who were all related and looked equal parts similar and differ-ent to each other, created a festive atmosphere unlike a Christmas I'd experienced before and I enjoyed a wonderful day of noisy good cheer and music and sumptuous tastes of the Caribbean. I learnt so much about being in a West Indian family that Christmas as Ayesha explained who 'belonged' to whom in the family and all of them made me feel a part of it.

Apart from Diane's five children, and four grandchildren, her sister Wally also had five children and four grandchildren. None of them were married and all of them were different shades of 'black' from the palest 'cafe latte' skin tones to the darkest of cocoa brown. I was at the paler end of the spectrum and more like some of the others there than I was my sister. The point was that their 'normal' was the same as I had grown up with as a mixed race child of an unwed mother who had sometimes been deemed abnormal and unacceptable by my childhood peers.

For her Christmas present I gave Ayesha a publicity shot of our dad from his film days when he'd been at his most handsome and least burdened. She was overwhelmed with emotion as she told me she didn't have any photos of Tony and she hugged me warmly in a bonding moment for us. I hadn't found my dad but I'd gained a sister who accepted me simply because we shared the same father. I'd also gained an entire West Indian family who made me one of their own because, as I'd discovered with both Ové's and Ayesha's family, that's the West Indian way and it made me proud of my West Indian heritage.

12. The Carnival

After the joy of spending Christmas with my West Indian extended family, I saw in the New Year with Obaro, who was back in town briefly for the holidays, Shola and their usual posse of Nigerian friends, Abi, Obi, Maje, Laolu, Kojo and Kunle.

On New Year's Day I found myself in reflective mode, contemplating everything that had happened to me since I'd arrived in London and realising that London almost felt like home now. My West Indian families in Camden and Hackney already felt like an integral part of my life and the Nigerians felt like old friends. Amongst all of these new people in my life being black wasn't an issue, it was just the way we were. I felt like I belonged as well as getting even more than I had hoped for in the way of cultural education.

And though my father's death had resulted in the greatest grief I'd ever experienced I was able to look at what had happened as a positive rather than a dead-end. Coming to London had been a journey of self-discovery and I'd gained a whole new outlook on the world, new extensions to my family and a growing sense of myself that no longer cared what colour I was. Through my West Indian and African friends I was learning a lot about identity and how it affected people differently depending on where they were from and the circumstances of their upbringing. I realised there was no single meaning to being black. Attitudes were as varied as people themselves and the shades of their skin. There were plenty of other people like me with skin that defined them but who identified themselves as resolutely British. I felt more comfortable in London than I ever had in Melbourne.

With the lease on our Pimlico flat due to expire in March, Mandy and I had a chat about what we'd do next. Mandy was keen to get moving again, complete our travels and return to Australia, but I was feeling settled and had new goals I wanted to achieve in London.

My job at HHCL & Partners had great potential for building my career in advertising and many of my work colleagues had become close friends, with the lines between work and play blurred due to the hours we worked, which naturally required collective decompression in Soho's pubs and late night bars.

I told Mandy I intended to stay in London and would never move back to Melbourne because I felt so much more accepted in London. I added extravagantly, and only half-jokingly, I'd never date another white guy.

My thirst for knowledge about black culture still wasn't quenched but it had become less about who I was and more about wanting a greater sense of my family history. Horace and Zak had captivated me with stories, films and photos from their lives in Trinidad so when Horace offered to step in for my dad and introduce me to his homeland I jumped at the chance. Horace invited me to stay with him and his wife Annabelle at their home in Port of Spain, so I booked a flight to get me there for the February Carnival.

When I stepped off the plane at Piarco Airport Horace was there to meet me. After a quick detour to eat some of Trinidad's spicier culinary delights he drove me back to his and Annabelle's house high up on the hill in Cascade with a view down to the 'Savannah' where droves of Trinidadians were jogging to get themselves fit for Carnival. Horace took me to the studio of the famous 'mas man', costume designer Peter Minshall, who was working on the epic costumes he'd designed for his 'Song of The Earth' band of 'masqueraders'. We stopped by the houses of Horace's nearest relatives to collect some other visitors from the UK and a journalist friend of Zak's from the States for the stunningly scenic mountain drive to the beautiful white sands of Maracas Beach. We indulged in Trinidad's famous Shark n Bake, washed down with Carib beer, and whiled away the afternoon sitting on the beach and swimming in the surf, reminding me of home. My Aussie experience in the surf came in handy when Bob, one of the other Brits Horace had introduced me to, got caught in a rip and I was able to keep him afloat until a lifeguard came to help.

Horace was sunbathing languidly on the beach when we returned and told him about our mishap. "That's why I don't go in the water," he said, chuckling.

Soon after, we gathered our belongings together to head back to Port of Spain. That night Horace took us to a bar and we ate delicious roti in the street before heading to a 'fete', the first of many parties we went to in the lead up to the Carnival parade.

The parade itself was an explosion of colour of feathered and sequinned costumes on an even grander scale than Notting Hill, some of them so big they needed wheels to carry them along with the bodies wearing them. Calypso and soca music and the sound of steelpans boomed out through the streets and it seemed the entire population of Trinidad had come out to party.

I followed Horace along in the throng and he stopped to introduce me to various people who'd known my dad, telling them I was Tony's daughter and it was my first visit to Trinidad. I had no way of knowing whether any of them knew about my father's death but each of them embraced me in a bear hug and welcomed me 'home'.

"It's amazing," I said to Horace, feeling quite emotional, "more amazing than anything I've experienced before in my life."

"This is your baptism, Aminah," he said.

★

After the Carnival, I left Horace and Annabelle's hospitality to follow the customary exodus to Tobago for recovery with the other visitors who had become friends and explored the smaller island that was more stereotypically idyllic, like postcards I'd seen of the Caribbean. I returned to London exhilarated by the rich assortment of my father's culture but was left wondering why he hadn't ever returned himself when his life in England had taken a turn for the worse.

13. Out of Africa

Having fallen in love with Trinidad, when I was invited to visit Lagos later in the year, the opportunity to experience the culture of some of my dearest friends first hand was irresistible. I assumed my long-distant ancestors had most likely come from West Africa as slaves so the idea of going right back to the probable origins of my roots appealed to my sense of discovery and desire to fill in the gaps of my history for myself.

I knew Nigeria was massively over-populated and that despite its oil riches the majority of the population was poor. But despite Trinidad being a poor country, the friendliness and joie-de-vivre of the Trinidadians had been exceptional so I was expecting a similar openness and warmth in Lagos.

On the plane journey I'd been asked by one man where I was from in Nigeria. "Are you Igbo?" he asked and thankfully I'd been educated enough by my friends to know he was referring to one of the three larger ethnic groups of Nigeria.

"No, I'm not," I said, not wanting to say any more in case he was and I might have offended him, and wishing the toilet would become vacant.

"What's your name?" he persisted.

"Aminah," I replied.

"Ah ah," he said in the questioning tone I'd become familiar with, "Ah-mi-nah? Are you sure you're not Igbo?"

"I'm sure, really?" I said, laughing at his disbelief.

"Ah-mi-nah what?"

I gestured to my friend Jason to save me but being an eternal shit stirrer he just watched on with glee.

"Aminah Hart," I replied, trying to hide my eagerness to escape.

"Ah! Ah-mi-nah Hart, you are from Rivers. I know of Aminah Hart from Rivers."

"No really, I'm actually not Nigerian," I said, shooting dagger looks at Jason.

"I'm from Australia."

"You are joking me now," he said, furrowing his brow in suspicion, "but you are black."

When he finally took his turn in the toilet I turned to Jason, asking with mock annoyance, "Why the hell didn't you save me?"

"Sorry, Ah-mi-nah Haat from Rivers," he said, laughing. "Just you wait until we get to Lagos!"

Nothing Jason said could have prepared me for arrival at Murtala Muhammed Airport. Peter, my Nigerian host, stayed close to me as an immigration official checked my passport before refusing to hand it back to me. He and Peter faced off for a moment before Peter discreetly unfurled a wad of Naira notes and handed a few over. The surly agent stared at him with disdain and nothing happened. Peter handed over a similar amount but this time when the official did nothing Peter threatened to make a scene and the man finally returned my passport.

We walked out into abject chaos in the baggage hall, with all manner of boxes, contraptions and luggage colliding and tumbling around the carousel and a sea of black faces jostling loudly for position amidst numerous official-looking men dressed in different military style uniforms and carrying firearms.

"What's with all the army guys with guns?" I asked Peter in alarm. "Or are they police? They're all wearing different uniforms."

"No, they're personal protection officers, not officials at all," he said.

"Bloody hell," I said. "Have I walked into a war zone?"

"Downtown Lagos can feel like one," he said looking at Jason and laughing.

My fortnight in Lagos was a very different experience to the two weeks I'd had in Trinidad. I couldn't really get a feel for the 'real' Nigeria because my friends were from such a privileged enclave. We were chauffeured from security patrolled luxury apartments and razor-wired compounds of opulence to boat clubs or restaurants, bars and clubs not so dissimilar to the ones we went to in London. When we weren't swimming or playing tennis behind barbed-wire fences we mainly stayed indoors in air-conditioned comfort. Other than one boat trip I didn't see much of Lagos at all, but the slums below the overpass as we drove back to the airport to fly home painted a grim picture of the vast discrepancy between my rich friends and the poor majority.

Though I'd enjoyed wonderful hospitality and had an amazing experience Lagos just wasn't what I'd envisaged of Africa and I returned to London with a much greater appreciation for Australia's wide-open spaces, freedom to roam and relative lack of poverty. But my affection for Nigerian people continued and a short time later Shola introduced me to another of his friends and I knew immediately he was special.

My attraction to Leye was instant. Apart from thinking him ridiculously handsome at first sight, everything about him appealed to me from the tenor of his voice and laugh that revealed a dazzling white smile, to his liquid dark brown eyes and expressive hands. From the moment Shola introduced us at the Atlantic Bar, Leye was an absolute gentleman, polite and utterly charming. Our first conversation showed him to be incredibly sure of himself but without conceit. I could tell immediately that he knew what he wanted from life and I liked his confidence.

Leye was living in the seaside town of Brighton at the time so I was disappointed that he didn't ask to see me again but he did give me his number and offer to show me around Brighton should I ever visit. He left a lasting impression that night but I didn't visit Brighton nor work up the courage to call him.

Almost a year had passed when we bumped into each other again at the Café de Paris where I'd gone with Shola and a group of friends after a birthday party at the King's Club. That night I got a sense from the vibe between me and Leye that neither of us wanted to let the other disappear again and we parted company with a definite plan to see each other again.

The day after our first official date he invited me on an outing with his young niece Adeola and seeing him behave so attentively and tenderly towards a child sealed my affection for him. From that weekend we were firmly together and I quickly saw that the qualities that had initially attracted me to Leye ran much deeper into a kind and thoughtful man who treated me inclusively and with consideration and respect.

Though we never stopped to discuss where we were going our relationship felt like it was on a serious footing from the get-go, perhaps because Leye was a serious guy who was building a serious career as a surgeon and had already charted his path in life hoping to become a pre-eminent urologist. We were quite different in that way because I'd never been much of a planner and my hedonistic lifestyle and penchant for all-nighters were both at odds with his need for early nights and to be on call to operate on people and save lives.

Our closeness to each other was intensified by disaster not long after we met. Leye arrived at my door and fell into my arms in anguish after receiving the devastating news that his older brother had been tragically murdered in a carjacking in Lagos.

I accompanied Leye to church that evening and despite being a non-believer I prayed with him for his brother and his mother, who had raised six sons and a daughter on her own after Leye's father had died when he was seven.

Later that evening back at my house I held Leye as he told me about his brother and recounted happy memories of growing up as the middle of seven children. As he confided in me and I offered him the little comfort I could, I knew I had fallen in love with him in a way I'd never felt before.

By this time I'd moved into a shared house in Baker Street with three bankers, one each from Norway, Argentina and Columbia via the USA. Mandy's lease had expired prior to going back to Australia for a holiday so I invited her to stay with me. It wasn't long before she'd fallen in love with my Norwegian flatmate, Axel. Their relationship soon turned serious, Axel subsequently proposed to her and they were due to marry in Australia early the following year.

When Leye finished his final exams he wanted to travel and I encouraged him to visit a fellow doctor friend in Australia, hoping he would like it enough to perhaps spend extended holidays there in the future with me so I could maintain my close relationship with my mum.

He arrived in Perth where he worked for a short time in a hospital and immediately loved the outdoor lifestyle and the climate. His trip coincided with Mandy's wedding so I flew out to Melbourne to attend her big day with Leye. We stayed with my mum, who thought Leye was much more down to earth than my previous boyfriends. She did question my suitability to be a doctor's partner, but I preferred to heed the approval of all of my friends who thought he was great and said we made a good pair.

Once we were all back in London Mandy and Axel moved into their first marital home and Leye took a house officer's job at a private hospital in Marylebone. I packed all of my belongings into storage and unofficially moved into the resident doctor's flat with him.

One of Leye's patients at the hospital was Omar Sharif and I pleaded with Leye to introduce us so I could ask him if he remembered my father from the set of *Lawrence of Arabia*. But Leye, being a consummate professional, refused to consider anything that went against the ethics of his profession. I felt more committed to Leye than I ever had to a boyfriend before and we were not to be swayed by our differing personalities and approaches to the future, so when Leye finished his term at the London Clinic we officially moved into a flat together in West Hampstead. I had no doubt we would always be together.

PART III

14. Home from Home

Life was always brimming in London, full of newness. New people, new clubs, new bars, new bands, new DJs, new restaurants, new airlines to fly to new destinations on the cheap. Life was so hectic at work and busy socially any momentary interval was quickly filled with something new to do. I'd been too busy living to pause for thought about the future and had barely noticed five years had passed by the time the turn of the century was suddenly upon me and a new millennium was about to begin.

The eve of a new century brought thoughts about the future to the fore for me and, having spent so many unplanned years in London, I started to wonder about whether I would always live there. I didn't miss Australia per se. During my trips there I hadn't felt any great sense of progress in racial diversity or integration in society as a whole. Then again, I'd spent only short bursts there so I knew it was possible I was a little out of touch. But I missed my mum terribly, and although our close relationship remained so from such distance the turn of the century seemed as good a time as any for a review of what I was doing with my life.

HHCL offered sabbaticals with the guarantee of a job on return so I decided to take six months off to spend some quality time in

Australia and reconnect in a meaningful way with the life I'd left behind as well as fulfilling some broader travel ambitions.

Leye couldn't join me in Australia because he'd travelled extensively the year before and was due to start his five-year urological rotation leading to becoming a consultant. So despite our love for each other we agreed to spend the millennium New Year apart and meet up in Asia during the second half of my trip. The thought of being away from him for so long made me realise how ingrained he was in my heart and shone a new light on the question of where home really was.

Leye was a man with a master plan. The loss of his father at such a young age had affected him deeply and so it was important to him to create a secure future for himself and the family he planned to have. He'd worked hard throughout his education to fulfil his lifelong goal of being a doctor, like the beloved father he'd lost. This had given him a very clear direction and pathway to achieve his ambitions. While he was a gregarious guy with many friends and we enjoyed a dynamic social life, he would never let frivolity distract him from his primary focus on his medical career and sometimes I could see that my propensity to prioritise good times frustrated him. It was daunting to my spontaneous self to be in love with a man who had already plotted his route on the map of life and placed such high value on maintaining tight control of its course. He had given me reason to look at a bigger picture so returning to my former life in Australia would be the ultimate test of my commitment.

Surprisingly I slipped effortlessly back into Melbourne life. The warm, fuzzy feeling of staying in the house where I'd spent my teenage years had the comfortable familiarity of sleeping on a favourite pillow.

I quickly recognised that both London and Melbourne felt like home. But Australia couldn't provide Leye with the international career he wanted, and continuing the legacy of his family name in medicine in Nigeria and maintaining a close connection to his own country were also important intentions for his future.

If our relationship was to be long term, London would be my permanent home and that wasn't accounting for the possibility Leye might some day want to go home too. To Lagos.

My fondness for Nigerians was at odds with my experience of Nigeria. The kind of crazy I'd seen in Lagos was not a lifestyle I coveted for myself or my loved ones. I'd never seen guns so commonly carried until I'd landed at Murtala Muhammed Airport for the first time. Coupled with the horrifying knowledge that Leye's older brother had been murdered in a carjacking in Lagos was enough to put me off living there.

Perhaps I was still a coconut after all. Despite having a greater appreciation of my blackness, I still felt like an Aussie at heart. The thought of living in a different country from my mum forever was painful and I felt torn.

In the search for my identity I'd attached myself to a personal fable of slaves sent from West Africa to the West Indies creating the lineage of my grandmother, but now, with a better sense of who I was, it felt okay to have my roots in Melbourne. Finally, at 30, a more self-assured black woman, I could define myself by the person rather than any need to justify the whys and wherefores of the colour of my skin.

I was grateful for the family I'd been given. No matter my blackness amongst their whiteness, they'd nourished my strong spirit and helped me thrive. I appreciated much more what a wonderful place Australia had been to grow up in bare feet and carefree. Mum had instilled in me a hardworking ethic, passion for the great outdoors and off-the-beaten-track sense of adventure. Also, I'd never experienced poverty, though there must have been times when Mum and I had very little. Mum always said she'd give me everything I needed but if there was anything more I wanted I had to go out and earn it for myself and since age 15 I'd done just that.

Nostalgia was pulling me back towards Australia but my heart told me to go back to London, back to Leye who loved me and felt like home for now. And I still preferred the feeling of being inconspicuous and ordinary – just another commuter on the train from somewhere else rather than the black girl who always stood out from the crowd in a city that still looked predominantly white to me. I also preferred the pace of London with its hustling bustle and language guessing game I played stuck between stations on the tube or gridlocked on a bus. By comparison the pace of Melbourne felt relatively staid. That said, I also recognised that despite London's vibrant cultural mix, racism, class divisions and injustice were alive and kicking.

My heart won out and after three months in Melbourne, I packed my suitcase and shipped it back to London, leaving just bare essentials to see me through South East Asia.

After a wonderful celebration to see in the millennial New Year on Sydney Harbour with friends, saying goodbye to Mum proved more emotional than ever before.

Mum in the swinging sixties

My dad in the movies

A Spanish sojourn

Daddy's number one

Just the two of us

Heading home via Rome

My Banchie and Louda

Life lessons

Cheers Davo

Soul sisters – Mandy and me

Surprise sisters – me with Ayesha and Kaynahn

Good fortune – with Jake in Thailand

Five fingers

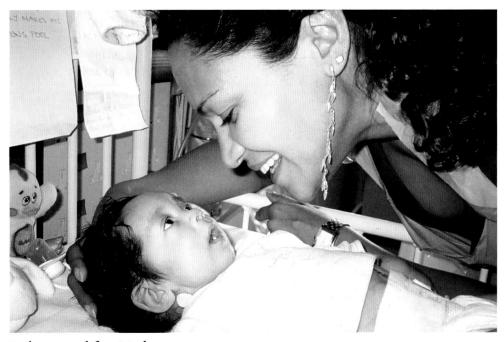

Light up my life – Marlon

Remembering Marlon

Strong sisters – Jules and me

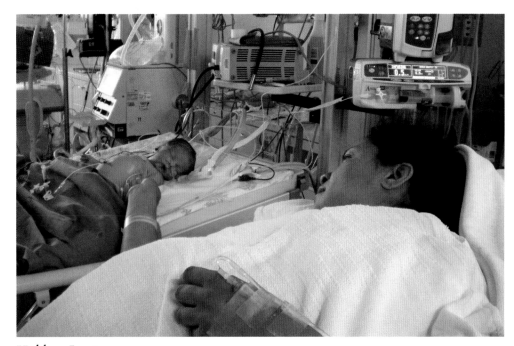

Hold on Louis

Mummy's boy – Louis

15. Adrift

My reunion with Leye was urgent and passionate as the missing of four months apart poured out into the tropical night. But, as the first day of our romantic rekindling dawned I sensed a subtle shift.

Something about my behaviour belied the happiness I felt at being back with Leye. I couldn't quite put my finger on a reason for the slight disconnect. He seemed different to the man I'd left in London but I wasn't certain what had changed, and I found myself veering between affection towards him and then wishing he'd never come.

One day Leye accused me of being too independent. "You always say 'I', Aminah, but never 'we'," he declared.

"Wouldn't it be presumptuous of me to speak for you or anyone else?" I protested.

"No, not when you're talking about us as a couple. Even then you only ever say 'I'. It's not something I'm used to and I don't like it, to be honest," he said.

He was right. I thought in the singular even when I had a boyfriend. So I took his comment on-board as one to work on if I was going to commit to him. The commitment game was all new territory to me so it stood to reason I'd be a work in progress.

We travelled overland towards the border of Malaysia, headed for the less frequented and commercial Perhentian Islands in the northeast. The hair-raising journey jarred our bodies in a mini-bus driven by a slightly manic Thai driver with a compulsive need for speed and I couldn't seem to get into a comfortable position or alleviate a growing pain in my left side as it careened and bounced along the pot-holed roads. I was very unwell by the time we got off and just as we boarded the ferry to leave the mainland I started having hot and cold flushes.

The next day I couldn't get out of bed to go scuba diving with Leye so he left me tucked up in our bungalow dosed up with Panadol but I slipped into delirium as the day progressed. Though I'd run out of water I didn't have the strength to get off the bed, never mind the clear instructions not to drink the tap water. At one point I'd banged my empty water bottle on the window ledge to attract attention and a Malay woman passing by came to my aid but as she neared and saw my fevered state she strode off in the opposite direction never to return, probably worried I was contagious with some dreaded infectious disease. By the time Leye returned that evening I was writhing with fever and excruciating pain. Alarmed at my condition, Leye wanted to get me to hospital immediately, worried I might have contracted dengue fever or worse.

Though it was going on dark with a storm brewing on the horizon Leye managed to convince a fisherman, either with bribery or charm, to brave the weather and take us back to the mainland in his tiny tinny. Leye then asked the bungalow staff to call ahead for an ambulance because I could barely walk and was wilting so quickly with dehydration he worried I might fall unconscious.

We set off with blackening clouds looming ominously overhead and I had to clutch at my side against the pain as the water got rougher. Then the heavens opened dousing the little boat, which pitched ever more precariously over angry waves. Between the sea spray, rain and sweat I was soaked, but I was too delirious to think about what would happen if the boat capsized. Despite being a strong swimmer I was so ill I would surely have drowned.

We finally made it to shore, where I was bundled into a rickety old ambulance van that carried us to a provincial little hospital in Kuala Besut. Once I was safely admitted with a drip in my arm Leye pounded the unfamiliar pavements in the dark to find somewhere to stay.

I was diagnosed with pyelonephritis, a severe kidney infection, and the next two days passed in a hallucinatory haze as the antibiotics failed to make me well. Between the old women threatening to cough up a lung and the mozzies flying freely through the louvred windows to feast at the entry point of my intravenous line, I feared I'd end up sicker than I started, or worse.

My stomach blew up like a balloon and I wasn't getting any better with the limited resources of the province so I asked Leye to call my travel insurance company for help. He managed to arrange a transfer to a clinic in Selangor where appropriate medicine set me on a fast track to recovery. But by the time I was discharged we'd lost a week of our holiday together and tensions had flared. I was angry our holiday had been ruined and Leye was an easy repository for my unspoken fear. He seemed angry, too, which was probably fair enough.

Things went from bad to worse and we slipped into a rift of silence in the cab to a hotel in Kuala Lumpur. As soon as we arrived, Leye dumped his bags in the room and left to go off on his own, barely saying a word to me or mentioning where he was going. Upset at being abandoned, I called reception and asked to be moved to another room, thinking we would both cool down by the morning and put an unfortunate experience behind us.

I was proven wrong when I went back to his room bright and early the next morning hoping for a fresh start only to find he'd checked out altogether and disappeared without saying goodbye or leaving an explanatory note. Bewildered, I found an internet connection and emailed him to ask where he'd disappeared to and whether he planned to return.

His response was thick with anger. He'd booked flights to Tioman Island to surprise me and make the best of our last weekend together and try to regroup but unable to find me when he returned the previous day he'd decided to go alone, unwilling to waste two airfares or indulge what he regarded as my spoilt behaviour.

Fair play, I thought, embarrassed by what I now saw as petulance on my part and I waited in KL for the weekend. Leye returned open to conversation but when we sat down to talk it became clear our relationship had hit the skids. Unable to delay his return to London for work, there wasn't time to resolve things further. A fumbled attempt in the airport only made things worse, bringing the romantic tropical reunion we'd envisioned to a decidedly icy end as we called time on the relationship right there in KL's airport.

I looked back over my shoulder as I walked away to continue my travels alone, unable to fathom that our relationship could be over for good, but Leye strode purposefully forward without so much as a glance back in my direction. There was little point standing there or spending more time in KL feeling miserably confused so I went to the sales desk of Malaysian Airlines and booked myself on the next flight to Langkawi Island to recuperate more from my illness and take stock.

I found a cheap little bungalow on the beach where I contemplated the implications of my failed reunion with a man I'd once assumed I'd be with permanently. My head reasoned that my feeling of vulnerability in the hospital had caused me to withdraw and my poor communication and a sense of helplessness had manifested itself in resentment. However, I also knew I'd been unfair to Leye and I remained perplexed about why I'd felt such a change in our relationship even before I got sick. It occurred to me I should have asked Leye what he might have been thinking about the difference in our dynamic. He'd always been very honest in our communication and would have given me a straight answer but maybe I'd been afraid of hearing his answer and now it felt too late.

I still needed time to think before I went back to London but I wanted to try and put things right with Leye before too much time passed so I sent him an email trying to convey my thoughts. His reply was distinctly detached and I considered getting on a plane to London to try and heal things but I was still incredibly confused and I knew Leye was a man of steely resolve. I also had the sense that, for now at least, he'd stubbornly dug his heels in. So I booked a flight to Manila and headed for the island paradise of Boracay wondering whether this said more about my level of commitment to Leye than my three-month visit to Melbourne.

The breathtaking beauty of the Philippines distracted me from my melancholy and a group of fellow travellers welcomed me into their multi-national posse. We gathered together for nightly congregations involving cold beers and street food. Every evening we watched the spectacular Boracay sunset sharing stories of our day's explorations. We'd then disperse to sleep or eat before reconvening in one of the nightclubs scattered along the shore, dancing under the moon until dawn. Thoughts of Leye and what I should do or say to him were pushed to the back of my mind and I was determined to have some fun before heading back to London and whatever lay ahead.

16. Crash Landing

Leye didn't want me back. I wasn't sure I wanted him either but I thought we'd done ourselves a disservice breaking up in such fraught circumstances, but Leye's mind was firmly made up.

Our breakup left me unsure about what to do next. My return to London felt more like a crash landing than a happy homecoming. I would have hightailed it back to Australia on the next available flight if I hadn't been committed to my job at HHCL. Thankfully they welcomed me back and it was a relief to be back with my familiar and friendly fellow 'HHCLers'.

As for somewhere to live I was back to square one. Luckily, my dear friend Alison was happy to put me up on a camp bed in the spare room of her Hampstead flat while I scoured north London looking at rooms for rent after work each night.

Post-holiday blues didn't quite cover how I felt starting from scratch again, and for the first time I questioned whether I'd made the right decision to come back to London, having drifted along on the flow of life without any definitive plans until my millennial decision. I'd been lucky to find family in Ayesha and my gorgeous nephew, Kaynahn, after I'd arrived in London and landing the job at HHCL had given me a ready-made life and friends, all of which had been the catalyst for sticking around.

I wasn't thrilled to be 31 and alone for the first time since I was 17, having pushed away the only man I'd ever envisaged as the father of my children. And over the last year or so I'd been hit with the realisation I really wanted a permanent relationship and family of my own. My newly single status without a partner to have children with or a home to raise them in made me feel lost and directionless. My unhappiness in London eroded a bit of its shine, the impersonal unruliness of the city sometimes felt harsh with my emotional defences down.

Ronnie, my workmate who I'd spent some time with in Thailand, had seen the beginnings of my relationship's demise and suggested gently that the uncertainty I'd felt at being reunited with Leye had been a sign.

"Maybe he's not the one for you, Means. I couldn't imagine you two being together forever," she observed sincerely.

"Really? What makes you say that?" I asked, intrigued.

"You're too different as people, I think you're too free spirited for him."

Ronnie's insight was spot on. Leye needed someone more grounded than I was, but I realised I'd buried any doubt under a veil of optimistic love for him and new investment in the future.

Now that Leye was gone and my options were open again, it was time for me to give more considered contemplation to whether I really wanted to raise a family in London when the time came.

Meanwhile I looked online at properties in Melbourne to see if I could afford to borrow the money for a house while I was still living and working in London. I resolved to rein in my excessive lifestyle and be more prudent in case it was my last year in London. Shortly after I moved in with a woman in Gospel Oak and put my head down.

★

With a goal set and a timeframe the weight lifted from my shoulders and I wondered ruefully whether I was finally growing up.

I quickly realised the woman I was sharing with in Gospel Oak was a little too quirky and neat for my liking and, around the same time, Ronnie was looking for a new flatmate so she invited me to live with her in Kilburn. Living and working together concerned me slightly but I decided to give it a go and my worries proved groundless because we got along famously. Ronnie was a caring, fun and easy-going flatmate who made me feel at home.

It wasn't quite as effortless keeping my promise to curb my spending and stash some cash for the future. I'd never been much of a homebody, preferring to keep a full social diary to exploit London's endless entertainments. I didn't intend to remain single for long if I could help it, so staying home on the couch wasn't terribly appealing although it would have been the more economical choice.

Ronnie and I often joined forces on Friday nights after work and if she wasn't available on Saturday night and I didn't have plans with other friends I usually went out by myself. I regularly ventured into the West End to a favourite haunt called Momo, which was an intimate, subterranean members' club tucked away under a Moroccan restaurant of the same name behind Regent Street. I could invariably find friends to party with amongst its loyal following. Nights always started out low key sipping Momo's signature vodka cocktails by the bar and chatting to people I might only ever see at the club. As the social lubrication worked its magic the DJ propelled everyone onto the dance floor with seductive Afro/French/Middle Eastern dance mixes and I'd keep moving until my high heels squashed my toes into sardines before falling into a black cab in the small hours. Sundays were invariably spent hungover, grazing my way through the day with friends who were also victims of Saturday night, watching a movie if the sun wasn't shining. Mostly always.

The single life was a pleasant surprise with a new breadth of people so much wider than when I'd been entrenched in someone else's social scene. There were attractive men aplenty but I didn't fancy starting anything new while I contemplated my future and remained uncertain of my next move. The thought of falling in love again scared me too so I just happily flirted without promise or obligation.

Ronnie was an agency producer I'd met while we were making a TV commercial for Guinness together which had taken us all over the country to audition everyday people to dance in the ad. A fellow Aussie of Peruvian extraction and another six-footer, she had the same love for drinking and dancing as me.

As a producer Ronnie was 'duty bound' to go to the Cannes advertising festival, one of the more frivolous perks of her job. She returned with stories of decadent indulgence and debauchery and a new fella in her sights.

"I met a nice guy over there, Means," she said. "I pashed him in the pool."

"That's great, Ronski," I said, laughing. I'd introduced her to Zak with whom she'd had a brief dalliance, and another guy, Michel, who'd become her boyfriend for a year or so but who didn't turn out to be 'the one' though she'd felt bad ending it, so it was great to see her putting herself out there again. Her grandmother in Peru kept asking when she would get married and have kids.

"I should introduce him to you though, Means," she laughed.

"Why do you say that?" I asked.

"Because he's black," she teased, knowing I hadn't been out with a white guy since I'd left Davo in Australia six years earlier, and I'd told both her and Mandy that I probably never would.

"Oh, very funny," I replied, laughing too.

They started dating after Cannes and when she introduced me to Jake I wasn't quite sure what to make of him. He didn't seem like any black man I'd met before, with none of the haughty self-assurance of a lot of the Nigerians I knew nor the proud proclamations of blackness of my West Indian friends. Jake fashioned himself as an enigmatic British fop in pinstriped suits and high-collared shirts accessorised with flat caps, duster coats, cravats and cigars which were offset by a dramatically expressive face and bushy eyebrows.

I was intrigued and irritated in equal measure by what I saw as Jake's slight air of affectation. But I soon learnt that Jake was an authentic, funny, kind and gentle soul, more sensitive than his image suggested.

It turned out Jake had been adopted in the seventies by a white couple, Pat and Derek, who'd also adopted a black baby girl a short time later. Pat was the daughter of Lord George Brown, deputy prime minister in the government of Harold Wilson, and Derek was a company managing director. Jake and his sister, Ria, had had a very middle class, white upbringing in north London. In many ways his life mirrored mine; his story certainly resonated with me and he was probably similarly struck by the parallels of our backgrounds. I wondered if he'd ever been called a coconut like me, but didn't dare to ask. Jake's father had died when Jake was seventeen, leaving him the man of the family, and his relationship with his mum was extremely close like mine with my mum.

Ronnie, Jake and I spent a lot of time together both out socially and at our flat with friends. The three of us got on brilliantly. Jake and Ria played in a band together and I met both Pat and Ria for the first time at one of their gigs. It was obvious to me that night that Jake was also especially close to Ria and both of the women in his family were exceptionally protective of him.

Initially Jake fitted comfortably into our household and it was friendly and relaxed until I noticed him watching me quizzically a couple of times with a look I found disconcerting because I couldn't work out what it meant and I wasn't game to ask. Gradually I noticed myself spending less time with them but I didn't give it much more thought other than to assume it was because Ronnie was less available to hang out with, until there was a discernible change in the vibe between the three of us. I decided there was something indefinable I didn't like about Jake and started actively trying to avoid them, which made it difficult for Ronnie, who found herself stuck between a boyfriend and flatmate who didn't get on. Jake's demeanour changed too and I got the impression he felt the same way about me but we tolerated each other for Ronnie's sake and continued to run into each other due to our mutual friends in the advertising business.

After six years with HHCL I decided to leave and take a short-term contract in another agency so I could escape the coming winter and go back to Australia for another extended stay. Around this time, unease spilled over into tension between Ronnie and me at home so it was a relief when the Christmas holidays arrived and I could get away to Australia. Though I'd once thought I'd stay in London forever, I intended to scope plans for a more permanent return to Melbourne. I resolved that if I decided to come back to London I'd find another place to live. I didn't want to jeopardise my friendship with Ronnie by living together uncomfortably and felt sure the friendship between us would return to normal as soon as I moved out.

I had a ball back in Melbourne and was gradually erring towards an eventual return but property prices had skyrocketed putting a nice house out of my reach so I decided to go back to London for a last hurrah. As soon as I got back I put out feelers for a new place to move into but in the meantime Ronnie and Jake's relationship faltered and I thought maybe I should stay put.

About a month later a small group of friends were celebrating Ronnie's birthday dancing the night away at Momo when I decided to call it a night. As I walked up the stairs out of the club I heard Jake's friend and business partner Jeff calling to me to stop.

"Aminah, wait," he said. "I need to talk to you, dude."

Slightly alarmed he might want to come home with me, I tried to beat a hasty retreat. I'd drunk one too many Momo specials and couldn't wait to fall into bed, so the last thing I needed was to be fending off unwanted advances or offending any more of Ronnie's friends. Yet another Aussie in London, Jeff favoured the same type of Savile Row suits and shirts as Jake, though with his skinny frame and bleached blonde hair that looked more suited to board shorts and a surfboard, he didn't quite carry off the look with the same urbane panache as Jake.

"Jeff, I'm tired, I just want to go home. Can it wait 'til tomorrow?" I said, edging away from him towards Regent Street.

"I just need to talk to you, dude. You know Jake. Well, you know. Don't you? You know."

"Jeff, spit it out. I'm tired and I'm going home," I said, turning to walk away.

"Jake loves you," Jeff blurted into the night.

"What the fuck?" I said, giving him a withering look. "I don't want to hear another word. This is not okay. Go back inside and we'll pretend you never said that."

"But, dude, I can't, he loves you. Like *really* loves you. He has for ages."

"What the fuck do you expect me to do with that information? Can you tell me that?" I snapped, thinking how puerile it was for him to be telling me this about his friend. "Does Jake even know you're telling me this? Actually, don't say any more. Tell Jake he better call me himself and explain what the hell I'm supposed to do now," I added before turning on my heel and storming off.

I shouldn't have shot the messenger, I thought wearily as I directed the cab towards Kilburn. I'd taken myself by surprise with the ferocity of my response and now I felt agitated and didn't want to go home and have to face my flatmate the next day. But it was too late to call Ayesha or Mandy to see if I could stay the night.

As the taxi drove on I couldn't make sense of the thoughts jumbling about chaotically in my Momo-special addled brain. I started to cry and by the time I got home I was so distressed that the cabby asked if I was okay before seeing me safely to the door. I called my girlfriend Rebecca in Sydney in a flood of tears and poured the sorry story out to her as an ex-Londoner and trusted friend who knew me well.

She reassured me it wasn't my fault and calmed me enough to take myself off to bed.

17. The Coconut Tree

I woke up the next morning with a thumping hangover and a mind awash with anxiety as my conversation with Jeff came crashing back. I closed my eyes, wishing I could go back in time, to before what Jeff had said.

I dragged myself into the shower, and as the cascade of hot water started to clear the fog from my brain, I finally conceded to myself why I had been so outraged the night before. Jeff's revelation had unveiled a secret of my own that I had been trying to bury in the hope it would go away. In truth I had retreated from Ronnie and Jake not because I didn't like Jake but because I liked him far more than I should. We had connected more deeply through our shared experience of growing up than I cared to admit and I was taken with the vulnerability I saw behind his dapper façade. And the enigmatic looks he had given me made me worry that he could see right through me and might even share the forbidden and unwanted feelings I was having. Having such thoughts made it easier to dislike Jake and avoid him than to face my true feelings. I'd known it but I couldn't acknowledge it even to myself until that moment in the shower. But even then acknowledgement didn't make it go away or tell me what I should do next.

I stood under the water for ages, stuck between the rock on one side of me and the hard place on the other. Getting out of the shower would mean having to figure a way out from between the two. I thought of fleeing to Melbourne and leaving the mess behind me for someone else to clean up.

I didn't want my friendship with Ronnie to be destroyed but I believed she'd inevitably think I was responsible for Jake's waning feeling towards her regardless of whether I felt the same about him.

On the one hand I felt I should tell her, but without any context for what Jeff had said or any confirmation directly from Jake it sounded ridiculously presumptuous to repeat it verbatim.

I also thought that if what Jeff had said was true, it should be Jake who told her, given the disclosure had come from his friend, whether he'd asked Jeff to speak to me or not.

The house was silent when I shut the faucet off and a wave of relief washed over me that Ronnie mustn't have come home. Maybe it would all be okay, maybe we could sweep the night before under the carpet. I threw on some clothes and slipped out the front door, walking the long way around to the station in case Ronnie was coming the other way. The motion of the escalators in the underground made me woozy and I felt nauseous but not as sick as when Jake called me and confirmed what Jeff had said.

"Jesus, Jake, I live with Ronnie. She's my good friend. What am I supposed to do now? You should never have told Jeff in the first place."

"Do you feel the same way?" Jake asked.

"How can you ask me that? How can I answer that?" I asked, incredulous.

"Well do you?" he persisted.

"Jesus, Jake, I don't even know what to say. What difference does it make? It's such a mess. We need to stay away from each other and hope it all goes away."

"That's a yes then," he said cheekily.

In the ensuing conversation Jake agreed we should avoid each other. Soon after, Jake ended it with Ronnie. I could see it on her face as soon as she walked through the door and her sadness made me want to reach out to hug her. She looked in pain and I couldn't bring myself to add to her anguish, but nor was I ready to sacrifice our friendship.

I kept my mouth shut and prayed, hoping maybe now she and Jake had broken up it would all just go away, and me and Ronnie could carry on as before.

It was farcical to think my truncated conversation with Jake would be the last time we spoke but thankfully he had to go away on a commercial shoot which helped with our promise to stay away from each other. For a brief time I convinced myself that the SMS messages Jake and I exchanged trying to unravel how we'd ended up in such a predicament and debating what to tell Ronnie were okay. But soon they reflected our growing feelings for each other and I felt conflicted about comforting Ronnie while communicating with Jake behind her back and knew it couldn't go on.

Jake and I felt we understood each other in a way nobody else could. It was as if Jake personified my inner self and I embodied his outer, and without even realising it we'd been falling for each other. Even if we managed to keep our distance the betrayal to Ronnie was in the feelings we'd hidden from both her and ourselves regardless of whether they were consummated.

Previously I'd always prided myself on honesty, believing the truth was better out than in, all cards on the table. But it was different this time with Ronnie and the tables had turned.

I wanted to help Ronnie through a tough time but I knew I wasn't being a true friend if I didn't tell her the truth, so whichever way I cut the cake our friendship looked doomed.

Meanwhile Jake and I had agreed by SMS that it would be better to speak in person to nut out a strategy that would keep Ronnie from further hurt. I thought maybe I could go back to Australia for a while and see if we still felt the same way in twelve months' time.

"We can't meet up in Soho," I told him. "There's too many advertising people with gossiping mouths who know us there."

"Yeah I know, what about if you come over to my place?"

"That's a terrible idea," I said, laughing. "What if Ronnie rocked up while I was there? We can't meet locally; if you try to be discreet in a city of eight million people you can be sure to bump into everybody you know."

"Yeah," Jake agreed, "it's impossible to get lost in London."

"I have to go to a wedding in Dijon," I said. "Why don't you come? Nobody will know us. I met the bride and groom in the Philippines when I was travelling. It would give us clear space to sort this out."

"I'm not sure it's a good idea," he said. "I don't think that fits with the agreement to stay away from each other."

"You're right," I replied. "We should just stop communicating altogether for a year and get on with our lives. We can see where everybody stands in twelve months and if we still feel the same we can make a plan then. Or maybe you'll meet someone else and I'll live happily ever after in Australia."

"I'd come and get you," Jake said teasingly.

"You're not helping," I said.

"I know, sorry, you're right, it's the only way," Jake replied.

Meanwhile back on the home front things took an ironic turn. In spite of Ronnie's melancholy she was managing to stay social and happened upon another black guy called Joseph. This time she insisted on introducing us, saying I'd been single long enough and suggesting a blind date. Given her selflessness, the secret I was keeping, and my agreement with Jake, I didn't really think I was in a position to say no when she asked if she could give him my number.

So next thing I knew I was fielding messages from Joseph trying to arrange a date. Then Jake called the following week, breaking the no contact rule to say he was coming to France.

★

On the way to Dijon, Jake and I avoided any heavy conversation. It would be nice to just relax and spend time together without fear of causing a scandal, but the feelings between us were palpable.

We arrived in France late Friday to find the bride and groom had arranged a pre-wedding dinner at a pizza restaurant. Jake was a very late addition and it was a good opportunity for them to meet each other before the wedding as well their other friends, some of whom we'd unwittingly shared our flight from London with.

The evening of the pizza dinner was balmy and the company was upbeat, with everyone in a celebratory mood. Wine flowed freely in the vine-canopied courtyard with much laughter and multi-lingual banter in what was an undeniably romantic setting. The new friends we made assumed Jake and I were a couple and we didn't bother to correct them, because we felt so at ease being in each other's company notwithstanding forbidden fruit.

But nothing could have prepared me for the moment when Jake broke all the rules again.

"It would be nice to just stay here," he said. "I've always wanted to live in France."

"Ha ha, yeah, wouldn't it just. We could just leave all our worries behind, but it's wishful thinking," I sighed. "We can't just run away."

"Let's worry about that on Sunday," said Jake, then paused and added, "So will you?"

"So will I what?" I said getting the giggles.

Jake held my gaze.

"So will you marry me?" he said.

"You're not serious?" I said.

"Well will you?" he asked again.

I paused to catch my breath. "Yes, of course I will," I said laughing out loud before planting a kiss on his lips. "Ask me again in the morning when you've had less rosé to drink," and with that we refilled our glasses and clinked them together.

I opened my eyes the next morning to find Jake staring at me intently, a look I recognised as the same one I'd failed to define months earlier.

"What?" I asked in mock panic.

"You said yes," he said.

"Well you asked!" I replied blearily.

"So will you?" he repeated.

"I will, Jake," I said, and it felt like the most natural thing in the world. "That is if you're really serious."

"I've never been more serious about anything in my life," he replied. "I want to be with you forever, I want you to be my wife."

"This is completely crazy," I said. "Now we really have a problem."

Suddenly a life exiled in France seemed far preferable to going back to London and explaining ourselves to Ronnie.

"I have to be the one to tell Ronnie we're going to be together, given you've broken up and I'm still her flatmate," I said when we got back to London

"Okay," Jake agreed, "do you want me to come with you?"

"No, it would be far too cruel to have us there together, it's going to be bad enough as it is."

I couldn't look Ronnie in the eye when I returned to our flat.

"How was France, Means? How was the wedding?" she asked as soon as I walked in the door, proffering me a hug. "Welcome back."

"It was lovely, thanks," I said, slipping from her grasp.

She sensed immediately that something wasn't right. "Are you okay, Means?" she asked with genuine concern as I averted my gaze.

"I'm fine, just exhausted," I said, then excused myself and scampered into my room.

I knew I had to tell her but I couldn't bring myself to do it, making excuses to myself about not wanting to tell her in the flat where we'd shared so many good times. But it was simply cowardice because I couldn't face the fact of what had transpired between Jake and me and when it came to the crunch I was chickening out.

Later in her typically selfless style, worried that something might be wrong with me, Ronnie knocked on my door and asked if I was okay. I pretended to be asleep and stayed hidden in my bedroom. I cowered there the next morning too so I couldn't be cornered into a conversation, but anxiety curdled inside me to the point that when she called me later to ask what was up I burst into tears on the phone.

"I have to tell you in person," I said.

"Means, what is it? Tell me. Are you okay?" she asked, her voice full of concern.

"I'm fine Ronnie. But, something has happened, I mean I've done something. I can't tell you over the phone, I have to tell you face to face. Can I meet you somewhere?"

"Sure. Let's meet at the pub across the road from my agency in Kingly Street," she suggested.

"Okay," I said despondently, unable to think of anywhere more private but knowing I couldn't put it off any longer. I hurried as fast as my legs would carry me off the tube into Soho to try to calm my anxious breath.

When I found Ronnie in the pub she had the same look of concern on her face, and I drew my breath in and held it. We hugged and I perched on the stool directly facing her as my stomach flip-flopped and my legs shook beneath me like jelly. I'd never had to look someone I cared about in the eye and tell them I'd let the side down, and it went against everything I held dear.

In the previous few years I'd finally reached a level of comfort with myself that stopped me wishing I was someone else and I'd proudly told anyone who asked that my name meant 'the faithful' or 'truthful' in Arabic. I prided myself on upholding its meaning. My mum had often said that friends are the family you choose and nearly all her female friendships had been lifelong, while men had come and gone. Yet there I was choosing my love for Jake over my friendship with Ronnie, who'd shown me nothing but loyalty and kindness.

"Ronnie, I don't even know where to start," I said, my lip trembling as I forced tears back. "I'm so sorry," I said starting to cry when I couldn't get words to come out.

"Means, it's okay," she said trying to comfort me.

"No it's not, it's not okay," I said, looking her in the eye. "Jake came to France," I sputtered.

"What?" said Ronnie, as if she must have misheard.

"Jake came to France with me. And we're together. We, well we want to be together," the words finally tumbled out untidily.

Ronnie took a moment to register what I'd said before her face fell open in disbelief and heartbreak crept across it. The way she looked at me cut to the quick though I felt it was no less than I deserved. But instead of crying or even asking the questions I'd been dreading, she stood up from her stool and embraced me.

"I'm so sorry, Ronnie," I cried. "We never meant to hurt you."

"I can't even understand 'we' to mean you and Jake," she said incredulously. "I'm sorry too, Means, I really am," she added and with that she walked away before I could finish telling her Jake and I were engaged.

As I watched her holding her body up proudly straight as she walked across the room and down the stairs I knew she'd never speak to me again.

I sat there in the pub for a while, gazing across at her office building, almost hoping she'd come back to continue the conversation. But it was finished as far as she was concerned and I wished I'd gotten the whole story out because now she'd hear Jake and I were getting married through the advertising grapevine and assume others had known before her.

I stuffed all of my belongings into a hire car that afternoon and moved in with Jonathan, a dear friend who'd offered me a haven for as long as I might need it. Jake lived in a one-room studio flat and we hadn't yet contemplated moving in together.

That night I called my mum and told her that I was getting married. She was taken aback at the haste of this development in my life especially as I hadn't told her that Jake was going to France with me. She sounded a little rueful when she said I would probably never move back home now but otherwise she was happy for me and gave her unconditional support as she always had.

By the next day the scandal had broken and it sizzled through the advertising scene for a little while and I lost the respect of some colleagues but my closest friends knew the whole story and how much I'd tried to avert disaster. They also saw that Jake and I were totally in love and committed to spending our lives together and they were happy for us.

After an annual pilgrimage to Ibiza with Jonathan and our usual party posse I bid a final farewell to my single life and moved in with Jake. We'd purchased a New York style loft apartment off the plan in the redeveloped Hartley's Jam Factory in London Bridge and we decided to hunker down together in his minute flat for the twelve months it would take to be ready to move into.

Our life together was blissfully happy. I took some time out of advertising to do a floristry course and accompanied Jake on commercial shoots abroad so that we could be together as much as possible. His family welcomed me into the fold and expressed their delight at seeing Jake so happy. We spent a lot of time social-ising with Ria and her partner Sam and I soon understood why Jake's close-knit family were so important to him as I quickly grew close to Ria myself and developed a good rapport with his mum.

My family embraced Jake with similar enthusiasm. Kaynahn in particular developed a special bond with 'Uncle Jake'. He'd often come over for a sleepover with us, getting to stay up late with Jake playing computer games before falling asleep on the couch. And Jake loved having a nephew.

Those months we were squeezed into the Devonshire Place bedsit were cosy and filled with love, conviction and optimism. We both felt like we'd found our perfect mate as we excitedly planned our wedding and our future, including possible names for the children we planned to have.

On Christmas Eve the following year Jake and I married in the Marylebone Registry Office with Jeff and Mandy by our sides and in front of our families, including my mum, who flew over from Melbourne, as well as friends from the northern hemisphere with a smattering of expat Aussies. We had a champagne breakfast to toast our union and then spent the afternoon with our guests in a Marylebone pub before everyone went off to their families to celebrate the Christmas holidays.

Waking up cosily on our first day of married life and the knowledge we'd be celebrating Christmas with our families together, life felt close to perfect, apart from the cold. Everybody we loved was around the same table for Christmas lunch and for the first time we got to spend Christmas with both of our mums. It could have been awkward to introduce Jake to my mum for the first time just days before we were to marry but his family had welcomed her to stay with them in Finchley and everyone seemed to get on very well. Mum admitted to feeling sad that I was unlikely to return to Australia to live but she was pleased to see I'd joined a loving family and Pat promised her that she would take good care of me.

It felt wonderful to be married, better than I'd imagined, having never dreamt of a fairytale wedding or being a princess bride in my younger days. Jake and I felt united in an idyllic bubble when we flew out to the warmth and sunshine of Australian shores on Boxing Day to continue our marriage celebrations with my Aussie contingent of friends, and three weeks later we topped off our wedding with a Buddhist blessing and a honeymoon on a tropical island. I felt happier than ever before in a relationship and I finally allowed myself to relax into the idea of a permanent commitment.

When the festivities were over and it was just the two of us gazing out optimistically over the Gulf of Siam, we contentedly looked forward to multiplying the coconuts on our freshly planted tree.

18. Marlon

Our tropical honeymoon thudded to an icy, early morning end as the plane landed at Heathrow on Australia Day no less. We should have been throwing another shrimp on the barbie rather than donning another layer of woolly clothes and I pondered why on earth we were back in London in January's biting chill.

"It's bloody freezing!" I muttered as I snuggled myself into the crook of my new husband's elbow weighted with the expectation that his warmth would protect me from London's drab, damp dreariness for the rest of my days. Jake concurred. He hated the cold and loved the summer as much as me, though he didn't rate Australia quite so highly because he thought it lacked culture and charm. I'd secretly hoped he'd put the feelers out for a TV commercial to direct in Australia to extend our time there but no such luck.

"So, what are we doing here again?" I asked as the bitter air assaulted my nostrils. Even the baggage carousel seemed sluggish.

Back home at the Jam Factory we battened down the hatches against the cold and sank into cosy nights accompanied by macaroni cheese and bottles of Macon Villages playing games of chess. But barely a week had passed before our thoughts turned to another holiday away from the Arctic chill in London.

Cuba rated highly for both of us and we hoped to get there before Castro died. Idyllic images of pristine Caribbean waters, brown bodies swaying to Cuban rhythms, rum punch and Havana cigars beckoned enticingly. We booked our flights and Jake gave me his dog-eared copy of Hemingway's *The Old Man and the Sea* to read before we left. With plans for holidays in place I settled more contentedly into the permanence of London life as the wife of a dyed-in-the-wool Londoner.

Cuba was all we'd hoped for, and more – the Cubans we met and their resilient joie-de-vivre was impressive given their closed borders and nominal fixed incomes, and everywhere we went we were welcomed with warm hospitality and curious charm. But we were unprepared for just how poor the Cuban people were and how little they were forced to live on in the charmingly decayed grandeur of Havana as well as the archaic towns that looked all but forgotten. Our tour guide took us to a carnival in her hometown of Hibara where the rickety old Ferris wheel was a relic from a bygone era that looked unsafe to ride.

It was Jake's first trip to the Caribbean and we agreed to return for further exploration of the West Indies when the holiday reached its end. Our Cuban trip was closely followed by a 'working holiday' on the French Riviera, punctuated by a brief stopover back in London. As a director, for Jake the Cannes Lions advertising festival was a highlight of the year, an excuse to glam it up and make like Hollywood types in the south of France.

No sooner had we cleared the Cannes hangover and refilled our depleted coffers than some friends of mine invited us to go sailing in Turkey, an offer too good to refuse. I'd met The Captain (aka Mark Piper) while we were working together at HHCL and since then we'd become firm friends with him and his wife, Kate. Now the four of us flew to Bodrum to set sail into the stunning Aegean with The Captain at the helm.

Eventually our extended honeymoon came to an end and, after booking tickets for our annual Boxing Day flight to Australia, we got back to work in London. With my penchant for holidays and Jake's buy-now-pay-later-with-interest approach to Savile Row shopping, we didn't make the ideal advertisement for fiscal planning and management but we committed to a combined effort to knuckle down and save our pennies until Christmas.

By then I'd left 'adland' and was working with Kate as a marketing project manager at Gala Casinos based in Nottingham, which meant waking with the birds and a two-hour commute every Monday morning. The only compensation was the outlook as the train rattled through the contrasting green space of the home counties, where my thoughts turned to the bigger picture and what life might have in store next.

Having ditched contraception after our honeymoon, and with September already upon us, I wondered whether I should reasonably expect to be pregnant, but we'd been so busy flitting about unencumbered that I hadn't given it much thought. We both wanted a family but planning per se hadn't featured in our profligate summer and neither had our lifestyle been conducive to pregnancy. It was time to clean up my act if we wanted to hear the pitter-patter of tiny feet, and no sooner had I insisted we stop smoking and drinking and replace all-nighters with a return to nights in than I felt a new and unfamiliar stirring in my groin as I lay in my Nottingham bed hundreds of miles away from my husband.

Back in London, a positive pregnancy test confirmed my suspicions with a due date on the fourth of July the following year.

By Christmas we heightened everyone's festive spirits with our happy news. And I was looking forward to sharing it with my friends in Australia.

We touched down in Melbourne on Boxing Day and discovered that while we'd flown across South East Asia an unrivalled human catastrophe had occurred. Almost a quarter of a million people had been killed across fourteen countries by tsunami waves that had swept across the Indian Ocean, obliterating most everything and everyone in their path of destruction. In that horrific context it was difficult not to feel selfish revelling in our own oblivious happiness and excited anticipation at becoming new parents, but our Australian family and friends shared in our joy and celebration.

Sitting on the balcony of a restaurant in beautiful Byron Bay, we agreed that as long as our child was healthy we'd be happy with either a boy or a girl. And after much debate and laughter at each other's outlandish suggestions for names, we settled on Marlon (as in Brando, not Marlin as in fish) for a boy and Remy for a girl.

Our return to London coincided with the critical 12-week scan which showed our baby safely nestled in and flourishing as it should. A single appointment with an obstetrician declared both mother and baby fit and healthy enough to be assigned to the care of a midwife despite me being of 'advanced maternal age' at 35. My sister-in-law, Ria, had been lucky enough to have a textbook natural delivery the previous April, giving birth to their first child Isaac without drugs or intervention. We shared Ria's touchy-feely, all-natural-birthing philosophy and made plans for an airy-fairy, relaxed and meditative, essential-oil-scented, water birth for our own special delivery.

With relief at passing the 12-week mark I continued my commuter life between London and Nottingham with the train journey providing time for contented contemplation about our new addition and imagining our life as a family of three. I passed the hours rubbing my belly and talking to the little person growing inside.

Though Jake and I agreed we didn't want to know the baby's gender before the birth, we relished the chance to see our baby on screen again at the 20-week scan. I happily settled back onto the bed for the ultrasound, eager to watch our baby come into view, when the sonographer said the baby must be asleep deep down in my abdomen. He prodded a little and probed some more, trying to wake the baby up but it appeared to covet its sleep so the sonographer dispatched us to walk around and try to wake our bub up.

Twenty minutes later we returned and the scan went ahead with all going well until the sonographer said, "The baby has slightly dilated kidneys."

"What does that mean?" we asked in unison, caught off guard by the sudden ambiguity in the sonographer's voice.

"Everything else seems okay so it might not mean anything. It could resolve itself," he replied, vaguely enough to reassure us that it wasn't serious. "You'll be sent an appointment for a repeat scan to check how the kidneys are going and they'll be monitored regularly through the rest of your pregnancy."

Jake and I gathered ourselves together in slight confusion at what we'd heard, distracted enough to barely notice his parting remark: "Good luck, I hope everything works out."

"Do you think dilated kidneys are anything to worry about?" I asked Jake, wanting him to reassure me as we walked out of the hospital, though he was as new to pregnancy as me.

"I don't know," he replied looking at me blankly. We grasped each other's hands falling into uncertain silence and caught the bus back home.

"We'll ask the midwife tomorrow," I said suddenly desperate for my first midwife appointment the following day, knowing a sleepless night stood between now and then.

When the midwife, Victoria Craig, arrived at our front door bright and breezy the next day, I greeted her feeling slightly ragged from the predicted lack of sleep. With her ready smile and cheerful manner she put me at ease immediately, striking me as having just the sort of calming presence a good midwife would need with women at their most vulnerable and exposed. I felt I already knew her by the time she asked me to lie back on the couch and lift my top to prod and poke around my already significant bump. Scanning for the heartbeat with her Doppler, she reassured us that she would be there with us every step of the way, including on or around the fourth of July, to help bring our baby safely into the world.

"All is well," she said wiping my belly clean and helping me up.

After sitting up I told her about the previous days' scan, including having to walk around to try and wake the baby up and the sonographer's comment that the baby's kidneys were dilated. "What does that all mean?" I asked her anxiously. "Should we be worried?"

"It can mean a lot of things, it's a non-specific finding," Victoria replied seeming unfazed. "But you shouldn't worry because dilated kidneys often resolve themselves by the time the baby is born. And babies spend most of their time asleep in the womb at this stage," she added, smiling as if to emphasise her point.

Somehow I trusted Victoria implicitly and her response meant I relaxed a little, either because she'd said what I wanted to hear or because I'd never been a natural worrier. After she left Jake and I quickly reverted to the blissful obliviousness of expectant parents who'd passed the halfway mark.

The follow-up ultrasound found the baby's kidneys unchanged, neither better nor worse and therefore still not a cause for concern, apparently. Monthly scans were scheduled to keep an eye on things.

Meanwhile my stomach grew exponentially with regular enquiries about whether we were having twins. Walking became a chore as I lumbered around with my enormous bump and I was wondering how much longer I could continue commuting between London and Nottingham. A scan at 29 weeks showed excess amniotic fluid – or polyhydramnios – explaining my gargantuan size with still 11 weeks to go and we were told that the baby's dilated kidneys might be the cause. Gestational diabetes was another possible cause so Victoria took a blood test to investigate. Regardless of the reason, it seemed to me that I had nowhere else to grow.

I was right.

Three weeks later I became short of breath with a belly so stretched that its surface shone tautly like a balloon. Jake took a video of me rubbing the caricature mound to send to Mum and though I struggled to catch my breath I remained jovial and upbeat while I explained the possible reasons we'd been given for my enormous girth to her, saying our medical supervisors had told us there was no cause for alarm.

With two parents of significant size it made sense to me that our baby would be a big bouncer and my biggest worry was how I'd push out such a big baby despite having child bearing hips that Mum had always joked I'd inherited from her side of the family. At our first birthing class we'd seen a demonstration of the contortions my pelvis would have to perform to birth our baby, sending a wave of doubt through my hippy-happy-clappy notions of a drug-free water birth.

The day after talking to Mum we went to the assessment centre for monitoring of the baby's heart, and as I lay on my back pain began permeating my abdomen making it impossible to lie still. Possibly Braxton Hicks contractions? I thought, alarmed by how much they hurt and making a mental note to accept whatever drugs I was offered when the time for real labour came. Though I'd been looking forward to checking out the hippy-happy-clappy, double bedded, bathing pool equipped, essential oil scented birthing suite at St Thomas's, there was no point in trying to be a hero if the pain I was in with Braxton Hicks was a sign of things to come.

We were released with a clean bill of health for the baby and told to go home, where I continued trying to work. However, I struggled to concentrate or sit still, pacing around the room and trying all manner of bends and postures to escape the pain of the cramps I was having. But by nightfall I was barely able to get up from all fours.

Unable to concentrate on anything or find a comfortable position to sit in, I decided to take myself off to bed, saying to Jake as I manoeuvred myself awkwardly downstairs to the bathroom, "I can't possibly go on like this for another seven weeks." My bathroom ablutions were rudely interrupted by an unmistakable sign that our baby had no intention of waiting until the fourth of July and finally the penny dropped.

"Oh my god, Jake, I've had a show," I shouted urgently up the stairs.

"What's that?" he asked, hurrying down the stairs.

"It means I haven't been having Braxton Hicks all day, I've been having bloody contractions. Real push-the-baby-out contractions. No wonder they hurt so much."

"What should we do?" Jake asked nervously.

"I don't know, call the hospital and ask them," I replied anxiously.

Ten minutes later we were in a cab to St Thomas's and once we were there I clung by a fine thread to calm as I explained our early arrival to the receptionist.

"I think my baby is coming and I'm only 33 weeks," I said as evenly as I could. "We called ahead and they told us to come in. I'm only 33 weeks," I added again for emphasis.

"Please take a seat," she said officiously.

John McEnroe popped absurdly into my head as I silently bellowed, "You cannot be serious." I mean I understood it might have been a regular, run-of-the-mill, daily occurrence for her but I was only 33 weeks pregnant. Did you hear me lady? Thirty-three weeks. It's. Too. Early. For. MY. BABY. To. Be. Born.

But I kept my mouth shut as Jake and I clutched each other's hands tightly, vicelike with nerves, as we waited. We were absolute beginners.

"Do you think everything is going to be okay?" I asked him, choking back the lump in my throat.

"Yeah," he croaked. "I mean, yeah," he said, deepening his voice and smiling to reassure me but failing to hide his doubt.

Fear tightened like a noose around my neck. Suddenly thoughts of the past week's events rushed into my head all at once – the soundly sleeping baby, dilated kidneys, polyhydramnios. I couldn't voice the question stuck in my throat. I didn't want to risk hearing the answer that something might be wrong.

"My water hasn't broken," I said to Jake. "Maybe they can stop me going into full labour."

Before he could respond a person appeared, whether doctor or nurse, male or female, I wasn't sure, such was the blurring effect of my rising panic. The medic led us to a room with a now familiar gurney and monitor and hooked me up to check the baby's heart. I struggled to control my dread as the person probed for our baby's heartbeat, fearing the only heart they'd hear would be the pounding, sweating beat of my own. Tears escaped as the person prodded and probed my stomach.

'Please, please, please, please, please, please, please,' I chanted silently in my head, the paradoxical silent prayer of a non-believer hoping someone might hear. I looked desperately at Jake, then at the monitor, then the medic and back to Jake again as a collective holding of breath weighed silently in the air.

Tears softened the edges of everything in the room, leaving me reliant on my hearing. Finally, faintly at first, we heard a soft heart-beat – dd, dd, dd, dd – and then a louder DD, DD, DD, DD, like galloping hooves. Jake and I collectively exhaled and the medic left the room. Our relief was short-lived as the thumping, loud and strong for a moment, disappeared again, along with my compo-sure without anybody in the room to reassure us. I willed myself to relax, telling myself that holding my breath wasn't good for the baby.

DD, DD, DD, DD, there it was again and I exhaled once more, trying to focus on breathing evenly as the walls closed in around me. The medic returned to check the trace, then tore a length of paper from the monitor and disappeared again.

Immediately another person appeared, who I could tell was a doctor because he spoke a foreign language.

"There is decreased variability on the CTG," he said earnestly, his furrowed brow signalling this wasn't good news.

I wanted to shriek at him to use plain English but didn't because I needed to hear what he said next.

"We need to do an emergency caesarean section to deliver your baby right now. Please sign this form," he said pushing a paper and a pen towards me without further explanation.

I looked at Jake but saw his confusion and fear reflected my own.

I swallowed down hard as more tears escaped at the knowledge that our baby was about to be cut out of me.

"It's too early, I'm only 33 weeks, the baby's not due until the fourth of July," I cried as Jake and yet another person helped me sit up. "Does Victoria know?" I asked hopelessly.

Nobody replied.

As Jake and I entered the theatre faceless people surrounded me. Jake tried to stay connected and keep me calm but the urgency of the voices around me was palpable as I was asked to bend forward as far as I could over my grossly distended belly.

"Try to stay relaxed, you'll feel a sharp prick and some discomfort as we put the anaesthetic into your spine so that you won't feel anything while we deliver your baby. You need to stay completely still," someone said.

As I bent forward, hot liquid cascaded to form a puddle on the floor. "I'm sorry," I sobbed.

"It's okay, just try to stay as still as you can, we're nearly done. Now, can you feel this, Aminah?" a person asked, pricking my back.

"Yes."

"Can you feel this?" they repeated, pricking me further down.

"Yes, I can," I said, aware that I shouldn't be feeling anything from the waist down and wanting to make sure they didn't start cutting while I could.

"Aminah, your baby is in distress. We don't have time to wait for the spinal to work. We're going to have to put you under general anaesthetic, I'm afraid. Unfortunately, Jake will have to wait outside until your baby is born," a doctor said.

Jake was ushered out of the room along with the last hope we'd be able to share the precious moment of welcoming our baby together. With me asleep and Jake outside, there'd be nobody to greet our baby I thought sadly as my mind faded to black.

19. The Other Mothers' Club

Bitter chills convulsed me awake some time later but I wasn't quite ready for consciousness and my awareness was limited to the cold sensation and a deep, throbbing ache that told me our baby was no longer inside me. Strange voices murmured unintelligibly nearby but there was no sound of a baby crying.

"I'm cold, I'm so cold, freezing cold," I moaned as I shivered uncontrollably.

Nobody came into view, just a single soothing voice trying to calm me while heated blankets were layered heavily across my body. But the tremors persisted and I felt a deep sense of something being wrong. "I'm so cold, freezing cold, please make me stop shaking," I pleaded.

"Try to calm down, Aminah, your body will naturally be in shock."

Then from the haze I heard Jake's deep and lovingly familiar voice warming me as he murmured into my ear, "We have a beautiful baby boy."

"Ah, a baby boy!" I repeated, still shivering as I slowly opened my eyes, feeling a glimmer of relief that he'd spoken in the present tense – but it was a fleeting moment of calm before my world was turned upside down.

"He's a bit sick so they've taken him to the nursery," Jake said gently, trying not to cause me panic. "He's a little bit floppy," he added.

Floppy? The word jolted my brain out of sedated stupor like a nuclear explosion. I knew it didn't bode well.

Marlon Louis Hart-Knowles was born at 12.57am on Wednesday 18 May 2005, almost seven weeks premature. His second name, Louis, was for my beloved grandfather, Louda. Hart was in tribute to my deceased dad and Knowles for Jake's dearly departed dad.

Even from my drug-haze I wanted to shout from the rooftops that we had a son, but first I had to find my way out of the post-operative fog in order to meet the little guy myself.

Eventually I was discharged from recovery and transferred to the maternity ward. Nightmares couldn't have conjured a more excruciating welcome to new motherhood than being forced to lie helplessly and in agonising spiritual pain next to cooing mothers and crying babies while I waited to meet my baby, chillingly aware and fearful that his fate remained uncertain.

Since the cord had been cut my only connection to Marlon had been Jake telling me that he existed. I'd been told nothing more about his condition or why he was 'floppy'. And whenever Jake disappeared to be with Marlon I'd wonder whether I might be trapped in a terrible dream I needed desperately to be awoken from. But my senses had returned with a vengeance leaving me all too aware and unable to retreat into sleep no matter how hard I tried, the crying babies around me serving as a punishing reminder that Marlon wasn't with me.

Finally, after some gentle coercion of hospital officialdom by Jake, I was given permission to visit Marlon in the nursery. Terror at the reality of seeing my sick little boy threatened to overcome me as Jake pushed me in a wheelchair through a maze of bleakly stark corridors towards the nursery and I hoped that perhaps I'd lost my mind and might be in a psychiatric hospital hallucinating.

When we got to the neonatal intensive care unit the nurse said he was still alive though he didn't look so to me.

My stomach took flight when I saw my tiny, helpless, hopelessly wilted baby draped over a rolled-up towel, flaccid and barely clinging to life in a tiny plastic cot. He looked more like an exquisite, mop-haired little ragdoll than a baby, with no signs of life other than the gentle rise and fall of his body as the ventilator pushed air into his lungs and gravity extracted it again. No other inch of him twitched or stirred and his broken little frame lay perfectly still shattering my fragile glass façade that splintered through my heart.

I wasn't allowed to hold my son, though my every instinct screamed that I needed to. The best I could do was gently stroke him and tell him I was there. I felt more like a spectator of a tragic unfolding drama than a new mum.

As I glanced around at the other tiny residents a symphony of monitors buzzed and beeped and their alarms drew corresponding looks from other parents hovering anxiously over their babies' incubators in a greenhouse of fear. Most of them kept their heads bowed with their eyes fixed firmly on their precious children, most of whom had arrived in the world too soon. There was no rejoicing in the gift of new life, just the occasional sad smiles of recognition shyly exchanged across the room. Every parent would rather have been anywhere but there.

Welcome to the NICU, the Neonatal Intensive Care Unit. Heartbreak hotel for babies. The other mothers' club.

For the first few surreal, otherworldly days in the NICU Marlon's life hung in the balance and Jake and I were his parents in name only as we sat disoriented by his bed, overwhelmed by all of the apparatus and machines needed to keep him alive. The rest of our parental duties were taken over by the nurses who vigilantly monitored his vital signs and watched for signs of deterioration.

All of my instincts to scoop Marlon up and hold him to my breast were put on hold, overridden by protocols and rules. The only maternal purpose I could fulfil was to make regular trips to the expressing room to try to pump out some milk. But even that didn't happen easily as my breasts were too rock hard to release even the tiniest drop.

Jake and I could only hope Marlon knew who we were and I hoped my smell might be familiar and that he might know my voice to recognise me as his mum.

"We're right here, my darling. We'll be here with you fighting every step of the way," I whispered into his ear. But my brave face belied the depth of the fear I was feeling inside.

None of the doctors could tell us anything apart from that Marlon was 'profoundly hypotonic', the medical term for floppy, but otherwise they had no idea what was wrong with our son and couldn't tell us with any certainty what would become of him.

Up until that moment I'd considered doctors to be oracles who had a name for every medical condition and I couldn't comprehend how they couldn't know and the not knowing was the worst part of all.

Meanwhile, Mum was stuck in Melbourne unable to get on a flight, having planned to be in London for the original due date. Ayesha was the first person to arrive who could really offer me comfort. As soon as I saw her I couldn't hold back the river of tears that had been dammed. She held me as I crumbled and told me it was okay not to be strong.

When Mandy came to meet her 'godson' I tried to give her ample warning before she saw him, saying, "He's a bit floppy, he looks in a bad way but he's just so beautiful…" before trailing off into more tears.

"Darls, he'll be a little fighter, strong just like his mummy, don't you worry," said Mandy in her perennially positive way.

Both Mandy and Ayesha were overwhelmed when they saw

Marlon for themselves. "You're right, he's so beautiful," Mandy agreed as tears welled in her eyes.

Tears were unusual for Mandy and she quickly stifled them. "I'm so proud of you, Means," she said, smiling and hugging me.

As she and I walked out of the NICU, I confessed the truth hiding under my bravado. "I'm so scared for my little boy. The doctors don't know what's wrong with him. They know it's bad but they have no idea why he's so floppy, they can't tell us anything at all. How is that possible? How can they not know?"

Usually one to run like the wind from heightened emotion, Mandy grabbed me in a tight hug like I'd taught her ten years earlier and we cried together.

"How could this have happened, Mands?" I pleaded. "Do you think I did something wrong? Do you think I'm being punished?"

"Means, you did nothing wrong, you've got to focus on being strong for Marlon, he needs you. They're doing heaps of tests, I'm sure they'll work it out, just give it some time," she said, regaining her composure to be strong for me.

"Thanks, Mands. I really wish my mum was here," I sobbed into her shoulder.

"I know, I wish she was here too," she said, knowing Mum would know what to say to comfort me.

Ayesha returned the following day armed with cabbage leaves and face washers. I was curious about the cabbage leaves, which she told me she would wrap around my inflated breasts to help get my milk moving. Then, like only a female family member would dare, she massaged and kneaded my boobs with hot flannels, squeezing, willing and coercing the backed-up milk to come out. The pain was beyond excruciating. "This is not something I ever imagined having a sister would entail," I giggled through tears of agony before she made me squeeze each of my nipples trying to break the invisible seal holding back my milk, causing me to scream in pain.

It was a split second of normalcy and humour that infiltrated our sadness and, as if the laughter had helped, a drop of milk appeared on the tip of my nipple, followed by another. Ayesha dripped the precious drops of golden colostrum into a container to be fed directly into Marlon's tummy. The colostrum glistened in the bottom of the jar I clutched and delivered to the NICU. I handed it triumphantly to Anne-Marie, a fair dinkum Aussie nurse who'd appeared just as the lack of information was starting to get me down and the enormity of our situation was finally sinking in.

As soon as I woke each day my mind accelerated with fretful thoughts, twisting my stomach into a knot. I couldn't calm myself down until I was back at Marlon's bedside. Whenever he was within my sight and reach I felt able to cope, so I returned to my room only to sleep and try to eat something in the hope it would help my milk.

One morning I was eating breakfast when I spied a file poking out beneath the breakfast tray and opened it to find the dramatic details of Marlon's birth. The words 'Possible Chromosome Abnormality' leapt off the page at me. I gasped for breath, thinking it couldn't possibly be right. I couldn't have read such devastating news about Marlon's condition on a randomly abandoned piece of paper. Surely the doctors would have discussed it with Jake and me in person.

My thoughts raced back over the pregnancy. His brain was all there in the ultrasounds. His heart was fine. They'd said he was a good size at each scan and he'd been a good size for his gestation when he was born. I wondered what sort of chromosome abnormality could have been completely missed in the scans. And then it hit me. Marlon's dilated kidneys. Had they suggested a chromosome abnormality? And if so, why did nobody tell us that dilated kidneys could mean disaster? Might his brain be affected as well as his body? Could he need a wheelchair? Would he be unable to walk or talk or eat or speak? Might he even…? I couldn't finish the thought.

I gripped my caesarean wound with one hand and the bar overhead with the other, levering myself out of bed and hobbling back to the NICU. Signing in at the NICU I was distracted enough by the receptionist's friendly enquiries to slow my racing brain and regain a semblance of calm. I needed information and had learnt doctors didn't do hysteria. So I assumed my best poker face and grasped at emotional control before I sought out the consultant to ask what the meaning of Marlon's possible chromosome abnormality might be.

"I need to speak to the doctors as soon as possible," I told Anne-Marie, trying desperately to assert calm authority in my voice.

Anne-Marie wasn't having a bar of my bravado. "Are you okay, Aminah?" she asked, genuinely concerned because I'd always maintained upbeat bedside banter.

Her Aussie-accented empathy instantly disarmed me. "I'm okay," I began. "Well actually I'm not, I've just read that Marlon might have a chromosome abnormality and now I need a doctor to explain it to me because it's the first I've heard of it."

Anne-Marie offered me comforting words in my distress and talked me through Marlon's 'obs' from the night before, reassuring me that he was doing well, knowing the distraction and focus would help me re-gather myself so I could talk to the doctors when they came on their rounds.

But tears bubbled out when she asked me, "Did you speak to your mum? My mum always knows what to say."

Anne-Marie handed me a tissue and quickly changed tack. "You know, Aminah, we do it a bit differently in Australia. I think you need to give Marlon a cuddle. We call it kangaroo care. You can hold him on your chest, skin to skin, it'll do you both the world of good."

I stared at her in grateful disbelief. "Really?" was all I could manage before being overcome again.

So, on the fourth day of my son's life I finally became a mother. At last I got the opportunity to perform my most basic role, the same one I'd taken for granted and looked forward to since finding out I was pregnant. Finally I got to hold my son.

Anne-Marie had to gather up Marlon's disjointed limbs and curl him into a ball and rest him on my chest. I inhaled the sweet smell of his dirty hair, which couldn't be washed yet, and delicately snuggled him into me as tightly as fear would allow. I savoured the moment, completely immersing myself in the feel of my baby and the warm heaviness of his weight in my arms as improbable love seeped achingly into my fractured mind. Finally we were real, Marlon was mine and I was his mum.

I felt whole again with my child in my arms and I couldn't imagine ever letting him go. Jake arrived as I was absorbed in my first cuddle and he sat down beside us to snuggle in close the way we'd never been able to before.

"He's trying to open his eyes," Jake said in wonder, looking down into Marlon's face nestled into my chest.

"Maybe he knows it's me?" I whispered tearfully.

"Of course he does," Jake replied.

"Of course he does," echoed Anne-Marie.

I let tears stream down into Marlon's curls as mixed emotions simmered over. I wanted him to feel the vastness of my love, devotion and strength as well as my profound sorrow for his struggle. I also wanted to inject my strength into him, to give him everything I had. My sense of purpose was fortified with a surging maternal protectiveness to keep him safe.

Eventually Anne-Marie bundled Marlon up to transfer him into Jake's arms and I saw the same combination of love and fear in his eyes as I felt. I tried to reassure him, as he had me, that his arms were the safest place Marlon could be.

Back in my room that night I collapsed under the enormity of it all. The doctors couldn't tell us anything more about Marlon's possible chromosome abnormality until the tests came back and sometimes his uncertain fate was more than my brain could conceive. Before

I'd held him that day I'd been too scared to let myself completely bond to him or acknowledge my overwhelming love but as soon as I felt him so still and warm in my arms my fears for the future grew.

As the stitches from my caesarean incision were unpicked ready for discharge I felt unprepared and petrified at the thought of having to leave Marlon behind in hospital. I sensed the hushed voices I heard were discussing me and my family and a dark realisation came over me that I'd have to get accustomed to pitying looks and being talked about, which had always been a pet hate of mine.

Before being discharged, Jake and I met with the leading consultant neonatologist, Dr Anthony Kaiser, and he reeled off a list of exotic tests still to be performed to try to get a diagnosis for Marlon. Each of the genetic conditions on the list sounded grave and depressing, with muscular dystrophy the only one I'd heard of. All but one were equally devastating and incurable: Prader Willi syndrome, spinal muscular atrophy, myotonic dystrophy and myasthenia gravis.

Our hearts heavy after speaking to Dr Kaiser, Jake and I went to kiss Marlon goodbye. I still felt wretched about having to leave him, though I knew he was in the best possible care. I whispered an explanation into his forehead as if he understood and, as if in defiant response, he chose that moment to lift his legs in the air for the first time.

"I think he's saying he wants to go home too. He's kicking his legs," I exclaimed to Jake as tears of despair turned to joy.

"He's telling us it's okay," said Jake, smiling back at me.

And for the first time since Marlon's birth five days before, I believed things were going to be okay.

20. Brave New World

Leaving St Thomas's I felt totally ill-equipped for what seemed like a new harshness in London. I'd watched its perpetual motion from the windows of St Thomas's, taking comfort from the fact that life was still going on outside, but as I walked out the intensity of the city startled me in a way it never had before and I felt utterly stripped bare.

While I'd been in hospital Jake had moved us into the new place we'd chosen to accommodate our expanded family, so I was venturing out feeling raw and vulnerable to a new home an hour's journey away in Hampstead instead of five minutes down the road from 'Tommy's'. And though I knew I'd go on breathing and thinking and being, I was uncertain whether I could actually walk away from the hospital without having my son with me.

It was a bewildering sort of reunion with my new and former lives as Jake turned the key in the front door of our new home and I had my first glimpse of its mostly empty rooms and little garden. The sadness of coming home without our son made me yearn for the life we'd left behind in London Bridge and I wished we could go back and start again but the lease was signed and our old home already had a new tenant.

No sooner had Jake and I sat down to a cup of tea than I was gripped by an urgent need to get back to Marlon for his next feed. I couldn't bear being so far away from him. I tossed and turned through that first night away from Marlon, unable to rest with the thought of him being without me and worried about how long it would take to get back to him if something happened.

The next day when Mum finally arrived from Australia I collapsed into her arms, seeking a top-up of strength from her as I'd always done. Before she had a chance to settle in or unpack her bags we were on our way to the hospital to meet her precious grandson. Having Mum with me and sharing the new development of Marlon's little horizontal jig from the previous afternoon lifted my spirits enormously.

"How long can you stay?" I asked Mum.

"Don't worry about that. Let's just get to the hospital and see what today brings," she said lovingly.

Mum always had the knack of making me believe that we'd deal with whatever happened when the time came, no point trying to foretell or control the future. And so we spent the day chatting by Marlon's bedside so he got to know his 'Nellie'. Mum was never going to be a 'Grandma', 'Granny' or 'Nanna' – such names were too suggestive of old age.

We spent each day after that in a routine of me dashing to the hospital as soon as I got up and Mum following later in the morning having attended to our neglected domestic chores. Jake would then come directly to the hospital after work while Mum headed home to cook dinner so it was ready for us as soon as we got back after tucking Marlon in for the night.

My milk had finally started flowing freely and our vigil by Marlon's bedside all day, every day, was punctuated only by my trips to 'the milking room' and the snatched breaks Mum and I took to eat.

As Jake and I rode the bus home of an evening I fell into him in emotional exhaustion and let my worries out. We both felt wrung out by still not knowing what was wrong with our son and our only consolation came from knowing he'd held stable through another day. Although we delighted in the tiniest of developments, Jake felt the strain of being separated from Marlon to go to work each day but his understandable desire to take time off work to be with Marlon made me feel pressured because somebody had to pay the bills. Because I needed to supply milk for Marlon it felt to me like Jake needed to provide the money. It was the first time we hadn't been fifty/fifty in everything and our conflicting emotions revealed the first hairline cracks we'd had in our relationship.

There was a certain inevitability that the stress under which we were living would get to us. The weight of uncertainty combined with unresolved grief that bubbled to the surface when we had to leave Marlon behind each night. Other than as an outlet for our fears, we had nothing left to give each other by the end of the day. We'd eat together with Mum before I'd fall into shattered sleep for a couple of hours before having to express milk again, but when night eventually fell and I needed to go to sleep, anxiety and panic invaded my brain instead.

Jake did his best to comfort me but he was suffering equally and the best we could do was to hold onto each other in the hope that we could stay strong by staying united.

The hospital chaplain offered counselling but her perspective didn't resonate with me so I attended Dr Kaiser's weekly support group for parents, where we shared our fears for our children and the tribulations and small triumphs of life in the NICU. Although there were other children with life-threatening illnesses apart from prematurity, we were the only parents of a child without a diagnosis. Marlon had a host of specialist doctors stumped as each of his tests came back negative and while they guessed at alternatives he was atypical for all the conditions his symptoms alluded to.

The best option on the list of doom was myasthenia gravis, which sounded ominous but was the only condition from which he could potentially recover. We hoped against hope that would be Marlon's diagnosis because he seemed to be getting stronger, moving his arms and legs against gravity and showing signs that he was improving. But no, a negative result took us back to square one on a diminishing list of increasingly rare disorders.

Meanwhile, with Marlon looking stronger we declined a muscle biopsy that would require surgery when the doctors told us that putting him back on a ventilator for surgery risked him becoming dependent on breathing support long term. A two-year-old girl, Carla, living permanently in the NICU required a tracheostomy tube attaching her to a bi-pap machine to breathe. Seeing her predicament made up our minds that we couldn't face a similar fate for our son. Instead we learnt from the nurses how to care for Marlon to prepare ourselves to take him home. We reasoned that if he continued on a positive trajectory the muscle biopsy could be done at a later date.

Anne-Marie had a knack for providing me with positives when everything else looked bleak. She gave us a great piece of advice that had helped accustom us to the bells and whistles of the NICU's many machines. "Watch the baby, not the monitors," she said. "Leave that to the nurses to worry about and concentrate on getting to know your baby's needs because when you go home you won't have the monitors to tell you what's going on."

"Do you really think we'll get to take him home one day?" I asked her dubiously.

"That's always the plan," she said, smiling at me.

It was hard to believe with Marlon still so fragile and prone to breathing problems but it gave Jake and me hope and kept us believing we'd eventually be together as a family. Our faith in our little family wasn't endorsed by Jake's mother, who heard Jake and me arguing one day and said to me, "You'll need to make time for your relationship, Aminah. You won't be able to go out once Marlon comes home because nobody will look after him."

The implication that she wasn't going to help us care for Marlon was devastating for me, having seen her jump at any opportunity to look after Ria's son, Isaac. But the implication that my marriage might falter if I couldn't meet Jake's needs was even worse for me in such a fragile state.

"Actually Ria's offered to learn how to care for Marlon and look after him if we're ever lucky enough to get him home," I retorted, barely disguising my disdain. With a few insensitive words she'd managed to highlight a key difference between my mother and my mother-in-law.

Meanwhile, I called the hospital as soon as I woke each morning, desperate to hear the word 'stable'. The overview of his overnight observations was all in medical jargon and it was a steep learning curve for both Jake and me, having never spent time in hospital before Marlon's birth.

On arrival at the hospital I'd wait for the doctors to make their round and provide any updates on their search for a diagnosis. Marlon's chromosome test came back normal with the 23 XY pairs of a healthy male contradicting the dire prediction on the green piece of paper I'd stumbled upon. But it also suggested that the answer to his condition could lie deeper in the complex web of his DNA and might prove impossible to find. Far from being all knowing as I'd assumed, geneticists had only touched the tip of the iceberg in decrypting the intricacies of the human genetic code and I was surprised when they informed us that a relatively small percentage of congenital conditions were easily identifiable by name and genetic origin.

And so the wait continued and we were kept strong by Marlon's tiny steps of progress, like staying awake for longer periods and interacting with us and his surroundings, his miniscule reactions in recognition of familiar voices, his first almost inaudible cry and, after many episodes of choking and turning blue, him gradually learning to drink from a bottle. Marlon's sheer will to survive also instilled in me the belief that having come so far he had to be okay, despite him regularly needing CPR.

It never ceased to amaze me how such distressing trauma as my baby turning blue and having to be revived with CPR could become so normalised in my mind having seen it daily and because the alternative was too unfathomable to comprehend.

By day Mum and I played with Marlon, trying to normalise his life despite its limitations, and taking turns to cuddle him until our arms became numb.

Jake and I had listened a lot to Coldplay's music since we'd been together. Ironically they released an album called *X&Y* shortly after Marlon's birth and Jake bought me tickets to their concert for my birthday. One particularly poignant song from the album called 'Fix You' became my anthem for Marlon and I hummed it into his ear incessantly as we passed the days waiting eternally for something to change.

At night, unable to sleep, I'd search desperately online for answers that the doctors couldn't give and go running in to Mum crying, interrupting her sleep with my latest discovery. Firstly I was convinced that Marlon had Prader Willi syndrome, which had featured as a possibility on his list, but once he tested negative to that I discovered cri du chat or cat cry syndrome and was convinced he sounded like a little kitten meowing when he managed to choke out a noise. I was sure he had all the physical traits consistent with cri du chat and collapsed in a heap of fresh heartbreak at the description of severe cognitive impairments, speech and motor delays, behavioural problems such as hyperactivity, aggression, tantrums and repetitive movements that characterised the condition.

Certain I'd solved the mystery one night I woke Mum in hysterics before she got me to climb into bed with her and proceeded to stroke my head until I eventually drifted into fitful sleep.

The next day when I told the consultants I believed Marlon had cri du chat, much to my relief they told me he didn't and that I should stop trying to do their job as I was only causing myself more unnecessary grief.

It was sage advice that I completely ignored as weeks turned into months.

Eventually Mum convinced me that I needed to get out more because she could see my mood was slipping into a more permanent despair. My natural disposition had always been upbeat and positive like hers but Mum feared the relentlessness of life in hospital without any prognosis or signs of diagnosis would eventually get the better of me if I didn't take time out for myself and to be with Jake.

So I ventured back into a social life of sorts with Jake, catching up with close friends and going to the odd party, but I felt like I was standing in a parallel existence that no longer resembled my life. The news of Marlon's birth and illness had spread through our networks and beyond but people who didn't know us well didn't really know what to say. Uncertain of what to say ourselves when people enquired about Marlon's health we'd reply that he was improving all the time. It all felt a bit false and contrived but at the same time it was good to have another dimension to life again and a respite from the hospital.

The date for the Coldplay concert was a couple of weeks after my birthday and any doubts I expressed about going were firmly rebuked by Jake, who said we needed time together and our shared passion for live music was just the ticket.

As we made our way off the train at Crystal Palace amongst the throng of concert goers, black storm clouds gathered overhead threatening to ruin our evening. The rain held off long enough for the crowd to fill to capacity and for a moment the music carried us away from our worries and back to a time when life had been easy and full of brightness. Then, at the very same moment the band launched into 'Fix You', there was a clap of thunder and the heavens opened, dumping a deluge of rain perfectly timed to blend with my tears.

It proved a spiritual moment to me as Jake and I held on to each other in the rain. It felt like the heavens were crying with me as Chris Martin serenaded our son.

21. Nurse in Charge

After ten precious weeks spending time with her grandson and doing everything she could to help Jake and me, Mum had to return to Australia. By then the doctors were planning Marlon's discharge so while it was so wrenching for Mum to leave and for me to see her go, she was hopeful we'd soon be taking Marlon home.

The doctors had run out of conditions to test for, so unless one final test for an even rarer form of spinal muscular atrophy with respiratory distress (SMARD) provided an answer, it seemed like the cause of Marlon's problems would remain a mystery until he revealed further clues.

Just as we were growing hopeful that his improved movement would continue, the consultants called us into a meeting where a doctor told us, "We think it's important you understand that Marlon's progress may have plateaued and he'll always be very disabled. We no longer think his hypotonia is benign because although he's shown some movement, he's still extremely floppy. We don't believe he will be able to hold up his head, certainly not crawl or walk. Unfortunately there's not much else we can give you in the way of a prognosis without a diagnosis but if the SMARD test comes back positive it is unlikely that he would have more than 12 months of life."

We'd been so built up by the doctors' talk of taking Marlon home, but now it felt like they were tearing us back down. It felt too cruel to bear that we were being cut loose with only bad news, no diagnosis and little information about what life would be like with such a fragile and susceptible little boy. On the upside the doctors told us that the NHS would fund us taking home a suction machine, which was used multiple times a day to keep Marlon from choking on his secretions. We were also told the management of Marlon's care would be transferred to the Royal Free Hospital in Hampstead, which was closer to our new home.

Frustrated at what I saw as the doctors washing their hands of any continuity of Marlon's care, I became determined to become the best nurse I could be, replicating Anne-Marie's caring, no-nonsense approach so when the time came to take Marlon home not only would I finally get to be his mum I'd also be the nurse-in-charge.

Ultimately it was three months before Marlon was stable enough to be discharged with his 'blue episodes' at a minimum and his progression to being fully bottle-fed, meaning his naso-gastric tube could be removed. On the fifteenth of August 2005 the auspicious day arrived when we were finally allowed to take our beautiful baby boy home and assume our rightful roles as his parents at last.

Over the previous three months I'd craved the chance to curl up with my son and cuddle him in bed rather than sitting uncomfortably upright and stilted in a chair. Grabbing the first opportunity to do so as soon as we got home, I reclined luxuriously into the pillows on our bed and snuggled Marlon into my chest, closing my eyes to cloister us in the moment. If time had stopped right then I'd have happily stayed suspended there forever.

Finally Marlon was ours. Finally we were home. Finally we were a family. Finally life could begin again.

I sucked in the beauty of the moment until Marlon fell asleep on my chest, then I lay him gently on the bed and busied myself with making up his cot. The anxiety I'd been feeling at home when I was separated from him evaporated and was replaced by a new sense of calm at having some control back in our lives.

Jake's family gathered to welcome us home making us feel even more complete, although I felt a tinge of sadness that Mum wasn't there to share the joy of Marlon's homecoming, especially after the endless hours she'd spent at his bedside. Apart from one or two little adventures outside the hospital walls with Marlon in a pram she'd never got to experience her grandson in a normal sense.

We sat outside in our little garden so Marlon could soak up some vitamin D but his eyes stayed closed against the unfamiliar glare of the sun while Ria nestled him in her lap and his one-year-old cousin Isaac poked at him curiously.

It occurred to me that I'd never seen Jake's mother hold Marlon in the hospital. "Do you want a cuddle?" I offered, not giving her a chance to decline before I placed Marlon in her arms. In any other situation I'd have forgiven her for looking so uncomfortable, especially as she wasn't a cuddly person at all, but as Marlon was her grandson I had to put the pity in her eyes down to fear.

After Jake's family left we bundled Marlon into his pram and went for our first walk as a family on Hampstead Heath. Ironically, as well as providing beautiful surroundings and long walks in its vast open spaces, we'd moved to Hampstead hoping to give our baby healthy breathing space from the smog and pollution of London.

That night the three of us snuggled onto the couch to enjoy our first night at home together doing something as normal as watching TV.

I'd researched therapists who might be able to assist with Marlon's development, rather than continuing the futile search for his diagnosis, and the next day I took him to a cranial osteopath who told me he'd seen other babies as hypotonic as Marlon who had gotten much stronger and gone on to gain head control and crawl. This left me with hope that I could have some influence over his outcome and his future. Doctors had been proven wrong before.

The first week was as normal as I'd imagined life would be with a newborn. With Marlon tucked snugly into his pram Jake and I wheeled him around our little village at South End Green, stopping for coffee and catching up for lunch with Jake's family and our friends. Passers-by would peer into his pram and exclaim at his beauty and thick thatch of hair.

Having reached a point resembling equilibrium I felt the need to get some help in processing everything that had happened and coming to grips with the vastly different picture of motherhood I was experiencing to the one I'd dreamt about. I knew I needed to monitor my state of mind with a future that remained so uncertain no matter how positive I tried to remain.

Jake and I also extended an open invitation to friends to come and visit us at home, which had been impossible in the hospital with only two people allowed at Marlon's bedside at a time. We soon enjoyed a steady stream of visitors bringing a new social aspect to my London life with its absence of the sort of drop-in culture I'd grown up with in Melbourne. It was different for Jake, whose life hadn't changed as dramatically as mine because he still went to work every day and socialised afterwards, whereas in hospital I'd been completely severed from most other facets of my life.

Before we could get too comfortable, however, Marlon's oral secretions increased so much during one day that I needed to suction him every fifteen minutes. I called the Royal Free Hospital to tell them and ask what the cause might be but was told not to worry unless there were other symptoms, because secretions could naturally change with the weather and environment. I'd never given a thought to how much saliva a person produced until Marlon was born and realised it must be gallons judging by the amount we had to suck out of his throat.

That night while I was feeding him a bottle of formula, his lips turned slightly blue and he seemed too lethargic to feed properly, causing me to worry we'd overdone the socialising or he might be coming down with something. He had copious secretions through-out the night and the next morning when I got him up and lay him in the living room while I prepared another bottle, I returned from flicking the kettle on to find him an alarming shade of blue.

I panicked and yelled for Jake, who immediately came running from the bedroom, dropping to his knees and starting CPR while I frantically dialled emergency. By the time the ambulance arrived Marlon seemed back to normal with pink back in his cheeks and lips. The paramedics took us to the Royal Free Hospital as a precaution and the emergency doctors admitted him to the paediatric ward to see if they could find a reason for his sudden setback. Jake's mum came to sit with me while Jake went off to work. The hospital did a round of tests but found no signs of illness or congestion in his lungs so after a day under observation we were allowed to return home.

Marlon was none the worse for wear but my confidence had suffered a blow and my nerves started fraying back to the edges again. Jake and I were shocked out of any false sense of complacency, heeding it as a warning of just how delicate Marlon's condition was.

The doctors said we'd done all the right things except forgetting to suction Marlon's airway before starting CPR, which increased the risk of aspirating liquid into his lungs. I was just grateful Jake had been there to take control as I'd panicked more than I'd expected and felt completely discombobulated.

"How did you stay so calm?" I asked Jake when we got home. "I panicked, what would I have done if you hadn't been there?"

"I saw he was in trouble and it was just reflex to save him. Don't worry, you would have done the same if you'd been on your own," Jake said gently, trying to reassure me. "You were just caught by surprise but you'd have been okay on your own."

"It's so scary," I cried. "It was so quick, I really won't be able to take my eyes off him when you're at work."

I'd been leaving Marlon in the living room while I went into other rooms in the flat but after that I put him in the car seat and took him into every room with me. I knew I had no other option but to carry on and hope that my confidence returned as I got back into a routine and dared to venture out of the house again. I took the portable suction machine everywhere we went and I tucked a catheter under the mattress in his pram ready for action should the same thing happen again.

The following weekend was the August Bank Holiday. Each year a fairground came to Hampstead Heath, so we invited some friends and their kids over on the holiday Monday to join us at the fair. Meanwhile we took a long and leisurely walk on the Heath on Saturday morning to check out the new sculpture of giant table and chairs before Jake's family joined us for brunch at a local café. Later Jeff came over for dinner and he and Jake went over to the fair while I stayed at home with Marlon. It felt like family life just as it should always have been.

I'd grown used to existing on minimal sleep, with Marlon still feeding four-hourly. Even when we were all asleep, Marlon rattled with secretions in his cot on one side of me and Jake snored away on the other in a symphony of reassuring noise. On Sunday, I gave Marlon his last bottle for the night and slipped into bed, looking forward to an extra day together the next day.

I fell asleep straight away but it must have been deeper than usual because I suddenly jolted awake and was immediately aware of the silence in Marlon's cot. I bolted out of bed and reached for Marlon. In the dim light of the bedside lamp, his face looked deathly pale and though he was warm to the touch he wasn't breathing.

"Jake, quick, wake up," I cried, trying to stay calm and lifting Marlon out of his cot onto our bed. "He's not breathing."

Without hesitation Jake started CPR again and I called the emergency operator and relayed our details for the second time in days.

The ambulance seemed to appear almost instantly and I swung the front door open and bolted up the steps to usher the paramedics in the right direction, almost pushing them down the stairs in my haste.

Jake stepped out of the way, allowing the paramedics to take over, and we waited outside the bedroom and then followed them out to the ambulance. Two minutes later we were back in the Royal Free emergency room where a team of doctors worked on Marlon while another person scribbled incomprehensible figures onto a whiteboard.

I had to run to the toilet before I lost control of my bowels. I tried to steady my breathing but started to hyperventilate when I returned to find the desperate attempts to revive Marlon still continuing. I knew it was taking too long and I couldn't catch my breath. Then everything went blurry when a doctor said, "I'm so sorry but he's gone. There's nothing more we can do to get him back."

Jake caught me as my legs gave out, the room swirling before me and nothing making sense anymore.

"No, no, not now," I cried as sobs wracked my body. "No, he can't be gone, we just got him home. Please no," I begged a final time before my voice petered out.

"I need to hold him," I cried into Jake's embrace and he led me to a stool beside a gurney where someone placed Marlon into my arms.

I looked down in disbelief at my dead baby who could have been sleeping peacefully in my arms and automatically I began singing softly to him the poignant lyrics from Coldplay's 'Fix You' as I had a thousand times before.

For a moment it was just me and my son in a bubble. And for that moment everything could still have been okay.

But I couldn't fix him. My beautiful Marlon had died.

And there in the emergency room of the Royal Free Hospital the world Jake and I had managed to stitch together since Marlon's birth unravelled and fell to the floor with the pieces of my heart.

The Royal Free community nurse, Rosemary, who'd been visiting us at home during the short time since we'd left St Thomas's, appeared from nowhere by my side and hugged me with Marlon still in my arms.

"He's gone, Rosemary," I cried. "He's gone."

Moments later, she suggested we needed to clear the emergency room for emergencies. Our time was up. I didn't want to leave Marlon because that would mean the end, but Rosemary promised me she would make sure he was well taken care of as we were led away to an office to call Jake's mum to pick us up.

A nurse explained that Marlon would go to the mortuary after we left and we would be able to see him there if we wanted to and could bring some clothes from home to dress him in.

The mortuary. My son.

My son was going to the mortuary.

The words didn't fit together in my head and I didn't want to make them make sense because then Marlon would really be dead.

Against my better judgement and every maternal bone in my body that ached to stay with Marlon, we left the hospital. I sat mutely in Jake's mum's garden and carelessly chain-smoked cigarettes wishing I could have a heart attack and die right there. Then they could put me in the mortuary with Marlon and everything would be okay.

Voices spoke but I heard no words. Every inch of me ached with sorrow but I felt nothing. Time kept ticking by, but my life had stopped.

I wanted my mum. I must have spoken to her or maybe someone else did, I couldn't recall, but somehow I knew she'd be coming to London on the next available flight and I had to hold on until then. It was only four weeks since she'd left.

Everything else was surreal. I wasn't really there. I was looking for Marlon in my mind, unable to process the images of him lying cold and alone in the morgue.

Eventually I couldn't stay there any longer. "Jake, we have to go home and get Marlon some clothes," I said as if he was there and had gotten himself dirty.

When we got home I selected a pale blue top with bunnies

on the front that had always suited him beautifully, along with a matching pair of pants.

"Would you like to see him and dress him?" the nurse offered gently when we returned to the same office at the Royal Free.

Her question winded me. "No. I mean, no, I can't see him like that. I just can't. I'm sorry," I began to cry. "Can you please dress him for me? I just can't do it, I'm so sorry."

"It's okay," she said softly, "I understand." But it wasn't her I was apologising to, it was Marlon.

"It's okay. I can't see him like that either," said Jake, trying to offer me comfort and reassurance. "It's better we remember him the way he was."

I handed the nurse some of Marlon's toys and the blue fleecy Marlon blanket my dear friend Sue had sent him from Australia personalised with his name. It was a struggle to hand over his clothes and I held them to me for the final time thinking of what Mum had told me about cuddling one of Marlon's jumpsuits all the way back to Australia on the plane. Finally I relinquished them to the nurse, knowing I'd never see my son in the sweet little outfit again.

22. The Inevitable Rupture

The torture of Marlon's death started almost immediately and continued to hunt me down and haunt me in my dreams as images of his life flashed back relentlessly through my mind.

The contractions I'd thought were Braxton Hicks. The moment I heard we had a boy. The moment I heard the word floppy. The moment I first laid eyes on his wilted body kept breathing by a machine. All of the times he'd turned blue and threatened to stop breathing altogether. The hopes and the hopelessness of the last three months. The endless tests that had found no answers. Our final night at St Thomas's gazing out across the Thames to Westminster, full of hope with Marlon in our arms.

It was hard to believe we'd only left hospital just 13 days before. Surely they didn't send us home for Marlon to die so soon?

Inexplicably my mind kept going back to images we'd seen after the Asian tsunami. The scenes of devastation were similar to how my life felt now, a survivor of some incomprehensible disaster, leaving me completely dazed and confused.

Marlon had needed undivided attention every minute of every day and now with nothing to do but sit in an empty house, my mind awash with flashbacks and memories, my sanity felt precarious. Jake tried to be strong but he was as wretched as me and we clung to each other in a treacherous sea. While Marlon had been alive we'd always had grains of hope to keep us going and we'd propped each up. When one was drowning the other would keep them afloat, but the epic wave of new grief inundated us both.

Marlon's funeral was the last thing we could do for him so we busied ourselves with practicalities and preparations to avoid the torment in our minds as we stumbled through the world of death. When the coroner released Marlon for burial we discovered from the death certificate that he'd died from aspiration pneumonia.

"How can that be?" I asked Jake. "He had an x-ray of his lungs on Tuesday."

"I don't know, nothing makes sense," Jake said forlornly, his face etched with bewildered pain.

"I suppose they had to put something because he doesn't have a diagnosis," I said. "They couldn't put 'mystery condition' down on the death certificate."

"Yeah," Jake said with tears welling in his eyes, "I guess he'll always be our mystery boy now. Maybe we'll never know what was wrong."

"I don't suppose it matters now he's gone," I said collapsing into tears again.

On our visit to Golders Green crematorium Jake showed me the resting place of his dad and maternal grandparents. I'd initially been horrified by the thought of cremating Marlon because we'd always buried our family members, but once I saw the tranquil beauty of the gardens where Jake's family were commemorated I felt reassured that Marlon should be safely interred with his grandfather and great-grandparents.

We sent notice of Marlon's funeral to all of our friends thanking them for their support and asking them to wear summer colours to help us celebrate his life. The beauty of our living room with the multitude of summer blooms silhouetted against the walls by the flickering candles was at odds with the dark desolation in our hearts.

"Do you think this is karma for how we got together?" I asked Jake solemnly.

"No I don't," Jake said firmly. "He was our baby boy and it doesn't work like that. I don't want you to say that again."

I fell into bed exhausted and crashed gratefully into a deep sleep, but my peace was fleeting as a recurrent nightmare of picking Marlon up under his arms like a normal baby and him slipping flaccidly through my hands ripped me out of sleep and my brain started whirring with recollections and guilt.

I wished someone had told me about the guilt, which cornered me in the darkness with its repeated roar of futile questions, like: "What if? How? When? Why?"

The decision not to see Marlon in the mortuary or dress him wreaked havoc with my conscience, with images of him lying on a cold slab in a drawer like I'd seen on TV haunting me while I was both awake and asleep. I blamed myself for his death because I'd been asleep and hadn't been able save him.

The regret was crippling and I desperately wished I could tell Marlon how sorry I was to have abandoned him when he needed me most, but it was too late.

Mum arrived just in time to save me from slipping further into an abyss of grief and exhaustion from lack of restful sleep. Once she was with me I felt strong enough to at least get through Marlon's funeral.

As we walked into the chapel the sight of Marlon's tiny white coffin was almost too much to bear. I thought a box so small shouldn't be allowed to hold a baby whose life had only just begun. The floodgates opened and I was unable to stem the flow as I sat down in the front row, and I couldn't muster the courage to stand up and speak to the assembly of our loved ones.

Jake was braver and did his son proud, reading from Khalil Gibran's *The Prophet* and choosing Procol Harum's 'Whiter Shade of Pale" and Louis Armstrong's 'What a Wonderful World' to honour Marlon. I chose Coldplay's 'Fix You' to play at the end of the service, which reduced every person in the chapel to tears. As the song reached its final bars the conveyor belt holding Marlon's coffin began moving backwards towards a door and Jake had to hold me back from leaping onto the conveyor belt to stop it. As the chapel emptied, leaving us with the echoing silence of our thoughts, Jake continued to hold me tight.

Eventually I reattached my brave face to join our friends and family who'd gathered in the garden of the crematorium. The sun peered out and I chose to think it was making its rare appearance for Marlon. Each and every friend enveloped us in love and condolence before Jake and I broke away to walk up to the plot where Marlon would be dug into the earth.

"I think I'd like to give Mum some of Marlon's ashes to take back to Australia. Would that be okay?" I asked Jake, feeling suddenly nostalgic that otherwise no part of him would ever make it to Australia. "That way Mum will have a part of him there when she visits her parents in the cemetery, and me too when I'm there."

"Yeah, of course," Jake said lovingly, pulling me in close as we stood side by side gazing down into the dirt.

I dreaded the thought of the funeral being over and having to return to the emptiness of our house and the life that stretched ahead without meaning in front of me. We implored our friends to come home with us after the service, desperate not to be alone with our thoughts. We drank to Marlon and I kept drinking into the night to numb the pain and ensure that sleep would come when my head finally hit the pillow.

The next day I received a message from my old friend Sue, who'd given Marlon the personalised blanket, to say she'd given birth to a healthy son named Jack and was now crying guiltily and apologising for having him on the same day as Marlon's funeral.

I told her not to feel bad and that I preferred to think of it as a beautiful coincidence and connection between our sons now that they'd never meet. "It's beautiful to me that as we were saying goodbye to Marlon, Jack was making his way into the world," I reassured her. "Now when we celebrate Jack's birthday, we will automatically think of Marlon too. We should only see the beauty in that."

"Oh Aminah, that is a beautiful thought," Sue said. "Thank you."

As the nothingness of the following days set in, my wheels started to fall off pretty quickly, beginning with the loss of my wedding ring down a crack in the bathroom cabinet, out of sight and out of reach.

Mum was still there helping hold me together and Jake was doing all he could to fix me but Mum couldn't stay forever and she was worried that I wouldn't cope after she'd gone.

"Darling, you've got Jake and you've got lots of good friends to support you. And I'm sure Ria will be a support," said Mum, trying to reassure me. "Although I think she's pregnant again."

"What?" My head snapped up to meet Mum's eyes. "What makes you say that?"

"She wasn't drinking at the wake," she said, "and sometimes I can just tell these things."

And as usual, Mum was right.

With Mum there to help support me, Jake was naturally turning to his family for comfort and one night he went off to dinner at Ria and Sam's house and didn't return until 3am. As had become the norm for me I was only dozing when he got home and asked him if he'd had a nice night, feeling resentful that he'd stayed out so late.

"Ria's pregnant again so we were celebrating," he replied.

I rolled over and pretended to go to sleep so Jake couldn't see the look on my face. I so wanted to be happy for Ria and Sam, and in a way I was, for them. But their news only compounded my sense of loss and made me feel like more of a failure.

I knew myself well enough by then to recognise that I was pushing my in-laws away because I felt they didn't care and I was taking my extremes of emotion out on Jake because I thought he was getting on with his life while I was floundering. Something had to give or our relationship was heading for trouble.

Just as things were becoming even more fraught, David, my close friend from our childhood in Carlsberg Road, invited Jake and me to his wedding in Bali and offered to fly us over to be part of the celebrations. It was just the change of scene we needed to give us something to look forward to.

Meanwhile Mum and I spent her last few days in London just being together and going through photos of Marlon, reminiscing and creating an album before her departure. As soon as she left I felt myself plummeting and as hard as he tried to stop me, Jake couldn't break my fall.

Once Jake and I left home to head to the airport I was finally able to exhale, relieved to be leaving the place where Marlon had died, with its vivid reminders of him in every room.

The close humidity of Balinese air enveloped me as soon as we stepped off the plane and the heightened senses of arriving in a foreign land made me feel alive and want to live again. The familiar smell of Denpasar took me back to my first trip to Bali with Mum as a ten-year-old.

For the next few days we immersed ourselves in the novelty of being away from London and I took pleasure in introducing Jake to Bali's charms. By coincidence my close friends Lisa and Dean and their three children, including my godson Cooper, were holidaying in Bali with friends and spending time in their familiar company lifted my spirits instantly, with their Aussie good humour. Their teasing reminiscences of the Aminah they knew so well made me want to find the woman I used to be and it felt like hope might be possible in the laughter my friends helped me dig out from underneath the pain.

Jake and I were still grieving deeply and between us we cried rivers of tears but I felt different to when we'd been in London after the funeral. Jake had tried to fix me but in London I'd felt so broken I believed myself unfixable, whereas in Bali I rediscovered the optimism I'd always had but thought I'd lost.

"I think we should consider moving somewhere, Jake, maybe go overseas, and I think we should start trying for another baby," I said, hoping he might take to the idea of a fresh start.

He looked at me forlornly. "I'm not ready to try again, it's too soon."

"I know it is. And Marlon can't be replaced," I said. "But I think having another baby would help us, give us a new focus, and if we move somewhere new we can rebuild our little family."

"No. It's too soon," Jake said resolutely.

"I feel the same fear as you, Jake, but the best thing to do when you're scared is exactly the thing that scares you most. And don't you think we should at least think about what's right for both of us?" I said, slightly irritated by his haste at shutting me down.

As Jake's brown eyes filled with pain and he shook his head sadly I understood that our approaches to grief were going to be as different as our approaches to life. Jake had always erred on the side of melancholy, which I'd seen as part of his creative well, while I'd always looked on the bright side before Marlon's birth. We'd been each other's yin and yang, Jake's sensitive soul to my gung-ho, his creative to my pragmatic, his cultivated gentleman to my rough diamond. We'd shared a myriad of interests in common but for the first time I wondered whether a more fundamental difference was coming to the fore.

I knew Marlon couldn't be replaced but I yearned to hold a baby again and feel that heavy warmth upon my chest. I felt like a mother but my child was gone, and Jake standing in the way of us having another child without space for further discussion left me questioning whether we'd hit a fork in the road.

Before I could dwell on it too much, Dave and his fiancée Sachiko arrived in Bali for the pre-wedding festivities, which often left us too drunk or tired to wallow. Surrounded by tropical beauty and Aussies with their zest for life and partying hard as well a crowd of Dave and Sachi's international friends, it was hard to ignore the vibrancy and diversity of life, there for the taking if we wanted it. It made me more determined not to fall back into a funk and I felt a distinct pull away from my London life and a desire to keep flying in the opposite direction.

After watching Dave and Sachi's romantic sunset wedding ceremony the celebrations were getting into full swing when I felt a vibration under my feet and looked around to see if anybody else had noticed. "Did you feel that, Jake?" I asked.

"The vibration?" he replied.

"Yeah, I wonder if there's an earthquake nearby," I said. "Or do you think it could have been a bomb?" I added, thinking of the 2002 terrorist attack aimed at tourists that had killed more than 200 people.

Murmurs began amongst other guests who'd felt the vibration too, with someone suggesting it might have been an earthquake, another a car crash. Then a phone call to one of the other guests confirmed that two terrorist bombs had gone off in Kuta and Jimbaran Beach before the mobile system shut down, leaving everyone incommunicado.

The next day we learnt of 20 more deaths at the hands of terrorists, making me want to reroute our flight out of Bali to Melbourne rather than London, where terrorists had recently killed numerous people travelling innocently on London transport. Australia suddenly felt like a much safer place to live and raise children.

I could happily have stayed in Bali and avoided reality indefinitely but as soon as we touched the ground in London so too did Bali's therapeutic benefits. Before we even reached the terminal I sensed trouble ahead.

I'd arranged to return to work on Monday to avoid the emptiness we'd left behind but Jake and I would have to get through the weekend first with just the two of us back in our empty house. Almost as soon as we got home it was clear that we needed help if we were going to make Christmas with our relationship intact.

Work was a blessed distraction but returning to the London–Nottingham commute was testing, with its memories of feeling so happy and hopeful while I was pregnant with Marlon. Now as I pondered the green fields of the Home Counties, I yearned for the greyer and yellower greens of Australia.

London felt to me solely like the place where I'd lost Marlon. I could feel myself being sucked down into the black hole that Bali had kept me from falling into and my mind again started swirling with the same images and flashbacks that had plagued me before we left.

"I can't stay here, Jake," I pleaded one day. "We have to leave, or at least move house. I'm going crazy with the memories and I can't just sit here watching myself fall apart."

Jake was resistant to moving, but I couldn't tell whether it was because he was grieving too much to uproot himself or because he actually didn't want a change. Either way he wanted to stay put close to his mum and sister and he didn't want to try for another baby and that was that.

"Okay, well what about Australia this Christmas? At least then we'll have another holiday to look forward to. Let's fly on Christmas Day this year. I really can't face Christmas without Marlon anyway. And with Ria pregnant again and little Isaac it will just remind us of what we're missing. I don't want to pretend to be festive, do you?"

"I want to be with my family for Christmas. That's what we agreed," said Jake, reminding me of our unwritten wedding contract.

"I know, but things are different now, I really can't face it and I don't want to bring everyone else's mood down. If we fly on Christmas Day instead of Boxing Day I can just take a Valium and drink red wine, forget it's even Christmas, and by the time we touch down in Melbourne it'll be over already," I pleaded.

"I don't want to leave my family," he said again.

"But I'm your family," I said plaintively. "Can't you do it for me? Or has that changed because Marlon's not here anymore?"

It was a low blow and I knew it but I believed that in getting married we'd created a new nucleus for our family and that Jake's mother and sister should now sit more at the periphery. Jake's insistence on being with them for Christmas made me feel like he had a far greater attachment to them than to me and made me question whether our family values had ever been truly aligned.

This wasn't the Jake who'd promised me we'd always be together and for the first time since we'd fallen in love I wondered whether I'd leapt before I'd looked deeply enough into his emotional well.

He looked at me and shook his head with a combination of resentment and distress. "That's completely unfair, Aminah. I just want to be with my family for Christmas. I'm not asking you to stay too. I can come on a later flight to Australia."

"Okay, fine. I just thought we should stick together," I said.

Thankfully we started counselling the same week of that fractious conversation, both together and separately, otherwise we may have parted ways immediately. I felt like I'd compromised by committing to live in London forever and that I'd always play second fiddle to Jake's mother and sister.

The first counsellor we saw was a marriage counsellor from Relate who said she couldn't help us and not to bother returning for another session, but then Rosemary at the Royal Free Hospital recommended another counsellor called Annette who we connected with instantly. Annette's first piece of advice was not to make any big decisions while the grief was still so consuming. She said it would take us on a journey that would see us end up at a very different place to where we found ourselves so soon after our bereavement.

Seeing Annette each week was like having a mediator in our marriage and it helped to have an independent voice of reason. She kept us from the brink of a marital implosion until Christmas arrived and we were able to take a step back from each other for reflection.

I'd started seeing another counsellor, Angela, on my own and she also helped keep me connected to reason and reassured me that everything that was happening to me was normal in the circumstances. She diagnosed me with post traumatic stress disorder, which she said explained my flashbacks, and she agreed with Annette that the disconnection between Jake and me was normal as we both grieved in different ways.

"Men and women do grieve differently, Aminah," she reassured me. "We've looked at the guilt you're feeling and how destructive it can be. Jake is probably feeling guilty about many things as well and men tend to want to fix the situation, so he may be feeling helpless because he can't."

"But what about our marriage?" I asked. "Where's his loyalty to me? How can he let me fly to Australia by myself when he knows how much I'm suffering and need to get away for Christmas? And he knows I don't think his family has been very supportive."

Angela understood my point of view but also tried to provide a take on Jake's perspective. She explained that he was likely feeling very vulnerable and scared himself, drawing him closer to his own family who had always known him, much as I turned to my mum. She suggested Jake probably felt very torn between me and his family, especially because I was feeling disconnected from them. And any sense of his family and me as separate entities at that time would be difficult for him to cope with.

I listened to her ideas before turning my attention back to Marlon and the indelible scars left by his death. Angela's reflections and observations helped me process the enormity of what I was feeling and kept me from sinking completely under the weight of the mental anguish I was fighting every day, but I remained annoyed with Jake for refusing to come to Australia with me.

By the time Christmas Day arrived I couldn't wait to get on the plane. The thought of fleeing London and a sedative-induced sleep for the 24-hour flight was the best present I could ask for, because it meant I'd completely miss Christmas Day in both the UK and Australia.

I half thought Jake might change his mind at the last minute but when he offered to drive me to Heathrow in his mum's car on Christmas morning all bets were off.

"Bye," I said, unable to muster much more to say as we hugged each other.

"Merry Christmas to your mum and David too. I'll speak to you tomorrow night and I'll see you in a week or so. Have a safe flight."

"Yeah, Merry Christmas," I managed as we parted to spend our Christmases apart.

As the plane took off I gazed down at London and pictured Jake and his family, the Christmas lunch table laden with the same festive fare we'd enjoyed the Christmas we got married: Jake's favourite vegetarian delicacies specially prepared for him by his mum, the excitement of Isaac at opening his presents, Ria's pregnant belly starting to protrude. I wondered if they'd miss me but thought they'd probably be relieved not to see my miserable face on such a festive day.

And with that depressing thought I popped a Valium into my mouth and sipped red wine until I drifted off into anaesthetised slumber.

23. In the Rubble

As soon as the plane landed in Australia my mood lifted immeasurably and I was tempted to bend down and kiss the earth, so hallowed it felt.

"It's so good to see you, Mum," I said, squeezing the air out of her lungs. "It's so good to be home."

"Home?" She looked at me quizzically. "London is home for you now, darling."

"I know, Mum, but you know what I mean, now let's go home," I said, feeling my smile returning for the first time in weeks.

The first thing I did when I got to Mum's was call every one of my friends to book in a date to see them in January after I got back from staying at a holiday house owned by my friends Lisa and Dean by the Murray River in Bundalong. I knew I'd find healing in Bundalong as it had always been a special place and the beauty of the view across the lagoon from their house on the water's edge made it impossible to feel sorry for myself or stay stuck in unhappiness for long.

Bundalong proved the perfect place to contemplate life and figure out where I might take it next. That was a fundamental question that couldn't remain unanswered if Jake and I were to move forward from the catastrophe we'd experienced and keep our marriage intact.

In the heat of the Aussie sun amongst family and friends and favourite places I felt myself getting stronger every day, finding enjoyment in simple moments and contentment in the mundane. I slept soundly through the night rather than waking with a racing mind at 4am, and my sleep wasn't riddled with horror-filled nightmares waking me in a cold sweat.

Having promised to join me in Australia straight after Christmas I was dismayed when Jake pushed his arrival out to the New Year and then found more reasons not to come. I suspected he was making excuses and couldn't bring himself to tell me that he simply didn't want to leave London.

The longer I stayed in Melbourne the more I felt at peace. As the weeks passed and I'd seen all my friends I began to feel more able to be on my own as I searched for and found old pieces of myself. I retraced my childhood, revisiting formative places that had remained vivid in my mind. Places where I'd learnt lessons. Places where I'd fallen down. Places where I'd gotten hurt. Places where I'd gotten back up. Places where I'd cried. Places where I'd dusted myself off and gotten on with life. Places where my grandfather had taken me and taught me about life. And there I found the belief in myself to find a way through the grief I felt at the loss of my little boy.

I changed my flight so many times that it was March by the time Jake asked if I had any intention of coming back at all.

"Of course I'm coming back," I said. "I'm feeling so much better, it's done me the world of good. And I think I feel ready to come back."

I hadn't realised just how much I'd detached myself from London until I landed back at Heathrow. Though I was happy to see Jake, doubts returned about his commitment to our marriage when I returned to the flat to find it exactly the same as when I'd left. By the time I got into bed that night my anxiety had returned with a vengeance and when I awoke at 4am the next morning I knew it wasn't just because of jetlag.

I did my best to avoid a sense of doom about the future and direct the reserves of energetic spirit I'd gained in Australia to good use.

I returned to work straight away to keep myself occupied and tried everything I could think of to stay positive. Jake and I stayed close to each other and talked about our feelings. We also organised for a memorial bench for Marlon to be installed in the children's playground nearby, giving us somewhere close to commune with him during restorative walks on the Heath.

When Mandy called with the news that our dear friend Jules' husband Karl had died on 28 April I grieved for Jules and their infant son, and his death at such a young age got me questioning my life again. I still felt so unsettled and somehow it renewed my own grief again to think of all that Jules had lost.

Afterwards I could be sitting on the couch watching TV or looking out of the kitchen window at the beauty of nature when the flashbacks returned to haunt me. They were particularly intense in the wee hours of the morning and sometimes my dreams were infiltrated with graphic images of Marlon falling out of my grasp from a barge into a London canal and me diving into the murky water after him only to break my neck.

I was falling into depression again and it felt pointless to try to fight it on my own. I could talk to Jake but his eyes only reflected the devastation I was feeling and despite endless counselling sessions with both Angela and Annette it was obvious I wasn't coping personally and we weren't coping as a couple. It felt like the foundations I'd started to resurrect from the rubble were crumbling around me again. And as much as I loved Jake as my husband and Marlon's father, I was losing my belief that we could bear the burden of pain and loss together.

I hated feeling depressed and emotionally out of my depth and it felt like I just needed the right environment to flourish again. My feelings of grief so dominated my thoughts that there was no space left for anything or anyone else and Jake bore the brunt of my frustration.

Ria and Sam tried to be supportive but I found it hard to spend time with them and Isaac, and I struggled with Ria's blossoming belly. Meanwhile Jake had got on with his life while I'd been away and felt cabin fever being stuck at home with my misery so he took every opportunity to escape.

One Sunday after I'd been rude to Jake and Ria about him going off to spend the afternoon with her and Sam I collapsed into tears, feeling terrible for the way I'd spoken to them. Jake deserved to have a life and had every right to spend time with his sister and brother-in-law. But since I'd gotten back I'd become unrecognisably clingy and needy.

Eventually I caved and decided to get a prescription for anti-depressants from my GP, who expressed surprise that I'd coped for so long without medication.

Five days later Ria and Sam welcomed a healthy baby daughter, but my despair was so pervasive I couldn't face visiting them or even raising a smile at their wonderful news.

Eventually the antidepressants kicked in and helped stop my mind getting stuck on the same traumatic thoughts and distress-ing images, though they also made me feel horrendous physically. I became jittery and sweaty, with a mouth like a desert, felt tired and drowsy during the day but couldn't sleep at night, and while I'd stopped ruminating on the past, I couldn't get rid of the intractable thought that I could get better without drugs if I could just get away from Hampstead. I kept on trying to give our marriage the chance to thrive again but it felt like going through the motions.

Because so few people had met Marlon in his 14 weeks of life, it could seem as though he'd never existed as we went about our daily lives. But the need to talk about Marlon didn't diminish for me as life went on; if anything, it intensified. Jake and I talked about Marlon all the time but the conversations were too fraught, with too much common misery for one of us to support the other while they let their pieces fall.

Day-to-day I was functioning, going to work and socialising or sitting numbly at home, but I felt more like an automaton than human, without any vision for a new phase of life.

Angela remained my lifeline and I looked forward to my weekly session with her. Our work together eventually started to take effect and slowly and painfully my recollections of Marlon's life started to fit into the bigger picture of my own. The minutiae of our days together finally became less manic in my mind. Eventually she led me out of the darkness and horror of my experiences into the light of my love for my son.

Gradually moments of joy snuck into our conversation as I shared more of Marlon the baby boy, with a growing personality and idio-syncrasies, rather than Marlon the patient with the mystery illness that killed him. And then I found myself laughing out loud at some of his antics, the way he could express himself despite his weakened muscles and how he could say so much through his expressionless face, how we learnt to understand him, to relate to him, to figure out his likes and dislikes.

My sessions with Angela not only helped me process the trauma of Marlon's life to keep the memories I could hold dear, it also helped me clear the way to see what I needed to do to rebuild my life. She helped me understand that I could only account for myself, I couldn't control what Jake did or force him to forgo his own needs. I realised I had to act for myself if I was to climb out of the pit and for me that meant leaving London.

But before I left I had to try one last time to save my marriage. Whatever happened next, I didn't want to live with regret and if I could convince Jake to leave London, even for just a while, I knew I could get my groove back.

At home I gently raised the idea of taking time away with Jake, though I took a slightly different approach, suggesting we could spend time in Los Angeles or New York where he could try to break into the movie business, something he'd always dreamt about. When that idea fell flat I even raised the idea of going to Dubai for a year to make enough money to be mortgage free.

"I can't leave right now, I can't leave my family and I don't want to leave London. This is my home."

"I have to go," I said to Jake, though I knew he wasn't going anywhere. "I understand you can't leave but I can't stay."

He looked at me with disbelief and I felt irked that he could really believe I'd be the one to compromise again.

"Don't look at me like that," I said, trying to hide the irritation from my voice. "I don't want to leave you, I don't want to leave our marriage, but if you're not prepared to even leave North London then what other choice do I have?"

"You could stay here with me, but I understand if you have to go and I'm sorry I can't go with you."

"But you won't even give it a go," I said, incredulous.

"I can't, I'm sorry," he concurred.

"Where will you go?" he asked.

"Well if you're not coming, I'll go home, I suppose. It makes sense given I was much better when I was there at Christmas."

"Yeah, you were," he said. "I'm sorry we couldn't make it work. I'm sorry I couldn't fix you."

"I'm sorry too, Jake, I really am," I said tearfully as we hugged each other.

So there in the living room of the house where Marlon had died, so too did our marriage and we agreed to go our separate ways, though we'd stay living together until my departure. I booked my flight home for the second of October – exactly one year since we'd attended Dave and Sachi's wedding in Bali.

A new grief enveloped both of us but for me it was coupled with relief that we'd made a decision, and for a little while we carried on almost as if nothing had changed. We still walked together on the

Heath and sat on Marlon's bench talking about all the hopes and dreams we'd started with and how our life and relationship could have veered so dramatically off course. We still cooked dinner for each other and played chess. We laughed one minute like old times and then cried the next because it was really over.

When Marlon's first birthday came around on the eighteenth of May, Jake and I hung onto each other, lost in mutual bewilderment that a year could already have passed. In that time he had lived and died and now our marriage was over as well.

I wrote a birthday note for Marlon that I took with us to the crematorium:

Happy Birthday Marlon. A year has already passed since the day of your traumatic birth and so much has happened since then that I barely know myself. But the love I learned that day remains and you, my little love, are imprinted on my heart indelibly like a footprint on the pavement. You're etched in my soul and branded on my every thought. Thank you for being born, thank you for being so strong, thank you for being my son. I love you for eternity. Always and forever your Mummy.

If there was a time I might have wavered, it was Marlon's first birthday because I realised that nobody but Jake could ever truly understand the way I felt and I wondered how I'd face Marlon's birthdays and anniversaries without him by my side. But I didn't change my mind that day, nor did Jake change his. I was still leaving and he was still staying and we reverted to our surreal existence of living together as a married couple who were separating. Jake lived his life and I lived mine, saying my farewells to London, spending as much time as I could with my treasured friends and Ayesha and Kayn, who I dreaded leaving having grown so familiar and close.

I didn't hear from Jake's mum so I was none the wiser as to whether she thought our separation was for the better or worse. I decided to let it go but was flabbergasted when Jake came home one afternoon after spending time with his family and asked if I could give back the ring his mother had given me to commemorate Marlon's birth, saying she wanted it because of its sentimental value.

I ripped the ring from my ring finger on my right hand where it had been since Marlon's birth and angrily flung it across the room at Jake. "Here. She can have the fucking ring back. What's she going to do with it, give it to your next wife who produces a healthy kid? When you give it to her tell her I don't want her bloody ring anyway, or her conditional love."

I could see protective ire flare in Jake's nostrils but he resisted the urge to fire back, and we both retreated into wounded silence.

I felt utterly bereft and alone after the ring episode and started packing my belongings up into boxes, ruthlessly discarding clothes and retrieving just a couple of the wedding presents my family and closest friends had given us. It made a stark image to see 11 years of my life squashed into a few cardboard boxes.

Angela was still providing a weekly sounding board for me to vent my emotions and share the complexity and confusion I was feeling in leaving a husband I loved. She provided what I found invaluable advice and I drew heart when she said that despite Jake's and my best intentions to support each other through our separation, sometimes the person that is part of the problem isn't the best person to salve the pain. This made perfect sense and I knew I had to move out immediately.

The Captain and Kate came to the rescue again, inviting me to go sailing with them in Croatia, and Jake and I agreed that I'd move out as soon I got back from the holiday.

When my feet hit the deck of the yacht and I dived off into the cool, clear Adriatic Sea the heaviness I'd been carrying washed away. That night I threw away my antidepressants, ignoring the doctor's warning not to go cold turkey. I didn't care and the feeling of liberation I got from knowing I would no longer live in the house where Marlon had died set me free. I knew I was going to be okay.

The first day of the holiday was unadulterated bliss but I soon learnt throwing away my medication in such haste hadn't been a sensible idea. Once my initial elation mellowed, I slipped into a more melancholic mood and probably wasn't the best company in the confined space of our yacht. Not wanting to spoil my friends' holiday I decided to leave and made my way back to Rijeka for my return flight to London three days later.

Being on my own again in a foreign country switched on all of my instincts for adventure and I found myself savouring the challenge that unfamiliarity presented. I felt more alive and hopeful there by myself than I had in months, though all the while a dialogue with Marlon ran in my head and I understood that I would always keep my little boy close and take him with me wherever I went.

Arriving back in London this time, I was more prepared for the angst that hit me as soon as I got back to Jake's. I knew it was just one more sleep before I moved out so I concentrated on making our last night together one to remember. The next day we went to lunch on Hampstead High Street and then had a final siesta at home before I packed the last of my belongings into my bag ready to move to Ayesha's.

"Do you think this is the most civilised parting in the history of separations?" I asked Jake, trying to keep things light before we went our separate ways.

"Probably," he replied sadly, "but most couples who separate don't love each other anymore."

"I'll always love you and Marlon, Jake," I said as a hint of lament pushed me off balance. I'll never forget or regret what we had."

"Yeah. Me too," he said simply, battling to maintain his composure. We held each other close.

"See ya," I said looking deeply into his eyes.

"Yeah. See ya soon," he replied.

★

HOW I MET YOUR FATHER

Ayesha and Kaynahn welcomed me into the cosiness of their flat, the air laden with the delicious smell of my sister's famous curry goat. Other family members had gathered to offer me support and, in the way of the Caribbean, enveloped me in goodwill and nurtured me with company, soul food and music on that first day of the rest of my life.

I cried myself to sleep that night and each night after that.

As the day of my departure neared I grew more eager to leave London and the losses it represented but I hadn't thought about what my impending departure might mean to Ayesha. We'd become sisters in most senses of the word and had spent more than a decade in the same city having grown up not knowing each other. She'd been so supportive since Marlon's birth and, in a culture where family was so important, I'd been so absorbed in my own grief and desolation, I'd never acknowledged that Ayesha had lost a nephew and watched her big strong sister fall apart. And now she'd be saying goodbye to me in the knowledge we'd probably never live in the same city again. As tension between us escalated into an argument it became clear I should leave.

I sobbed as I repacked my bag, wondering why I seemed to be arguing with everybody, and arranged to stay at the home of an ex-work colleague and friend, Cat.

I spent my last days in London in a round of final goodbyes and realised I'd made as many close friendships in London as I had in Australia. I would always have my heart in two places and it was a wrench to leave people who'd become so important in my life. Apart from my British contingent of friends, many of us had come to live in the melting pot of London from some-where else, whether it be Africa, Asia, the Middle East, Europe, the Americas or the Caribbean. I'd formed a veritable United Nations of true friendships.

I moved to Mandy's to spend my last few days with my best friend and the person I'd started the adventure with almost 12 years before. It seemed a fitting close to the circle of my life in London and we stayed up drinking, talking and reminiscing until five in the morning just like old times and it felt comforting to know that some things would never change.

During those last days in London, Jonathan held a farewell party for me at his house where my nearest and dearest friends gathered together to send me off with a good hangover.

The next day it was time for my final goodbye with Jake. We'd deliberately not spent much time together since I'd moved out – apart from a couple of counselling sessions with Annette to make sure we weren't making an irreversible decision that we might later think was a terrible mistake. Annette seemed to think we might still be able to salvage our marriage in the future, even if it meant taking some time apart, but I knew that once I left London there'd be no going back.

Jake and I wandered around Hampstead High Street chatting and catching up on each other's lives, but for the first time it felt like a distance had settled between us. It didn't mitigate the sadness when it came time for our final goodbyes and we hugged each other in an embrace that held all the love and the loss and heartbreak of our little boy and our broken relationship between us.

"I don't want to let go," I cried into Jake's collar, knowing I was about to walk away for the very last time.

"I don't either," he said, holding back his own tears. "If it's too hard I'll come and get you."

"Okay," I said, laughing and crying simultaneously at Jake's die-hard romanticism.

We finally pulled ourselves apart and I rushed away without stopping or looking over my shoulder in case I changed my mind.

Mandy and I stayed up drinking again that night, drowning my sorrows and laughing at the irony that we'd always imagined it would be me who stayed in London forever. Mandy had once joked that I'd marry a black guy and have black, fuzzy-haired babies and she and Axel would end up back in Australia with a blonde-haired brood. Alas, my side of the story hadn't quite panned out, but there was still hope she and Axel would come back to Australia one day and live out her part of the happily-ever-after dream.

The next morning Mandy scraped my hungover pieces into her Porsche to take me to the airport. She was the perfect friend to deliver me safely onto my flight. We'd been friends for almost 20 years and, regardless of whether she stayed in London or came home eventually, we knew we'd be friends for life. Not one to stand on ceremony but having perfected the art of the hug she wrapped her arms around me and said simply, "See ya, mate."

"Bye, Mands, thanks for everything, you're…" I began, starting to get emotional, but she stopped me before I could cry.

"Means, don't start, you'll get me going. And don't worry, knowing me you'll probably see me in a month." And with a wink and her signature grin she was gone.

As the plane rose in the air I looked down on London with a sense of finality, a mixture of good and bad memories crashing together and tumbling around in my head.

I'd always felt tied to London by my dad and as I left I felt overwhelmed by all that it had come to represent in my life. I was thankful to escape it but I knew I'd always feel connected to the city, no longer because of my father but because of my sister and my son.

I'd come to London to find my dad and although he hadn't been there I'd eventually found myself. Now, as the plane flew further away, I thought about my dad left standing at the very same airport 36 years before while his partner and child had flown away. The words from the first letter he'd written to us after we'd left echoed in my mind:

My darlings Helen and Aminah

I received both your cards and letter, you had me worried for a while and I couldn't understand why I didn't hear from you. It seemed such a long time. Anyway I phoned Stuart to see if he had Marion's phone number and found there was a strike in Rome.

Helen as you know writing is not one of my best forms of expression, however I would let you know what happened on my way back from the airport. I kept seeing you push Aminah in that little pushchair thing and I know I really wanted to take her out of it and cuddle her real tight, and take her home. I felt so upset I had to stop the cab and do some bawling so I could feel better, the little old man must have been so shocked, he started whispering some consoling words which sounded very kind but all I could hear at that moment was something or somebody telling me I did not have the guts to take both of you out of the airport and return to the flat. Maybe I shouldn't be telling you all this but my feelings is something I refuse to suppress because although you profess not to understand me sometimes, I believe you know how much I do care about the both of you. Again, I would like you to know it's not my fault that the world we live in it seems it's not sufficient to love and this is why I couldn't get it together to stop you from leaving.

However my unhappiness will probably make a few other people happy, that's life. I got Aminah a gold bracelet for her birthday and do hope you like it, it's adjustable and should be useful for a few years. I hope you have a party for her with lots of kids on the scene. I think she would love it. I miss her so much I can't really explain. If the bread scene is okay I will phone on her birthday. This is all for now give my regards to your parents and give plenty of kisses for my Aminah and you darls.

Love to you both.

Tony.

PART IV

24. From a Broken Home

Home bittersweet home. Melbourne had always provided a soft landing into the loving arms of my mum and reconnection with wonderful friends. My many Melbourne friendships had remained strong over the years I'd been away in London. But that was then, before Marlon. This was a very different time and a very different me. Though I may have appeared my perennially positive, optimistic self on the surface, inside I couldn't find that person anywhere.

Desolate thoughts that everything was broken and lost besieged me as I flew across the vast wilderness of Australia. But it was no happy homecoming like the ones I'd dreamt of, returning each year with my growing family. It felt agonisingly different with my arms empty. This was more a bitter déjà vu of coming back alone, like Mum had done 36 years before.

I felt defeated by the interminable crushing pain that overwhelmed me. I wanted to land and then hide away and lick my wounds in the healing bosom of my mother, otherwise I feared I might not survive. My firstborn son was dead. It still seemed too terrible to be true.

As we neared Melbourne, grief about my broken marriage came flooding in. Visions of our short time as a little family of three played over in mind. I thought I'd been a good mum, as much as I'd had the opportunity to be, but we'd hardly gotten started before Marlon slipped from our grasp. Now my marriage to Jake lay in tatters.

I questioned what sort of ___ ___ ___ nning away. I wished Jake and I ___ ___ trayed the marriage vo ___ ___ 't been able to hold on ___ sed. My enduring love ___ tralia. Then again, Jake ___ 'd always made it clear ___ im. He appreciated i ___ each but never as a pl ___ f our marriage deal. At ___ foreseen ever wanting ___ e.

As th ___ e terminal at Tullamar ___ r my life in London a ___ ow only sad reflections in the sliding doc ___ ...ght have been.

It still felt like it was a given that I'd make my own family someday. I'd assumed life would go down that path of its own accord and I'd have a bigger and more conventional family than Mum and I had had. Despite having had a happy childhood in my family, for the next generation I wanted to provide my children with the stronger sense of belonging I thought two parents and siblings could bring. I didn't envisage a big brood, but at least two kids or maybe even three. Now that the foundations of such a future felt obliterated, the realisation hit me of just how much family meant to me. What if...? Maybe...? I should have...? I must...? All the punishing unanswerable questions wrought chaos in my mind.

In the past when I'd walked through Mum's front door it had held the snug feeling of a security blanket but this time it felt more like a bunker to hide away from the world until I could heal. I wasn't moving back in with Mum aged 37 just for fun. I was simply too brittle to be on my own and it seemed the obvious place to start again.

The upside of coming home in November was the fortifying feeling of spring, the warmth of the sun on my skin and the promise of the summer to come. It was the perfect time of year to catch up with friends and get lost in the party atmosphere.

Once I'd settled in at Mum's I drew in the people closest to me and recklessly clutched at old vices like alcohol and cigarettes to help me through the mire. Loyal and loving friends welcomed me back to Melbourne life with open hearts and invitations into their social scenes, but it was difficult to share the details of the hell I'd endured. A couple of good friends had met Marlon but I didn't want to unload my trauma on anyone else.

The alcohol seemed to hold me afloat and infuse me with artificial good-humour but the grief was still there underneath, like the ocean with its currents and tides. One day I'd be floating in the shallows, the next a wave would crash over me, suck me back under and drag me back out to sea. It was pointless trying to avoid it – eventually I had to look into the murky deep of a future without my son.

A tragic twist in fortunes brought me closer to an old friend, Jules, who I'd known since PLC. Although in different years at school, we'd remained in overlapping circles of friends and our paths had crossed regularly through the years. Coincidentally she'd grown up next door to Mandy and the three of us had a lot in common, with a rebellious side, as well as love of adventure and a penchant for all-night carousing. So when Jules had moved to London the three of us often partied together, and by the time she left London to return to Australia again we'd become very close.

After Jules had come back to Australia she'd quickly found a partner in Karl and the two of them had fallen fast and furiously in love. A few months later Jules was pregnant and Karl had proposed to her on a mountain top in the Austrian Alps.

However, soon after Jules gave birth to their beautiful, healthy son, Marlow, Karl began complaining of headaches. He was away in New Zealand when a brain haemorrhage struck him down. With their 12-week-old, breastfeeding baby in her arms Jules flew to Karl's bedside. The doctors thought Karl had an arteriovenous malformation which had caused a blood vessel to bleed, but his prognosis was good and after a couple of weeks he'd recovered sufficiently to fly home to Australia. But Karl had continued to suffer severe head pain. A subsequent MRI revealed that he had glioblastoma multiforme grade 4 – the most aggressive type of brain cancer. The doctors said he might live 12 months at most or as little as three.

Karl wouldn't take the diagnosis or such a shattering prognosis lying down. He had everything to live for with a newborn son and a forthcoming marriage to the love of his life. He and Jules committed to fighting his cancer together and to keep their wedding date in November, so they attacked his disease with a double barrel of chemo and radiotherapy. After finishing his treatment and diminishing the tumour, Karl and Jules, both intrepid travellers, took Marlow on a trip to East Timor.

Karl had always been an adrenaline junkie, the first to leap off an alpine ledge and disappear off the piste, showing up in the pub afterwards with a hair-raising story to tell. He took the same approach to his cancer, facing it with bravery and defiance, expecting a bumpy course but stubbornly positive he'd come out the other side.

After brain surgery, he made it to his wedding, a triumphant celebration on the beach at Palm Cove surrounded by family and friends, but by the following month he and Jules were counting time because his tumour had returned. Jules and I shared a moment together looking out across a park pondering how our lives could have veered so wildly off course. Shortly after, Karl died aged 33, leaving little Marlow without a father and Jules a shattered widow at only 35.

After my return to Melbourne Jules and I banded together in our misery and despair, supporting each other as we fell apart and struggled to put ourselves back together again. And though we learnt that the new couldn't resemble the old we were grateful to have each other's support through our grief.

Jules had always been trustworthy and loyal but I couldn't have imagined how tireless a friend could be in sharing the minutiae of our tragedies and bearing witness to my pain. Our friendship blossomed in those darkest of days when it felt like the world was moving on without us. We talked, reminisced, cried and found dark humour in our sorrow, providing mutual counsel amidst countless bottles of wine. When I was down she lifted me up and I tried to do the same for her in a therapeutic alliance that eventually pulled us up from the bottom of the black hole.

I knew I also needed professional help, having trodden the fine line between melancholy and depression before, so I reached for a guiding hand. SIDS & Kids was like an oasis for people like me whose children had died, offering counselling and peer support, social gatherings and group therapy, as well as creative outlets for feelings of grief and loss. It quickly became another source of support and eventually I became a Parent Supporter myself, channelling my own experience of grief into supporting others going through similar pain.

Being more than a year down the track from bereavement made me a 'survivor', and I gained a new sense of purpose and discovered a knack for providing a comfortable space for others to share their stories without obligation or judgement. And after a while my work with others pointed me towards a more fulfilling new career.

As the new year dawned with no sign of Jake I knew it was time for me to propel myself back into life. I decided to combine my desire to help others with new learning and started a course in life coaching, focusing on the power of positive self-reliance to retake the helm of my life and help others do the same.

Though I'd returned to advertising and the people in adland were as lively and fun to be around as ever, the work itself had lost its shine. I gave it a hundred percent of my effort but my mind was elsewhere and I'd get home exhausted feeling empty and unfulfilled, as if what I'd seen of sick children   advertising hollow an   permanent job offers   cow while I forged al

Life coa   t inevitably loneliness c   missed me and I still f   he would ever come   reunion. I didn't want   led to get proactive an   r actually dated before   through social avenue   nds were married or in   potential new partner.

Lonely Hearts Ads

Once I put myself out there it wasn't difficult to find a date, but finding someone to fill the cavernous space left by my husband was more challenging. I tried blind dates and online dating and even the direct approach when out with friends, picking out someone I found vaguely attractive and asking him out. A few were genuinely lovely but more were drifters or socially awkward types. The common thread was a lack of that distinctive something I was looking for, and the more dates I went on the more disillusioned I became that I would find someone with the elusive x-factor. I wondered what I'd expected as I veered towards 38.

25. Hope and Fresh Heartbreak

Just as it felt like it was getting too hard, the numbers game paid off when I met a six-foot-three and three-foot-wide bloke in a Melbourne pub. It wasn't just Simon's impressive footballer's physique that struck me; the sincerity in his eyes immediately set him apart. We got chatting and his gentle manner as well as the indefinable something that had been missing with the other men I'd met since returning to Australia made me feel that I wanted to know him better. We drank and talked into the night and I liked his country-boy lack of pretension.

Our first meeting segued naturally into a regular thing and before I knew it he was introducing me as his girlfriend. The presumption didn't bother me; he was the first and only guy I'd imagined having a relationship with since Jake. Perhaps his lack of enthusiasm for protected sex should have sounded an alarm but I still had enough of a devil-may-care attitude not to force the issue, and resorted to the morning-after pill. It was a relief when I started bleeding but Simon caught me completely off guard when he declared, "It wouldn't have mattered if you were pregnant. I'm ready to settle down and have kids, so I'd be happy if you got pregnant." Those tantalising words added tenfold to his appeal. He couldn't have found a more willing mate or one more vulnerable to such a suggestion.

While Simon and I were still in the first flushes of a new relationship, I had to fly to New Zealand for work, to shoot a TV commercial with an agency producer called Melissa who I'd become friends with on another job the previous year. Melissa and I decided to fly to Auckland a few days early to enjoy a weekend of leisure before the shoot started. After an indulgent day of shopping and spa treatments, I was back in the hotel room when I noticed peculiarly familiar sensations in my groin.

I lay on the bed and tuned in to my body, feeling the same unmistakable twinges I'd had before I discovered I was pregnant with Marlon. I wasn't sure whether to laugh or vomit because I hadn't expected anything to happen quite so soon. Whether reckless or wishful in my actions, I should have known better because getting pregnant had happened easily before but I'd have to wait a week to be certain and in the meantime I needed to abstain from drinking, which was unheard of after a day on a location shoot.

"I'm pregnant," I said to Simon when I got home then handed him the evidence of a positive pregnancy test.

"That's great," he replied, a grin spreading across his face.

Simon and I were stunned and ecstatic in equal measure. And though I didn't love Simon exactly – there'd been no time to establish such complexity of feeling – I quickly attached myself to what he now represented and was all up for making it work. If only I could get through the pregnancy with a healthy baby at the end, I'd be happy and the rest felt within my power to influence.

While Simon's happiness at the prospect of a baby remained absolute my initial delight was soon replaced by nagging anxiety which grew more intense with each day. I didn't want to dampen Simon's joy but my innocence had been taken. While Marlon was in the NICU I'd seen too many horrendous complications that could blight pregnancy and birth to be as naively optimistic as I'd been before Marlon was born. The reality of his life and death loomed larger now and I found it impossible to relax and approach the pregnancy with the same eagerness or joy as Simon.

Easter came upon us and instead of Easter eggs Simon came home bearing baby clothes. I felt a flicker of annoyance that he could be so premature with such an optimistic gesture because I'd shared my worry and the reasons for my fear with him.

Having never met Simon's family, other than the younger sister he lived with, he arranged for us to visit his parents for their Easter family gathering. His elderly grandparents would be there and his older sister's family, but none of them had any inkling of our news. Simon seemed to have no concept of my nervousness and announced our pregnancy to his family while we were there.

Simon's family didn't really have much of a choice but to accept me given I was pregnant with their grandchild, and they were graciously hospitable, expressing sincere happiness at our news. But being good Catholic country folk I was sure they didn't really welcome the haste with which Simon and I had tied ourselves together with the commitment of a child. I was still incredulous myself and even Mum, who'd always gone with the flow of my life without judgement or reproach, wondered at our haste, though she knew the depth of my longing for a family and remained supportive, keeping any reservations to herself.

In truth I was still in love with Jake, or at least the idea of him and true love, but I'd taken us to the point of no return by getting pregnant to someone else. If he'd turned up on my doorstep I'd have had to send him away with the hurtful truth, so it was time to officially conclude our relationship. I found a how-to guide for divorce online and – with enormous sadness – ended our marriage. I sent Jake a message telling him what I'd done but I wasn't ready to tell him I was expecting another baby because I hadn't fully accepted it myself and I knew it might add unnecessarily to his pain.

All of my early antenatal tests were perfect and my obstetrician, Michael, said all the right things. However, the geneticist I consulted couldn't guarantee that what had happened with Marlon couldn't occur again. She could only reaffirm the statistic of less than five percent that the London geneticist had given me, saying, "A recurrence is highly unlikely, especially with a different dad."

The geneticist's words didn't completely reassure me; I needed a watertight warranty to allay my fears. Simon chose to bury his head in the sand and simply couldn't conceive of anything other than nine months of glowing and growing expectancy followed by a bouncing bundle of joy. I understood his blissful obliviousness but desperately needed his reassurance and support. He couldn't appreciate my fearfulness and insisted I should be more positive.

Needless to say, I was already trying my best to be optimistic. I constantly played affirming mantras over in my mind and attempted to convince myself that the long odds of a recurrence of Marlon's condition should be enough but it proved exhaustingly futile to overcome my anxiety. To deny the worries only exacerbated my fear – I worried that if I didn't worry I'd be more vulnerable should something go wrong.

What I saw as Simon's lack of understanding resulted in me withdrawing into self-protection mode. I focused on my coaching studies which served a productive dual role in teaching me how to support others and tap into my own resources.

To appease Simon's pleas for optimism, he and I spent a few weekends looking at houses we might potentially buy, but quickly realised that the market for family homes was beyond our means. And when Simon made no offer for me and the baby to live with him, a distance settled between us, and our communication with each other deteriorated as we each retreated into our protective shells. We met for lunch one day in an attempt to bridge the gap but the conversation only widened the breach between us and we lacked the means to reconnect that might have come from knowing each other better.

Meanwhile, I started to look for a place of my own to buy and happened upon a cosy art deco apartment which I immediately put down a deposit for. When I told Simon I'd found a place to live he was furious that I'd acted independently.

"Where else will I live when the baby comes?" I asked him incredulously. "I can't keep living with my mum and we can't afford to buy a house together right now so what choice do I have? And you could move into the flat too, at least for the time being until we can save for a bigger place," I added uncertainly.

"It's too far away from work," he replied, bringing the conversation to a fractious halt.

I drove him home in awkward silence and when we arrived he flung the car door open, got out without looking at me and muttered, "Call me if you need anything," over his shoulder before slamming the door and walking away.

It floored me that he could stalk off like that and I found his sulkiness infuriating given he'd offered no alternative for housing our child. With anger thrown into the cauldron of hormonal fretting and anxious fear, I started crying, so instead of getting out of the car and taking the initiative to try to solve the impasse, I sped off in a flood of tears, leaving each of us to stew.

A stalemate of stubbornness and avoidance ensued and our communication descended into patchy and perfunctory exchanges. Simon continued to attend antenatal appointments but our mutual pent-up frustration often overflowed into anger and argument when what I desperately craved was reassurance and a hug. Instead his exasperation compounded my fears that our conflict might negatively impact on our baby's wellbeing, deepening our estrangement.

With the halfway mark of my pregnancy approaching I'd hoped my confidence would improve but I couldn't feel the vigorous kicks from the baby I'd hoped would differentiate it from Marlon's pregnancy. The movements were stronger but not robust enough to put my hectic mind at ease. The critical 20-week scan suggested everything was exactly as it should be and the obstetrician who performed the scan said the baby was moving just fine, saying, "Everything looks beautiful."

I wanted to know the baby's sex because of the niggling five percent chance the geneticists had given for the same problems occurring should I have another boy. It felt like a finger-in-the-air statistic to me given Marlon's lack of diagnosis and it remained a sickening worry. Simon wanted a gender surprise but we were contrary about everything by then so I went ahead and found out for myself. When I told him I knew the baby's gender he was incensed. "You don't give me a say in anything, do you? Everything has to be your way, doesn't it, Aminah?"

"It might be different if you tried to understand how hard this is for me," I replied, knowing the chasm between us would widen with my increased anxiety at knowing our baby was a boy.

The months dragged on and my apprehension escalated so I tried to focus on anything and everything else in my life, but buried my head in the sand where my relationship with Simon was concerned. The best I could hope for was that we could maybe fix our relationship once the baby safely arrived.

I moved into my new apartment, happy to think it was opposite my beloved grandfather, Louda's, alma mater, Scotch College, and taking pleasure that my great-grandfather, Reverend Dr Alexander Marshall, had been instrumental in securing the tract of land for the school to relocate to from East Melbourne. One day Mum and I looked across the road from the apartment's windows, imagining a time when my little boy would continue the family tradition and go to school at Scotch College, our conversation drifting towards a happily imagined future. It was a precious moment of normalcy and optimism and I decided then and there that I would name my son Louis, in honour of Louda.

I knew it wasn't fair to Simon to make such a fundamental decision as the baby's name without consulting him but by then I felt like a solo parent-in-waiting. When I called to tell him I'd decided on a name and the reasons why, suggesting he might like to choose a middle name, he exploded, "You're a complete bitch, Aminah, you don't just make that decision by yourself and tell me."

"I already have. His name will be Louis. Louis Hart," I said before ending the call without saying goodbye.

My obstetrician was planning a normal delivery despite my previous emergency caesarean, hoping to make my second experience of birth as natural as possible with minimal intervention. "I'd like it to be a happier experience for you this time," he said confidently.

His confidence was contagious because I started attending birthing and breastfeeding classes as my due date neared. I allowed the prospect of a full-term pregnancy to take root and began to divert my thoughts away from Louis' health to how I'd cope as a solo mum. Though I was sad not to have a partner to share the highs and lows of parenthood with, and exhausted by the perpetual need for emotional self-sufficiency, having been raised by such a strong and independent single mum I knew I had it in me to do it alone; I just didn't relish the prospect of isolation and loneliness it might bring.

Simon and I made some vain attempts to bond as Louis' birth loomed. He generously bought a car seat and a pram, but we tiptoed around other issues to avoid further fights. We shared a stilted brunch one morning and I got tearful as we went our separate ways. Maybe it was hormones but the longing to bring Louis into a warm and protected family life felt beyond my reach. The tentative connection we'd tried to regain was irretrievably broken.

Marlon's third anniversary and a new wave of wistful reminiscence arrived on 28 August. I'd come so close to achieving everything I'd wanted with Jake and Marlon but it had all gone so horribly wrong. Now, with the way things were between Simon and me, life was even further from ideal but I had to hold onto the growing hope that Louis would be safe and well in order to create the foundation of a new life structure.

During the final trimester I allowed myself to look forward to meeting my second son. Passing 33 weeks, the stage of Marlon's premature arrival, boosted my confidence and although my fears weren't completely assuaged by Michael's repeated assurances of Louis' health and vigour, I surrendered to an attachment to Louis I'd tried so long to deny.

I passed the gestational diabetes test and the final countdown had begun but all of a sudden I blew up and my weight spiked off the scale. Michael said, "It looks like polyhydramnios, you've got too much amniotic fluid."

The mere mention of the word that had caused Marlon's early entry sent my fear spiralling upwards again.

Michael ordered further tests and I grappled with an alarming sense of doom, my heart racing uncontrollably as I lay on a hospital bed hooked up to a trace on the baby's heart. Waves of nausea rolled through me and I held my breath until I heard the reassuring rhythmic beating of his heart, but even with that and another scan to be sure Louis was okay, the seeds of doubt had been resown, turning me into an emotional mess destined to survive six more weeks without sleep or respite from worry.

26. Louis

With four weeks to go before my due date, I was dozing fitfully one night when I felt a gush of liquid leak out onto the bed. As I waddled to the bathroom I realised my waters had broken.

Somehow staying calm, I called the Mercy Hospital and was told to come in, then I called Mum to alert her too. Without any pain to signal labour I declined her offer to pick me up and tottered out to my car with a towel between my legs and drove to the hospital, trying to stave off panic until I found out what was happening. I pulled up in an ambulance bay, shuffled inside and managed to keep an even voice as I explained things to the nurse, who quickly admitted me to a room by myself in the labour ward.

I lay on the bed stock still, frozen by fear as I was hooked up to a monitor to monitor the baby's heartbeat. Though barely audible at first, familiar thumping like horse hooves reassured me he was alright. The more disturbing concern was that I could no longer feel him moving and there was no other positive sign that he'd be making an appearance any time soon.

Michael came in the next morning and said, "He seems comfortable in there so I'd like to wait and see if you go into labour spontaneously rather than rushing you in for a caesarean."

"Really?" I said, surprised at his hesitation. Knowing my history I'd assumed he'd want to deliver Louis posthaste.

"The longer he can stay in there the better for his lungs," said Michael. "I'll come by again this afternoon to see how you're getting on."

Hours dragged on interminably as I lay there tormented by the ghosts of the past. I started to feel I might lose my mind as two nights passed.

Finally Michael called time to bring Louis into the world because 36 hours without amniotic fluid meant there was a risk of infection setting in. As I was wheeled into theatre fear mixed with a frisson of excitement at the prospect of finally getting to meet my little boy. Once the spinal block did its job, Mum took up her seat beside me, gently stroking my head.

I thought guiltily about not letting Simon know I was in hospital, unable to tolerate the idea of spending hours with nothing to say to each other. I knew I was depriving him of seeing his son come into the world but after a lifetime of unwavering support, Mum was the only person I wanted with me when I held Louis for the first time. After the pain she'd helped me through with Marlon I wanted to share the joy of Louis' birth with her and have a memory we could treasure together.

We held our breath collectively after Michael made the incision but it seemed to take an inordinately long time for Louis to appear and I sensed a struggle was going on. Mum and I looked at each other fearfully as the pulling and tugging continued until finally Michael broke him free.

Rather than the anticipated cry of a newborn, ominous silence filled the room. Louis was held aloft just long enough for me to register he wasn't squirming and pink but a deathly shade of blue.

Time stood still with the realisation that history had repeated itself and Louis looked barely alive. Everything went black for a moment and I thought perhaps I'd passed out. Then all hell broke loose as a siren rang out an urgent Code Blue.

A terrible awareness came over me that Louis was stricken with whatever Marlon had suffered from, as well as the undeniable realisation that the affliction had come from me. There was no other explanation given their two different fathers that I'd passed something genetic onto my kids that rendered them barely able to survive their births.

The guilt that had taken such a long time to overcome came raging back with a mighty force. I felt it was my fault that Marlon had been so sick and died and now Louis was suffering too.

I looked at Mum as our eyes filled with tears of despair.

"I'll never have a healthy baby. The same thing's happened again," I whispered, searching her face imploringly, begging for it not to be true.

"Oh my darling," was all she could say as we clung tightly to each other.

The room erupted into a frenzy of barely controlled chaos as the rescue team arrived and doctors set about trying to perform the miracle needed to give Louis life.

Mum and I could only look on helplessly at the screen showing the heartbreaking scenes of my lifeless son and doctors' hands trying frantically to get his heart pumping and a breathing tube down his throat. Louis was so limp and loose limbed that I was convinced he was already dead and asked, "Has he died?"

All the while terrifying flashbacks to Marlon peppered my mind as the rescue team desperately continued their attempt to get oxygen to Louis' brain.

"No, he's not dead but he's in a very bad way," said Michael.

"It's happened again, hasn't it?" I asked, in the vain hope I might be wrong.

"It looks like the same thing," Michael replied as he stitched me back together.

Suddenly the camera was shoved aside, turning the screen to black, and I assumed the worst because it was taking too long to revive Louis than he could possibly survive.

"Has he died now?" I asked again, tears streaming down my face, as I silently begged Louis to take a breath. I just wanted the chance to hold him once before he died. It seemed like hours since I'd seen the telling blue tinge of his face and I knew his chances were fading with every second.

"No, he's still alive but only just."

Suddenly the tension in the room eased slightly as one of the doctors said, "They've got the tube in." A ventilator could now breathe for Louis and I hoped he might hold on long enough for me to cuddle him.

I said a silent thank you as Louis was wheeled away to the NICU then tried to regulate my breathing to slow my heart and alleviate the shock.

At least I'll get to say goodbye, I thought as my heart shattered into a billion sharp-edged fragments.

"Please go with Louis," I said to Mum. "I'll be okay, I'm in good hands, but I want him to know his family is there. Tell him I love him and Mummy will be there soon."

In the recovery ward I tried to disappear into sleep, squeezing my eyes closed and pleading hopelessly to be woken from the nightmare holding me captive. But there was no escaping the searing new pain of a broken heart, which far outweighed any physical pain from the caesarean.

I couldn't understand how something so catastrophic had been missed during my eight months of pregnancy. Nor could I come to terms with the possibility that the momentary glimpse I'd had of Louis all blue and barely there might be my only memory of seeing him alive. Time warped and things took on a surreal hue as

I desperately ached to see my son, though I was in no rush to get back to a life so unrecognisable from the one I'd hoped for.

Eventually an orderly came to wheel me to the NICU where Louis was clinging precariously to life. Lying on the gurney next to his intensive care bed I reached for him. He looked more like the victim of some horrifically violent accident than a newborn baby freshly plucked from the sanctuary of his mother's womb, with every inch of his body puffy and bruised red and blue with scabbing blood coagulating where they'd pushed the breathing tube down this throat, needles under his skin and catheters into his veins. Wires were attached all over him and tubes protruded from where breath and food should go.

I took his tiny hand in mine, saying quietly, "Please don't go, Louis," as I tried to swallow down my tears and will him the strength to hang on. "Mummy will come back again, I promise, please hold on, darling boy. I love you, Louis. I know you can do it. Be strong, little one."

My heart broke all over again as the words 'little one' slipped out of my mouth, the same term of endearment Jake and I had used for Marlon, which were now etched into his memorial bench. Looking past the wires and medical paraphernalia keeping Louis alive, all my maternal eyes could see was my perfect son desperately needing a cuddle from his mum.

Beneath the bruises, every part of him was exquisitely formed, his flawless body belying the devastating floppiness of his muscles, which were leaving him so perilously close to death. I imprinted the image of his face in my mind and the feeling of his hand in mine in case it was the only lasting impression I ever had. He felt cold to my touch and I couldn't help but think that he was closer to death than life.

As I lay there, suffocating sadness descended on me at my inability to fulfil my desperate yearning to nurse my broken little boy. But the more wretched part of my sorrow wasn't for myself but for

Louis that such implausible cruelty could be inflicted on him. And it wasn't only Louis I saw lying there but Marlon too, ghostlike in the replica bed. Both of them wrenched pitifully into the world only to cling onto life by a thread, two vulnerable little beings forced to fight for every breath.

Because I needed to be under medical supervision my first visit to Louis was fleeting despite my protests. I grasped Louis' hand again before I was wheeled away, saying, "Hold on, little boy, you're doing so well, just keep going and Mummy will come back very soon."

I was obscurely grateful that the gruff and bearded director of the NICU, Andrew Watkins, was a straight shooter. He didn't mince his words when he gave me Louis' brutal prognosis. "We're doing all we can," he said gravely, "but it took 20 minutes to get him intubated so a hypoxic brain injury is highly likely, notwithstanding his muscle problems. His lungs have collapsed and with the amount of time his brain was without oxygen we don't expect he'll survive much more than 24 hours…but we will do our very best."

I knew that if his prediction played out my next visit would be to a private room where they'd take Louis when he died so that I could have some solitude in which to say goodbye.

Dr Watkins explained that Louis was being given 'TOBY therapy' which meant cooling his body to slow down all of its functions and let his brain focus on healing itself. That explained why his hand had felt so cold. I kissed my fingertips and touched them to the parts of him I could reach before I was trundled away to my room to be alone again with my tortured thoughts. The best I could hope for was that Louis might share the same dogged determination as his brother to continue his valiant fight for life.

As I hugged Mum tight after talking to Dr Watkins I told her, "You'd better call Simon and tell him he needs to get here fast. You should probably say it's not looking good and that Louis has whatever Marlon had."

★

It turned out that Louis had the determination I'd hoped for, defying the doctor's prediction and tenaciously holding onto life.

Simon was with Louis when I hauled myself out of bed and shuffled back down to the NICU. Simon had always tended to keep himself coolly composed and had rarely shown emotion but his red-rimmed eyes conveyed his anguish at Louis' dire state.

And though a small part of me wanted to shout, "Do you get it now? Can you see what I mean? Can you understand why it was so hard for me to overcome my fear?" I didn't because Louis needed both his parents by his side.

I sent a message out to all of my friends announcing Louis' early arrival, trying to sound as upbeat as possible as I delivered the news of his condition. I knew everyone who'd been so eagerly antici-pating the start of a new and happy chapter of my life would be stunned and saddened. The messages of love I received lifted my spirits as did the arrival of my closest friends in shifts to meet Louis and show their support. They came bearing gifts and food parcels and offers of anything that might help lighten my load, sitting with me by Louis' bedside and taking me out to eat.

Even Simon was supportive in those early days and we managed to maintain something of a truce for a while. Our families united at Louis' bedside, willing him to soldier on and overflowing with pride at his stubborn fight for life. For a short time I imagined things could be different between Simon and me as we cherished our son together, and my feelings towards him softened as I saw his love and devotion to Louis. He showed tireless dedication, spending hours at the hospital talking to Louis, reading stories and massaging his tiny feet. He whispered encouragement and willed physical strength to his son – bringing a huggable Mr Strong to the hospital to be Louis' mascot.

Despite the doctor's dire predictions Louis began to show unexpected improvement which contradicted the conclusion he'd suffered catastrophic injury to his brain during his birth. His MRI was normal and his brain was fully functioning, so either the TOBY therapy had worked or he'd simply defied the odds. Marlon had done the same after a prolonged period without oxygen during his delivery, so maybe it was something about their condition that allowed their brains to remain intact. While it wasn't cause for celebration it was a significant hurdle for Louis to have jumped, though we still needed a diagnosis of his condition to reveal whether anything therapeutic or curative could be done.

The geneticist I'd seen for counselling early in the pregnancy appeared quickly and said that because Louis' presentation at birth was so similar to Marlon's his condition was highly likely to be one of two genetic diseases of the muscles known as congenital myopathies. I'd researched atrophies and dystrophies but never myopathies, as there hadn't been one on Marlon's list of possible diagnoses.

After being discharged from hospital, I went to stay with Mum, whose house was just a short five-minute walk up the hill from the hospital, which I could see from my bedroom. It gave me comfort when I tucked Louis in each night knowing I could get back quickly if he got into strife. Despite defying all expectations he was far from out of the woods. He still needed breathing support, couldn't swallow and struggled to tolerate milk in his tummy. He also remained profoundly weak and susceptible to any infection.

I should have learnt my lesson from the fruitless hours I'd spent searching for the name of Marlon's condition, but I couldn't help myself and searched online for information about Louis' illness at the first chance I got, searching mitochondrial myopathy and X-linked myotubular myopathy respectively. Both were inherited maternally, both were passed on only to sons, and both had the shattering prognosis of death in early infancy. Any glimmer of hope I'd taken from Louis' demonstrated determination was shattered.

27. X and Why

Seventeen days after Louis' birth we received his catastrophic diagnosis. His condition was called X-linked myotubular myopathy and his life expectancy was two years at best. After hearing this I fell apart all over again, obliterating any chance of lasting harmony with Simon, who couldn't cope with my emotional state. And though I finally had the knowledge I'd so craved with Marlon, instead of providing relief or hope, an overwhelming renewal of loss overcame me along with a feeling of being totally out of control.

After receiving the news I went for a walk to try to catch my breath and regain some sort of composure. Eventually I found myself sitting on a bench by the railway station where I was gripped by the urge to jump on a train and run away, though in reality there was no way I would ever abandon my son. Instead I rested my head in my hands and asked the universe for a renewal of strength. It was my version of praying, despite believing God didn't exist. When I looked up again I was astonished to see a sign I'd never noticed before, which said:

"For the unlearned, old age is winter. For the learned it is the season of the harvest. If we had no winter the spring would not be so pleasant. If we

did not sometimes taste adversity, prosperity would not be so welcome. In the depths of winter I finally learned, there was in me an invincible summer. There are stars whose light only reaches the earth long after they have fallen apart. There are people whose remembrance gives light in this world long after they have passed away. This light shines in our darkest nights on the roads that we must follow. Anon."

Somehow reading these words recalibrated my thinking and gave me the slap I needed to snap out of self-pity and dig into my reserves of fortitude to find a way forward for my son. Louis was alive and he was perfect, it was my expectations that needed adjustment and the onus was on me to make them.

We had a cause for Louis' muscle problems and a reason for him being so sick but not a single doctor or nurse in the NICU had ever heard of X-linked myotubular myopathy, let alone worked with a patient afflicted by it. Even the geneticist had never seen a newborn suffering from it firsthand. However, she did offer a ray of hope when she told me she'd spoken to Associate Professor Andrew Kornberg, who was a neurologist at Melbourne's Royal Children's Hospital specialising in neuromuscular disorders and had seen the condition before, and he'd agreed to see Louis as soon as he could. She hoped he'd be able to give me further information and something in the way of a prognosis.

I thanked her gratefully, telling her that none of the doctors in London had been able to provide me with any sort of real prognosis for Marlon. She then organised for a sample of Marlon's DNA to be sent over from London, which she dispatched with a sample of my blood to the only molecular testing centre for MTM in Australia. When the results came back they showed that Marlon, Louis and I shared the same variation in one of our genes. Amongst the tens of thousands of genes in our genetic code one minor glitch was all it had taken to dislocate the boys from a normal life. Much like a typographical error in a single word can change its meaning, a

G transposed for an A in a single string of genetic coding on one of my two X chromosomes had caused the life-threatening condition Louis had.

I learnt that X-linked myotubular myopathy only affected boys because the XY genome that made them male denied them the backup that a second X chromosome provided to girls. So while women could be born with the genetic flaw but not necessarily suffer any symptoms, they could pass the disease onto their sons. With a carrier mother both of my sons had had a fifty/fifty chance of having the condition, depending on which X chromosome they inherited, so it was just tragic bad luck that both Marlon and Louis had both gotten my dodgy X.

At a molecular level the faulty gene caused problems with a particular protein that resulted in the cells in the muscle fibres not developing properly, leaving the boys in a profoundly weakened state. Despite the miracles of modern medical science, the increased understanding of genetics, and the constantly advancing treatments and cures when genetics went awry, there was nothing that could alter the immediate course of Louis' condition.

It was impossible not to blame myself for the rogue gene I'd passed on although I well knew the futility of guilt. I was burdened by the knowledge that despite Marlon's monumental fight for survival he'd been destined to lose his battle and die. Now Louis faced the same struggle and the knowledge that I had absolutely no control over his fate was almost too much to bear.

Despite my pain I developed a defiant resolve that his fight to survive wouldn't be in vain, and I would do whatever it took to keep him going for as long as possible and give him a full and happy life.

So, by day Mum and I would sit by Louis' bed and do whatever we could for him: massaging his limp little limbs to try to infuse them with power, bathing and cuddling him, singing and reading to him, putting on finger puppet shows, pulling faces and performing antics to try to make him smile, and tickling his feet, which he seemed to love. I also pumped breast milk regularly to sustain him and whispered endless words of encouragement to him, telling him all the good reasons he had to stay alive and all the wonders he'd see if he got to come home, and willing him to keep getting stronger every day.

By night I scoured the internet for more insights into MTM, finding inspiration in people's tales of survival in the face of seemingly unbeatable odds. The further I searched the more positive examples I found to fuel my fire, to never give up on Louis and to never give up hope. I forced myself to look outside the statistics and the medical approach to reason, to ignore the dire mortality rates and not give in to negative thinking. And I also reminded myself of Anne-Marie's wise words about Marlon, focusing on Louis rather than his condition.

Louis gave me every reason to be hopeful, and concentrate on what he achieved rather than getting lost in the mire of his disability. He passed one milestone after another, first surviving the muscle biopsy operation that confirmed his diagnosis, then getting off the ventilator and not becoming dependent on the machine like I had feared he might. A couple of weeks after birth he required minimal breathing support and then learnt to breathe on his own. Despite his physical limitations, I forced myself to believe Louis had unlimited potential in his non-physical qualities which could fill his life with goodness and fulfilment. If I looked deeply into his beautiful liquid brown eyes all I could see was my bright and strong-minded child.

Once again, life in hospital was a balancing act between hope and despair with Louis stable one moment and then teetering on the brink the next. And though I'd been through it before there was no getting used to it, in fact experiencing it the second time around was bleaker because of the diagnosis we'd received.

The medical team looking after Louis had expertise with premature babies but were essentially flying blind with a child with Louis' particular needs. But he fast became a popular long-termer and the nurses were obviously very fond of him despite his daily blue episodes keeping everyone on their toes.

When Louis was around three weeks old, Associate Professor Andrew Kornberg came to see us at the Mercy as promised. A warm and compassionate doctor, he gently told Simon and me that there was some validity in the statistics on mortality and premature death in infants with MTM. But he also provided us with a glimmer of hope when he told us he knew of boys with MTM who hadn't died as babies, and in fact there were children living with the disorder well into childhood and beyond. He also said that though peer-reviewed research into MTM was scant, anecdotally it appeared to be a spectrum disorder with varying degrees of severity, meaning it had unpredictable outcomes too. Andrew believed that if Louis could get through the precarious early months of his life then we could expect to take him home and look after him with support from the multi-disciplinary team of neuromuscular specialists at the Royal Children's Hospital to care for his special needs.

Andrew's words immediately cast Louis' future in a new light for me and increased my resolve to value the quality of his life over its length. Andrew also offered to introduce us to another family in Melbourne whose little boy had been born with MTM nine months before Louis.

As a result of that meeting with Andrew I knew there must be other children with MTM around the world and when I went online to check I found an article about a boy in the US called Joshua Frase who'd been born with X-linked MTM. Joshua had well and truly passed the two-year life expectancy for children with MTM and was still alive at 13. I was heartened to read that Joshua was a happy, vibrant, funny and intelligent schoolboy and although his body didn't work properly he'd learnt to breathe on his own and there was nothing wrong with his brain. On the contrary, he excelled at academic pursuits and by all accounts was a popular kid whose peers took special care of him but otherwise treated him just like their other friends. It was a story that offered a tantalising germ of hope and gave Louis' life a more optimistic outlook.

I also read about a boy in the UK called Zac Hughes, who seemed to have a milder form of X-linked MTM. Zac was another story of survival from fragile and tentative beginnings and he too was a smart and successful achiever at school who, despite his physical challenges, embraced life with guts and gusto, showing strength lay in determination rather than muscles.

I reached out to both Joshua's mother, Alison Frase, in the States and the founders of the Myotubular Trust in the UK, who embraced me virtually and took me under their wings with kindness, understanding, experience, information and introductions to the global online MTM community. It was another parents' club I had no desire to join but I couldn't have been more grateful to have found them and been given their lifeline of support.

There were several other MTM boys around the world and although they were few in number, they were living rich and happy lives despite their significant challenges, limitations and vulnerability. Their families spoke universally of gentle and happy dispositions similar to that of Marlon and Louis, and they seemed to share positive cognitive traits along with similarly stubborn wills. There were three-, five- and eight-year-olds as well as boys in their early teens. If they could do it I determined we could too, and I was incredibly grateful to the other amazing families who offered me mentorship, guidance and advice from their firsthand experiences of the difficult early days.

With a new village to help me raise Louis I decided he could have a good life, and while he might not win any running races his mind could be his might.

28. Back to the Future

While it was all well and good to find strength and look to the future it didn't change the reality of the present or remove the daily ordeals. After winning the early fight for survival and coming off ventilation to breathe on his own, the threat that Louis' secretions would obstruct his airway or leach into his lungs and cause pneumonia remained very real.

The doctors put him on a drug that was supposed to reduce his secretions but it only seemed to make them thicker and more likely to plug his throat. He continued to have regular blue episodes, during which he'd change colour and struggle for breath to the extent that on a couple of occasions I was sure he wouldn't survive. During one emergency I watched on helplessly as Louis went through the rainbow's spectrum of reds and blues and purples until they were finally able to suck out a globule of sticky goo the size of a ping pong ball. Once they'd succeeded I dashed from the NICU to find Simon, who I knew was somewhere nearby, I was so sure another episode like that would take Louis out.

Mostly, I managed to stay relatively calm and somehow detach myself during what were regular daily occurrences including a close call when the nurse on duty with Louis was unable to clear his airway and had to press the MET call button for help. The ensuing alarm saw doctors come running from all directions and swing into action. My stoicism wasn't due to desensitisation, I just knew all eyes were needed on Louis to keep him breathing.

Afterwards I'd need to unleash all the emotion I'd held in while glued to the spot unwilling to leave Louis' side in case he slipped away. It was only then that I could let the gut-wrenching fear and shock and distress of witnessing my helpless child almost suffocate on his own mucous erupt out of me in uncontrolled, hysterical sobs and I'd hide in the bathroom, allowing it to flow out of me until I could compose myself again.

There were positives to each day too. I delighted in his first smile, and was overjoyed when I saw him achieve weightless movements in his legs in the bath, and thrilled by his unmistakable look of recognition when he heard my voice. Such precious moments helped me to push through the frightening times when I wasn't sure he'd make it through the day. We did as many normal things as his bed-bound condition allowed and I spent countless hours each day just snuggling him in my arms.

I gradually gained confidence that the medical staff would do right by Louis. Because of his diagnosis they didn't attempt risky things like feeding him orally because of the danger of aspiration pneumonia, but I also had the sense that I understood Louis' needs more than them. Against a doctor's advice I asked them to take Louis off the drug that caused the mucous plugs to obstruct his airway and within a couple of days there was a noticeable reduction in his 'blueys'. I realised I'd sometimes need to second guess and question Louis' carers because of the rarity of his disorder. I needed to be his advocate and head nurse as well as his mum.

Running on pure adrenaline to get through the long days in hospital meant that as Christmas neared I was exhausted and desperately in need of respite from the monotonous sameness of every day. It had been almost two months and Louis had never been outside

HOW I MET YOUR FATHER

the NICU. And though Andrew Kornberg had promised that Louis would be transferred to the Royal Children's Hospital for rehabilitation so we could eventually take him home, the holidays and skeleton hospital staff at Christmas resulted in further delays.

I couldn't fault the care the nurses provided to Louis. Their kindness and compassion went above and beyond their duty, especially at Christmas time. They'd become like extended family in a way and eventually I heeded their advice to leave Louis safe in their hands and take more time out for myself to catch up with friends. These snatched moments of normality were all that remained of my life before his birth.

With Marlon, his discharge from hospital had been a positive step towards being a 'normal' family at last, which Jake and I had embraced with blind optimism, certain we wouldn't have been allowed to take him home if the doctors didn't think he was ready. We'd had no clear idea of what lay ahead, let alone that he'd be gone in the blink of an eye.

Louis had a diagnosis and the specialist team at RCH were going to provide us with a management plan. My challenge this time was to redefine normal and get my head around the physical and emotional challenges of being the single mother of a profoundly disabled child whose survival required 24/7 care. I came to realise I needed to be selfless enough to focus only on Louis and stay in the present.

Despite my determined hopefulness it was sometimes hard to watch parents walking out of hospital with their new bundles of joy, off to start the next chapter of their lives while we languished in the hospital for months counting vital statistics like oxygen saturations, tachycardia, bradycardia, number of suctions, administration of medicines, the miniscule millilitres of milk Louis had kept down and the other surreal markers of the quality of our days. Three friends had given birth to babies around the time Louis was born so it felt as though robust and healthy babies were all around me. Even the extremely premature ones in the NICU were gradually going home while we waited for graduation from the NICU into the hospital mainstream.

The delicacy of my resilience was compounded by the ticking of my biological clock, the wreckage of my broken relationship and the fact that my single status was unlikely to change.

With the best will in the world the stress and strain inevitably took its toll on my interactions with Simon and we started disagreeing again to the point he completely stopped speaking to me and the atmosphere beside Louis' bed whenever we were there together was unbearably tense and awkward.

When Louis was in my arms I could watch him sleeping peacefully and my world felt safe and intact, my overwhelming love for him the only guide I needed, but when I walked out of the NICU into the reality of an out-of-control life and the enormity of the responsibility I bore, the vulnerability of my coping powers was exposed. With Marlon I'd had a husband to share the load and give me the hugs I needed and reassurance that we were in it together, but the isolation of the journey with Louis filled me with loneliness and despondency.

In danger of becoming an emotional wreck despite my best intentions and the knowledge that it wouldn't help Louis, I reached out to a counsellor from SIDS & Kids who I'd met soon after my return to Australia from London.

With a counsellor I trusted coming to my rescue at the hospital I was able to share my fear about the challenges I was facing, my fear of being a mother without children, my values about life and death and where my boundaries lay in regard to Louis' quality of life, the painful dilemma of not wanting to get my hopes up for Louis but needing to hold on to hope, and how sad and angry I felt about the sorry state of things with Simon. It was a huge relief to be able to talk these things through openly and honestly with a professional who could truly understand my feelings, having lost a child herself.

Christmas Day was more miserable than any I could remember. Louis was stuck in hospital and leaving him there while I attended our family lunch made me feel like I was missing a limb. It was all I could do to stay for Christmas pudding before rushing back to the hospital, unable to bear the thought of him without me on Christmas Day.

By the New Year my life came to a grinding halt, and while I knew we'd get to the Royal Children's Hospital eventually, I realised I needed to act in Louis' best interests before he faded into oblivion waiting for the wheels of public health to turn.

I viewed a move to RCH as a lifeline for both of us because Louis would have a specialist team looking after him there and I'd be in a place where I could meet other parents in similar situations. I hoped to be able to both give and receive comfort with others who lived in fear and understood the rollercoaster of having a longed-for child without knowing if they'd live or what quality of life they'd have.

Reading *Time* magazine one afternoon while Louis was asleep I happened upon an article about how in Buddhist-dominated Thailand, people understood the concept of a long cycle of suffering before salvation comes. The notion appealed to me and while I had no idea what my salvation might be, it reminded me that time was in perpetual motion bringing with it constant change and made me think about the third world countries where Louis wouldn't have survived his birth.

When the day of Louis' transfer to RCH finally arrived it felt to me like a giant step towards the time when I could take Louis home. The Mercy nurses showered us with affection and wished us luck before Louis was gingerly placed in a mobile incubator for his auspicious ride. I wondered how the nurses and even the doctors felt saying goodbye to such a sweet little boy who they'd looked after for so long knowing they'd probably never see him again.

The nurses on the neurology ward at RCH were lovely and very sweet to me and Louis but they were run off their feet with so many sick children and it quickly became apparent that Louis wouldn't have the undivided attention he'd enjoyed at the Mercy for the previous two months and I'd need to be his voice and take on a more proactive role in his care. This turned out to be a positive thing because it built my confidence that I was capable of taking him home. And I needn't have worried that he wouldn't get enough attention because within a week Louis had worked his charm on the neurology ward team, flashing his winning smile when a nurse cleared the gunk from his throat or gave him the slightest attention. It didn't take much to make Louis happy, he gave no trouble apart from his 'blueys' and it wasn't long before he was counted a model patient and the nurses were vying for his attention.

It became clear he had two favourite nurses on the ward – Alyssa and Belinda – and Danni, the neuromuscular nurse co-ordinator, was his favourite special guest. Whenever they could spare a moment they'd lavish him with affection and cuddles. When I declared them all Louis' 'girlfriends' it was as if he was in on the joke because he managed to make each of them feel special. As with our time at the Mercy it became easier for me to come and go and create a life for myself outside the hospital knowing that the nurses would look out for Louis, though my main goal was still to get him home with me. The problem was that discharge planning couldn't start until he stopped having so many 'blueys' requiring resuscitation. And I didn't want to take him home before he was strong enough and risk him dying like Marlon.

The move to RCH also fulfilled my hope of being inspired and fortified by the parents of other children who faced equally confronting obstacles and decisions. For a while, Louis shared the room with conjoined twins, Krishna and Trishna, who'd been rescued from Bangladesh by their adoptive mother, Moira Kelly. Their lives remained uncertain as they prepared for an operation to take them a step closer to separation. Moira seemed so positive, despite having no way of knowing whether either or both of the girls would survive each surgery they endured.

Then there was fifteen-year-old Shira who was discharged from Intensive Care, where she'd clung to life after being hit by a train. Against almost impossible odds she'd survived and her large family rallied around, learning to care for her despite the devastating consequences of the brain injury she'd acquired.

I also met an exquisite little blonde angel called Skye who was only three years old when she took up residence in the adjacent bed to Louis after Shira moved on to rehab. Skye was another miraculous survivor who'd clung to life by a thread. When she arrived at the High Dependency Unit she still had drains protruding from her skull, which had been smashed when her mother's drug-addicted lover hurled her against a wall. Sweet little Skye personified the resilience of a child.

Another child whose tragic end would stay with me forever was an innocent little girl who landed at the hospital by helicopter on a sweltering hot January morning. Her dad had been driving her to her first ever day of school when he'd inexplicably stopped on top of Melbourne's highest bridge and dropped her 58 metres into the water below. She was declared dead at the hospital in the arms of her destroyed mother. I often thought of her mum after that day and wondered how she was faring.

Around the same time as that horrific incident, hundreds of fire-fighters were battling out-of-control bushfires around the state in blistering hot weather. For days and weeks the fires continued to scorch the earth with such intensity and velocity that many people lost their lives, entire communities were razed to the ground, with numerous homes and countless livestock also lost. The fires of Black Saturday were on a scale not seen since 1983, when the Ash Wednesday bushfires had created headlines in the UK, prompting my dad's last ever phone call to Mum.

Those were just some of the multiple human tragedies I saw that summer but it was the triumph of human spirit out of them that stayed with me and demonstrated the indomitable nature of courage. It was the parents of the children in that hospital and the survivors of the devastating fires who made me grateful for what I had and inspired me to make the most of every day.

I felt less sorry for myself bearing witness to the traumas of other people and was feeling more resilient by the time a shocking call came from an old friend. I'd left Louis at the hospital and was about to sit down to drinks with friends when my friend Lisa called with the unbelievable news that Davo had suffered a massive heart attack and died at just 42. Sorrow washed over me at Davo's early death. It was another timely reminder to stay in the moment and cherish every minute I had with Louis.

Amidst all the tragedy and trauma going on around us Louis continued to have his own near-death experiences. One minute he'd be blue, with his oxygen levels plummeting, and the next he'd be all smiles again or looking up at me from the safety of my arms oblivious to the emergency he'd triggered. On one occasion the nurse administering CPR was about to stop and declare him dead only to have him splutter back to life with her final compression of his chest.

Soon enough Louis and I were long-termers in RCH and I was desperate to get us home so we could get on with life in a less clinical environment with some semblance of normalcy.

At the same time I was acutely aware that because of the level of care Louis would require if I took him home I'd be hard pushed to do the work of a roster of nurses. In the hospital there was always someone to watch him, so when one nurse went to the toilet there was another to babysit in her place, and at the end of a shift one nurse was replaced with another nurse who was rested and ready for action. At home I'd be Louis' main carer, though I knew Mum and my close friends would be happy to help out too.

I was grateful when the hospital offered the support of trained carers for three overnight shifts per week once Louis was discharged, but Louis' care needs were 24/7. That meant I'd have to fend for myself the other four nights of the week and I knew the level of sleep deprivation involved wasn't sustainable or safe. I understood the funding problems of supplying overnight care on more than three nights but I'd already lost one son at night while I was sleeping and I wasn't about to let falling into an exhausted sleep put Louis' life in jeopardy. As a result I dug my heels in and told the RCH's home and community care co-ordinator that Louis would need to live at the hospital indefinitely if they couldn't provide a carer every night of the week. After telling her about my experience with Marlon I said it would be better for me to help take care of Louis at the hospital during the day and then go home each evening to get a good night's sleep.

Eventually the hospital agreed to my request for a carer every night of the week as a one-off exception given I'd be Louis' sole carer.

Delighted and thankful for their decision, I interviewed a shortlist of five agency carers, making it clear to each that Louis' life would be in their hands if there was an emergency and I was asleep or out taking care of the necessities of life, so they needed to be prepared and stay calm under pressure. I also told them they might need to administer CPR and call an ambulance to save his life in my absence so if they didn't think they could handle it they'd be better to say so.

My direct approach had the necessary effect, and three wonderful carers – Ashley, Barb and Gaye – became Louis' guardian angels.

After 128 days in hospital with Louis, in addition to my time in hospital with Marlon, I'd seen most iterations of how to save a baby's life and felt confident about going home. I was ready to make every day one to remember with a focus on what new experiences Louis could have rather than what he couldn't do.

The seventh of March was decided upon as Louis' discharge day, and I felt unexpectedly mixed emotions about leaving our RCH family and especially the nurses, who'd firmly entrenched themselves in our hearts. It was a wrench to leave the security of the hospital but Louis was as ready as he'd ever be and so, despite my nervous trepidation, I finally took my precious son home four months and one week after his birth.

29. Carpe Diem

My apartment soon resembled a mini hospital and Louis' bedroom a private High Dependency Unit, with tanks of oxygen and resuscitation bags and masks beside his customised hospital bed, which tilted up and down to stop secretions settling on his chest. We had a suction machine with catheters and tubing, a manual foot pump for backup in case of power failure, a pulse-oximeter that would ring an alarm at the first sign of breathing or heart rate anomalies and a feeding pump to deliver his nutrition. CPR instructions were mounted on the wall and binders were close at hand containing the manuals for all of Louis' care needs. The carers and I kept a record of every observation and intervention to ensure Louis was getting everything he needed. I'd regretfully given up expressing milk before bringing him home as there wasn't time to do it as well as keeping up with all Louis' other needs and I wanted to minimise stress so I could enjoy every moment of finally just being his mum full-time.

It was another bittersweet homecoming but I focused on the joy of being free and having my son with me at home.

Four days at home without incident was just enough to lull me into a false sense of security before Louis had his first 'bluey' as I was attempting to put him in the car. We were about to head off to the children's hospice, Very Special Kids, which Louis had miraculously been accepted into despite their long waiting list. VSK is the only hospice for children in Victoria and one of only two in Australia so we were incredibly fortunate to gain access to their support. No sooner had I buckled Louis into his seat than his lips turned blue and his face took on an alarming pallor.

With no time to grab the oxygen tank that I'd packed into the car, or to get him into the recovery position, I squashed my mouth over his face as best I could and blew oxygen into his lungs. As soon as some colour returned to his face I wrenched him out of his seat and dashed back into the house to lay him flat and get him breathing again. Thankfully his airway wasn't obstructed and his colour returned to normal, indicating that he was okay, but I wondered if I should call an ambulance anyway. I composed myself but was struck by the sinking feeling that I'd failed in my very first attempt at a solo expedition.

Simon's older sister called that afternoon to ask when his family could visit. She'd long since decided my failed relationship with her brother was entirely my fault, and her condescending tone as she spoke about Simon not having seen his son for days immediately infuriated me in the wake of such a stressful event.

I replied "You've chosen not to appreciate how this might be for me and you've really got no idea what it's like to have a child as fragile as Louis. I've lost one child already and I'm doing my utmost to get everything in place to care for Louis at home and ensure it doesn't happen again."

Off she went again about Simon's equal rights as Louis' parent, at which point I retorted, "Simon hasn't done his training. Never mind being a parent, unfortunately, with Louis' condition he needs to be a carer too. When he does the training, then talk to me about parental rights."

Then I hung up in her ear before she could hear the worst of what I had to say.

Relations between Simon and me had thawed a little from frozen silence during the latter days at RCH, and we'd been vaguely on speaking terms when Louis was discharged. But the thought of having to invite him into the sanctuary of my home filled me with resentment and dread. I was desperate to keep it as a place where I could retreat from conflict and the relentless rollercoaster life had become, but because he'd still not trained in all of Louis' cares and resuscitation, I had no other option but to let him come into my home.

I never had the intention of keeping Simon from seeing his son but all of my focus, energy and attention was on figuring out how to make things work at home with all the medical people his life was contingent on. There were the carers and the registered nurses to train them in the home, the case manager, family support workers, the social worker, the counsellor, the physio, occupational therapist, speech therapist, as well as numerous other care-in-the-community people. I'd barely had time to take a shower or eat since we'd gotten home, which was something I'd expected with a newborn, though I'd never envisaged all the extra people necessitated by a child with a life-threatening condition. I had no idea where or when I'd find the time or space for Simon to come and visit and he didn't seem in any rush to give me a break.

When I finally arranged to meet Simon I was only prepared to do so on neutral ground. I bundled Louis into his pram and walked him down to the park. Louis' face lit up when he saw his dad, triggering a twinge of guilt in me, but it didn't erase my anger that he could demand equal rights but not share equal responsibility. We managed to be civil to each other but tension and reactions simmered close to the surface, with Simon angry at his loss of freedom to come and go as he pleased as he had while Louis was in hospital.

It wasn't long before he demanded to know when Louis would be able to go and stay with him.

"How do you expect to have him at your place when you haven't even done the CPR training?" I snapped. "You're all care and no responsibility, Simon, and if you really want to co-parent Louis then you have to learn how to take care of him properly. Do you know how to put a nasogastric tube into his stomach if he pulls it out and can't feed?" I asked him. "And do you know how to use the bag and mask to give him oxygen if he turns blue? No you don't," I answered for him.

I could see the pained expression on his face that spoke of fear and maybe guilt. I knew that he loved Louis and never questioned his dedication as a dad but I felt he avoided the harsh reality of having such a severely disabled child.

"Just do your training," I said in a more gentle tone. "And in the meantime you can see Louis at my place whenever you like if you let me know when you're coming."

After that Simon came by most evenings until the season began to change. With the end of daylight saving Louis' bedtime was earlier, so by the time Simon arrived at seven Louis was already tucked up in bed, which led to further friction between us. It suited me that he went into Louis' room rather than sitting with me on the couch as the only other alternative was to give him the living room and retreat to my bedroom. I couldn't go out in case something happened that Simon couldn't handle, but in such a small and cluttered space as Louis' bedroom and with Louis ready for sleep he couldn't really make the best of their time together, which caused further argument.

"Is he always going to be in bed now when I come?" he asked accusingly. I explained that it was because daylight saving had ended rather than me being obstructive and we agreed to change his visiting time to 5.30pm. That agreement only lasted 48 hours before he delivered a sledgehammer blow to our newfound cooperation.

"I'm seeking legal advice about the time I get with Louis," he said and with that I told him to get out and never bother coming back.

It was hard to believe he could be serious in threatening to take me to court. It was clear he couldn't see past his own needs in order

I'll be there – Mum is my hero

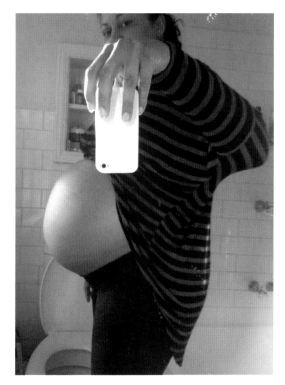

It's a girl!

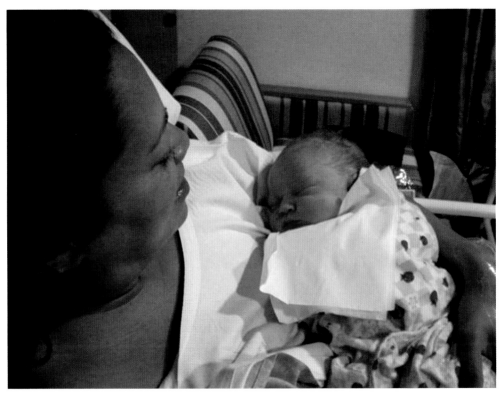

To have and to hold – Leila

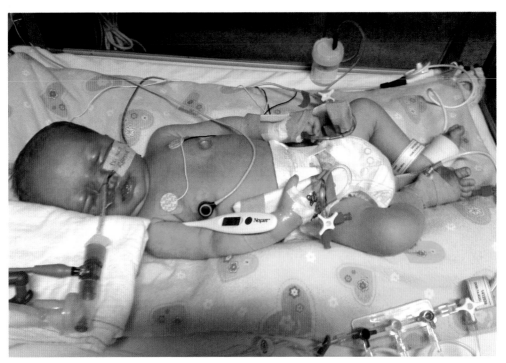

Be strong my baby girl

Healthy

Happy

Just the three of us

The Godfather – Jonathan

We are family – Ayesha and Kaynahn

On the road again –USA

Call me dad

Andersen family Christmas

My Belle

We made the news

Master counsellor

She's not heavy, she's my daughter

My big brothers

The farmer gets a wife

I got you babe

to put the safety of our son first. My stress levels detonated an explosion of confusing thoughts and the four hours' respite I'd have the next day couldn't come soon enough. I still wanted to protect Louis from the ugly dissonance between his father and me so I needed to be out of earshot when I let out my frustrations and disappointment at Simon and the pent-up grief that constantly bubbled beneath the surface threatening to boil over whenever Simon turned up the heat.

I wandered down to the Yarra River to a peaceful spot in Riverside Park I'd reserved for my few hours of weekly respite to meditate or vent my spleen before making my way back home to Louis. Afterwards I felt a little lighter of step.

That seat by the river saw my regular pilgrimage to sit and let out my feelings when the confines of life got me down; it helped having such beautiful surroundings and the nature earthed me when the static in my head became too loud.

On the flipside, once I had a few solo emergency responses under my belt I felt more confident I could deal with Louis' episodes wherever we might find ourselves so we started to get out and about more, with Mum's place our most frequent destination though we gradually ventured further afield. My closest friends extended open invitations to visit and would give the all-clear that their kids were free of contagious bugs, knowing that the common childhood infections could put Louis back in hospital or worse.

Simon followed through with his threat to hire a lawyer who served me with a summons to appear in court over Louis' custody. As far as I was concerned Simon had missed the point entirely, which was that he just needed to pick up his equal share of Louis' care. Once he'd done his training I'd be happy for extra time to myself but there was no point in trying to explain this to him again because he clearly didn't understand.

A few thousand dollars later the lawyers agreed visiting terms without any need for a judge to intervene. Simon would see Louis every Sunday for less time than we'd agreed previously for free. The solicitor's intervention marked the end of any civility between us whatsoever and any hope that Louis might someday have a united family. I resorted to communication via email only to keep our communications businesslike and concise. I drove over to Mum's every Sunday so she could hand Louis over to Simon and I could avoid him altogether.

With Louis at Simon's every Sunday I was able to have more of a social life with friends and for the rest of the week I made the most of every day with my little guy. As biased as any mother, I thought he had the sweetest, most easy-going and serene disposition of any baby I'd ever known. He never cried, not that he could cry out loud, but he never complained or whinged, and between his two families and his carers he had people everywhere catering to his every need. Louis wanted for nothing and while it probably wouldn't have augured well for a future wife, in Louis' case I decided he could never be spoiled enough.

Once Louis could tolerate the car seat I took him everywhere with me, and everybody who met him admired his gentle zest for life. People who offered him their time and attention were rewarded with a beautiful smile that shone out through his eyes, and if you listened closely with your ear against his mouth you could hear the faintest sound of laughter that could melt the hardest heart. Louis didn't know he was different. He was happy to just be and as aware of the people around him as any other child. His body didn't work very well but he still intuitively did the things that babies do, learning to lift his legs up off the ground and eventually finding his toes and playing with them incessantly until his nappy was removed after which, like any little boy, he'd grab his other bits. He learnt to roll from side to side when he didn't have his helmet or leg brace on, and once he rolled himself right over onto his tummy though he had to be rescued by my mum when he couldn't roll back again.

Anything that involved being upright, like holding his head up or tummy time was beyond his capability, but we celebrated every little milestone he achieved. Despite his physical limitations it was obvious his brain was fine as his reactions conveyed understanding and he interacted with his eyes. His happiness was contagious, he enjoyed the simplest of things and he got to watch more TV than any able-bodied kid would be allowed. He'd be glued to the screen for hours watching the most annoying TV characters like Barney and BJ and Baby Bop who could make him laugh all day while the theme song nearly drove us adults to distraction played on such frequent rotation.

Those were happier days for us as well. My mum and her partner David both learnt to take care of Louis and when Louis laughed we all laughed along with him. It would have been easy to slip into a false sense of complacency as a new normal settled in but I lived in a permanent state of hyper-vigilance to ensure he wasn't exposed to germs. We avoided other children when they were sick and stayed away from enclosed spaces where he might be exposed to bugs. I dreaded him catching an infection that might get into his lungs and possibly take him out.

30. What Lies Beneath

And then it happened.

Louis caught a cold which quickly worsened and one night Barb woke me up when his oxygen levels dropped and stayed down despite her repeated attempts to clear his throat, following all of the procedures we had in place. He'd begun to struggle for breath and as soon as I saw him I knew it was bad so I bundled the three of us into my car with his equipment at the ready and drove to RCH as fast as I safely could. Barb sat in the back with Louis, and he was immediately admitted as a member of the group of vulnerable children in the Accelerated Care through Emergency (ACE) program. He was rushed into the Paediatric Intensive Care Unit or PICU, where a chest x-ray revealed that one lung had collapsed entirely and the other was full of pneumonia.

I took up vigil by his bed again as he deteriorated. I wasn't ready to lose him, having just gotten the hang of being his mum and enjoying our life together regardless of the bumps in the road.

Louis showed the same steely determination that had got him through his early days. He eventually got back to full health after a fortnight before being discharged home again but it was an ominous sign of how easily he could succumb.

It was his only serious illness that winter so he got through it relatively unscathed but the stress took its toll on me and I couldn't say the same for myself. A symphony of symptoms began to wear me down and had me feeling I might be losing control of my mind, which I thought made sense in the circumstances. I'd never been prone to anxiety before I'd had the boys, always remaining fairly laid-back and not worrying too much about anything until it happened. I was mostly able to reason with myself but the anxious and depressed reactions I'd had during Marlon's life and after he died made me realise something now didn't feel quite right. I was having emotional mood swings, crying frequently and feeling a strange jittery sensation all the time. My head and skin itched and I became kettle hot in bed at night, my heart racing with palpitations, and I was exhausted but unable to sleep. My hair was falling out faster than it could grow back and my fingernails were splitting and flaking away. The only upside was that the 'baby weight' that fell off me finally had me fitting back into my old skinny jeans. Even so, that didn't feel quite right either because no matter the amount of food I stuffed into my mouth I was constantly ravenous, but I looked emaciated because I was losing muscle and my body couldn't seem to take any nourishment from the endless supply of food.

Thankfully our wonderful family GP, Dr David Doig, had always been on the ball and said my symptoms suggested I might be hyper-thyroid. "It could be thyroiditis but it's more likely you've developed Graves' disease, a simple blood test will tell us," he told me. "It's quite common for women to get thyroid problems after pregnancy. I'll refer you to an endocrinologist for management."

Dr Doig explained that Graves' disease was an auto-immune disorder in which antibodies attacked the thyroid gland in the neck, making it overactive and producing the symptoms I was suffering from. There wasn't really a cure and I'd need to manage the thyroid hormones or the thyroid could be removed or ablated with radio-active iodine. He said I should have blood tests before we considered anything drastic. In the meantime he gave me medication for the worst of my symptoms, to help me feel better and get some sleep.

The blood test confirmed Graves' disease and I was sent off to see an endocrinologist called Dr Elif Ekinci, who I decided was the second nicest doctor in the world after Dr Doig. When I shared a little of the stress I was living under she couldn't have been more compassionate, showing me more empathy during the first appointment than I'd imagined a doctor to possess. After prescribing me anti-thyroid medication she said, "It might take a while to get under control and I strongly advise you not to get pregnant while your thyroid is overactive and you're taking this medication."

"Oh don't worry, I won't be falling pregnant," I said, laughing ironically, not having mentioned that I was a solo parent who hadn't had sex in eighteen months.

When the medication kicked in my symptoms mostly dissipated and the hair in my sparse patches gradually started to grow back.

As I started to get my mojo back Louis had his first birthday and we invited a big gathering of friends and family to celebrate at Mum's house. For a boy who'd been expected to live only 24 hours it was a momentous milestone. An unseasonably sweltering hot day made the heat outside unbearable for Louis so we all squashed into the dining room and put the giraffe cake my aunt Jane had lovingly shaped into a numeral one down on the floor so Louis could see the single sparkler from where he lay. It meant the world to me to mark an entire year. Louis had surpassed those fragile early days and although he'd had one life-threatening infection, he'd otherwise done surprisingly well and Andrew Kornberg was happy with his progress.

Life continued on a rollercoaster track. On the upside we were in a good place and starting to look to the future, exploring special schools that could cater to Louis' needs and attending hydrotherapy classes, which he loved. On the downside I was tasked with developing a palliative care plan for him that forced me to confront where the line was to be drawn in attempts to save him if the worst should happen. At the start of Louis' life Simon and I had decided together that we wouldn't risk hypoxic brain injury again or keep him alive on artificial ventilation if he were to become dependent. I thought I still adhered to that, though it would be an impossible decision to make.

I'd come to know other families with disabled children and bonded closely with Michelle and Russell, whose son George had a similar condition to Louis and was also looked after by Andrew Kornberg.

Later I met Danielle and Richard through a hydrotherapy class Louis attended with their sons, and by happy coincidence they lived just around the corner so I could push Louis to their place in his pram. Serendipitously they were all my kind of people – warm, open, honest and generous. The time I spent with Michelle and Danielle was as much for us mums as anything else. The boys couldn't interact much although George and Louis would lie side by side on the floor staring curiously at each other and reaching for the other's hands while Michelle and I discussed the daunting new world of congenital myopathy.

Life wasn't easy but it felt like Louis and I finally slipped into a steady groove which I had a half-decent handle on. There would always be a constant stream of appointments both at home and at RCH, but with Louis' carers providing respite and Mum and David babysitting, to give me a break, I'd managed to get into a routine of taking time for myself to socialise and have a life. But I couldn't shake a perpetual underlying grief and melancholy. Maybe it was even depression, though I didn't think so, but the sadness centred on the hopes and dreams foregone and the life and children I'd never have, as well as the constant knowledge and fear that the child I did have was living on a knife's edge. Louis might be happy and healthy on any given day but I knew our situation could change like the wind.

I didn't allow such thoughts to take root often but occasionally I needed an outlet so I continued to see a professional counsellor regularly and keep an eye on my mental health. My Graves' disease had made me realise the importance of finding a balance between attending to Louis' constant needs and finding time to nurture myself.

With the support of Very Special Kids and their respite house, which was located conveniently up the road from my place, I was able to take an entire weekend off eight months after bringing Louis home. Emma had themed her fortieth birthday party around the music of the sixties. Between Mum and Aunt Jane, they fitted me out in an original mini-dress Jane had made, relic platform shoes of Mum's and a giant Afro wig that perfectly captured Motown. With Louis safe at VSK, I forgot all of my worries for that weekend and partied from Friday night through to Sunday morning as if I didn't have a care in the world. It was liberating and uplifting, but by Sunday morning I missed Louis terribly and my heart nearly exploded with pride and joy at the smile that lit up his face when he saw me approaching his hammock where he'd been gazing out the window.

Em's birthday signalled the countdown to Christmas and the end of another year, and I looked forward to Louis' first Christmas at home. Having a child gave a touch of magic to the festive season and Louis had a special love of all things sparkly, just as Marlon had, so the tinsel and lights of Christmas tickled his fancy. We stayed at Mum's on Christmas Eve and woke up to share in the joy of Christmas stockings filled with goodies from Santa. Louis was oblivious and the ritual was more for Mum and me than him, but he got a swag of shiny new trinkets. Afterwards we went to Aunt Jane's for our customary family Christmas lunch and I briefly thought of Jake, who'd never been to one of our family Christmas lunches.

Louis sat at the table in his special chair, his feed pumping into his tummy as we all overindulged on beautifully prepared turkey with all the trimmings. That Christmas Day did have a touch of the magical, with Louis spellbound by the lights on the tree, which was the same one Jane had put up every Christmas since my childhood. It was jam-packed with presents under its branches. I'd shopped preposterously for Louis, not caring if he was spoilt, to the point that he was swamped by the wrapped gifts surrounding him on the floor. He couldn't open them or really understand what it was all about but we delighted in showering him with glistening new things and seeing him smile and delight in the wonder of it all was the greatest gift I could have wanted.

That festive season was a truly memorable time in the life of my little boy. I forgot his fragility for a little while and gave his carers a couple of days off so we could all be with our families. I'd agreed that on Boxing Day Louis would have his first sleepover at Simon's, and if all went well every fortnight after that Louis would stay with Simon for the weekend. For me it was a big step towards a more equal sharing of Louis' care and I hoped it would create greater harmony and equilibrium in all our lives. There were conditions, of course. I asked Simon to always make sure Louis' cousins weren't sick if they were going to be around Louis. And he could take Louis to his family home in the country but otherwise he needed to keep Louis as close as possible to the Royal Children's Hospital and not take him out of town. Simon was infuriated by my conditions and instructions, and accused me of being a control freak, but I didn't care what he thought of me by then. My only focus was on Louis' health. I believed that if Simon could show the same vigilance as me we could maintain Louis' good health and keep him going for another year.

I planned to make the next year much more balanced. With Louis spending more time at his dad's I would have the chance to get away for weekends myself. I'd booked Louis in at VSK for February and planned a week at the Golden Door health retreat in the Gold Coast hinterland to reinvigorate and indulge myself.

Louis seemed exhausted when he returned from Simon's. I hoped he was just tired out by the Christmas festivities, but I couldn't help worrying he was coming down with something as his secretions were copious and he looked rundown. I emailed Simon to ask whether Louis had been exposed to any lurgies but was given short shrift and accused of trying to make trouble.

Nothing sinister seemed to manifest itself by way of a high temperature or respiratory problems so I kept a date to join in New Year's Eve celebrations with Emma and a small gathering of her friends while Mum and David looked after Louis. The low-key tone of the evening hit just the right note, with nothing too triumphant or optimistic or filled with shallow resolutions. We raised a glass and wished each other a great year to come and my friends made another toast to Louis as well, after which we praised his tenacity and drank to his continued good health.

31. On a Clear Day You Can See Heaven

I greeted the New Year by waking up beside Louis on our makeshift bed on the floor of Mum's living room and wishing him a happy New Year with a kiss. I lolled around with him in bed for most of the morning, reading stories and helping him play with his new Christmas toys until Aunt Jane arrived for lunch. It was a balmy New Year's Day so we sat outside to eat, with Louis sitting up in his special chair.

"What do you see up there, Louis?" I asked as he gazed up to the sky.

He brought his gaze back to meet mine and smiled, then looked back up again. I scanned the sky myself to see if I could see what had captured his attention but there was nothing, not even a bird, so I assumed he must just be daydreaming. I wondered what went through the mind of such a small child who'd seen so little of life and the world. We went out walking often enough so Louis had seen plenty of nature but I had no idea whether he'd already have an imagination. It was just another of the unanswerable mysteries of having a child who couldn't vocalise or even really utilise his hands to gesture.

We whiled away the day together with our little family and I'd have happily stayed another night at Mum's but I'd rostered Barb back on duty to care for Louis.

I fell asleep deeply that night until Barb jolted me out of my slumber at 5am with a firm knock on my bedroom door. "I'm really sorry to wake you, Aminah," she said, urgency in her voice, "but Louis' heart rate has shot right up high."

I rocketed out of bed and into Louis' room and couldn't see anything glaringly obvious in his appearance to suggest an emergency. While I took Louis' temperature Barb reviewed her overnight observations, saying his heart rate had been up and down through the night and he'd become restless before she woke me. His temperature was normal as was his respiratory rate, although his heart rate remained high, so I thought he might be brewing something and hoped it wasn't serious. After giving him some medicine I watched him with Barb for a few minutes while he drifted back to sleep.

"Let's withhold his 6am feed for now just to see what he does," I said, worrying that if he was getting sick and vomited his formula up he might aspirate into his lungs. "I'll go back to bed for an hour but you did the right thing waking me, and don't hesitate to wake me again if you're even the slightest bit worried."

I nodded back off as soon as my head hit the pillow and woke again just before seven for Barb to do her handover.

"He's been peaceful since you gave him the medicine," she said, "but his heart rate is still up and down and he's been coughing a bit."

"Thanks so much, Barb, I'm so lucky to have you, Ash and Gaye, otherwise I'd never get any sleep," I said as she left.

After farewelling Barb I sat in the reclining chair to watch Louis as he slept. He was sound and peaceful as Barb had said but his heart rate kept shooting up. He definitely wasn't in respiratory distress and it wasn't an emergency so I couldn't take him to hospital if he was just getting a cold. He'd had other sniffles and gotten through them on his own, but his elevated heart rate was something new and I wasn't sure what to make of it. After a while I took his temperature again. It was still fine and his heart rate was back to normal so I left him to sleep, not feeding him until he woke to avoid digestion adding extra effort to his body.

At 10am Louis' pulse oximeter alarmed as it always did to signal he was awake. Walking into his room he responded to my "Good morning, Louis," with a beautiful smile. When I bent down to kiss him on the forehead it felt slightly clammy so I took his temperature again but it was still normal.

I decided to give him a bath before his feed in case it made him vomit. He loved the water and I thought it might make him feel better if he was feeling unwell.

I'd just immersed him in the water and was soaping up my hands to wash his body, when his lips assumed the blue tinged edges indicating something was wrong and I needed to get him to a doctor.

I whisked him out of the bath, into a towel and back into his cot to suction his throat but nothing came up. I turned the oxygen tank on and put the mask over his face to pump it in with the bag. His lips went pink again. I unwrapped the towel and got him into a nappy when the colour drained from his face again. I suctioned again but there was nothing blocking his airway and he wasn't struggling for breath.

I snatched up the phone and dialled 000 frantically asking the operator for an ambulance.

"Hold on please, I'll put you through," the operator said, but Louis was turning blue so I needed both hands to bag him properly so I hung up the phone and reattached his pulse oximeter. His heart was beating at 220 beats per minute.

Panic rose in my throat as I continued to force oxygen into him and simultaneously answer the ringing phone. "Did you call an ambulance?" came the voice down the line.

"I did, it's my son. He's turning blue. He has a neuromuscular condition."

"Okay try to stay calm, what's your name?"

"Aminah Hart."

"Okay, Aminah, thank you, what's your address there?"

I gave her the address and then answered her questions with the phone balanced between my shoulder and my ear as I continued pumping, but it wasn't Louis' saturation levels that were concerning so much as his heart beating way too fast.

"I have oxygen here I'm giving him and everything I need for resuscitation but his heart rate is 220 and he keeps going blue. I've suctioned him but there's nothing blocking his airway. He's with the ACE program at the Royal Children's Hospital so I need to get him there quickly please."

"Okay, Aminah, I'm going to stay on the line but you can put the receiver down to keep doing what you have to. The ambulance is on its way."

I kept giving Louis oxygen from the tank while desperately trying to stay calm as there was nothing else I could try. Somehow Louis was showing no signs of distress in his demeanour despite clearly not getting enough oxygen in his blood. He was almost serene when I looked into his eyes and I had to divert my gaze so as not to lose my composure. I stopped what I was doing and raced to the front door to leave it open for the paramedics then ran back to pump more oxygen but it made no difference, his heart rate stayed up in the 200s.

I heard the ambulance pull up out the front and yelled to the paramedics to alert them to which room we were in. Once they were with me I managed to stay calm and give them a full briefing on Louis' condition and presentation throughout the morning. The male and female paramedics took over from me and hooked Louis up to their monitor. Though I was relieved to have them there I just wanted to get him to the hospital as fast as possible.

The paramedics seemed to stabilise Louis enough to transfer him to the ambulance. After that I rushed back inside to grab the bag I kept on standby in case of an emergency departure and slammed the front door behind me.

Stepping back up into the ambulance the female paramedic said calmly, "His heart rate has come right down."

Momentarily I thought that was my cue to take my seat for the journey to RCH but in the same moment I caught something in her eyes that told me otherwise.

"What do you mean, what's his heart rate now?" I asked urgently, unable to keep the panic down.

"It's around 70," she replied quietly.

"That's too low," I said as my blood ran cold.

"What would you like me to do?" she asked softly, knowing I knew.

"Please just let me hold him now," I replied, and she placed him gently into my arms.

"I'll leave you with him," she said stepping out of the ambulance onto the road and gently closing the door behind her.

I held Louis in my arms and gazed intently into his eyes boring my love as deeply into him as I could, thinking, *Please don't go, Louis, please stay with me,* but I didn't let the words come out. I could feel his heart beat on my hand nursing his back, b-bm, b-bm, each and every distinctive beat as it slowed down. I forced my tears back so they wouldn't be his last image of me. I wasn't sure what to say to him but I knew I needed to tell him it was okay.

"Brave little boy of mine," I said. "You've done so incredibly well. It's okay if you need to go. Thank you for giving us Christmas, sweetheart. Thank you for giving us another New Year. Thank you for giving me so much time. Thank you for coming home with me. Thank you for all of the cuddles. Thank you for choosing me to be your mummy. I love you, Louis. I always will. It's okay, my baby boy, your mummy's here."

I felt the very last beat of my beautiful Louis' heart and then he was gone. Just like that. His eyes continued to gaze up at me, but I knew he couldn't see me anymore so I gently kissed his forehead, closed his eyelids and hugged him more tightly than I'd ever dared when he was alive, knowing I couldn't break him now.

Then the truth overflowed with the tears that I couldn't hold back any longer. "Oh no. Please no. Please don't leave me, Louis. I can't lose you. I don't think I can do this again. Please don't go."

I let the tears stream down onto the face of my son as I etched his features into my memory, much as I'd done the day he was born. He'd changed so much in 14 months, his face more elongated, a full head of hair, eyes that were fringed by thick black lashes and eyebrows that had filled in. I rocked back and forth gently with him in my arms until numbness finally descended.

I placed Louis gently down on the ambulance bed where the paramedic had tried to save him and stepped out to speak to the paramedics waiting patiently on the footpath.

"Do you think you could call my mum Helen for me?" I asked, thinking I wouldn't be able to get the words out myself. "And can you ask her to call his dad Simon? I have an arrangement for Louis to go to Very Special Kids House instead of the mortuary, so I wonder if you could possibly call them for me too?" I said, then gave them the phone numbers for Mum and VSK before getting back into the ambulance and taking Louis back into my arms.

I rocked back and forth and side-to-side as a mother does to comfort her baby, but it was more to comfort myself as I tried to comprehend that Louis had just died in my arms and that New Year's Day 2010 had been his last day on earth.

I conjured Marlon into the back of the ambulance with us and held him in my arms too. Everything I'd lived to regret about Marlon's death I would put right with Louis. After Marlon was taken out of my arms in the emergency room at the Royal Free, I'd never seen him again. I hadn't been able to face going to the mortuary and

HOW I MET YOUR FATHER

I'd hated the fact that I hadn't dressed him in his final outfit. Louis wouldn't be in a morgue, cold and alone. Instead he'd go to VSK House where I could stay with him till his funeral if I wanted to. I intended to make up for what I saw as my neglect of Marlon when he died with attention to every detail of Louis' death. I needed to do that for both of my boys, I needed to do it for myself.

The female paramedic came to the back of the ambulance, having made the calls I'd requested, and said, "Unfortunately we have to take Louis to the Royal Children's as there's no doctor at VSK on the weekend to certify his death. A doctor at the hospital will need to certify him and then you can take him to VSK."

"Okay, thank you," I replied, in a daze.

"I spoke to your mum, she's very distressed and worried about you, but I told her we'll take care of you. She's going to meet us at the hospital. If it's okay with you we'll get going now?"

"Okay, thank you," I said again.

I clutched Louis to my chest as the ambulance weaved its way slowly and silently through Melbourne's Saturday morning traffic, the familiar streets blurred. I felt almost detached from reality, numb and disbelieving as I sat with Louis cocooned in my arms. When we pulled into the ambulance entrance to Emergency at RCH, the female paramedic gave me a blanket to wrap around Louis' body and I carried him through to a private room where Mum was waiting. She took one look at Louis and me and collapsed into hysterical sobs.

There was a bed in the room and I lay down on it with Louis snuggled into my chest. I closed my eyes and tried to imprint the feeling of his heaviness in my arms while his body still retained a little warmth. Then I left the room to give Mum the chance to say what she needed to say to him and hold him for the final time.

A doctor eventually came in with the paperwork and, going above and beyond the call of duty, the paramedics offered to drive us back across town to Very Special Kids.

"Thank you so much for everything," I said to the paramedics when they dropped us at VSK. I would always remember their kindness and that they were the last people other than me to see Louis alive but I didn't even know their names.

The family suite at VSK was waiting for us and I tucked Louis into the bed and lay down beside him. The room had to be kept cold to preserve the deceased so eventually I got under the covers with him and used the privacy to tell him everything I wanted him to know as well as some messages for his brother too.

I wasn't religious and didn't believe in an afterlife or heaven but I took comfort from the thought that maybe my two sons might be together and that Marlon would take care of his little brother.

A big part of me briefly wished I could go too. I didn't want to kill myself but I just couldn't face the pain of losing another child. I didn't have an ounce of energy left and there was nothing to fight for anyway. I wanted to doze off in the bed with Louis, never to awaken again.

But sleep didn't come and I wanted to give Louis a fitting send-off, celebrating his fourteen months of life and his strength and fighting spirit.

When Simon and his family arrived at VSK I went home to contact my loved ones to tell them Louis had died and make preparations for his funeral. I called on my stalwart friend Jules to help me pull plans together to commemorate the life of my beloved little boy.

I dressed Louis in the jumper that had been my favourite on him, with a black puppy on the front and matching linen trousers. He looked so smart and grown up. I had no idea that there were photographers who took photos of sick and deceased children but the VSK team called a photographer called Gavin Blue, who was the president of the Victorian chapter of the Heartfelt charity. He came to VSK House with his camera equipment and took a beautiful set of pictures of Louis and me which were so sensitively arranged that if you didn't know Louis was deceased you couldn't tell. One shot in particular of me kissing Louis on the forehead captured my love for him so flawlessly and encapsulated the final moments we'd had together that I decided to make it the thank-you card I would send to everyone who'd known him.

Andrew Kornberg came to VSK to say goodbye to Louis and offer me comfort, which made me feel that Louis was special to others too.

Somehow I found strength in the practical things I needed to do. I spent many hours of each day at VSK with Louis, much as I had by his hospital bed, and when I wasn't there I ran around getting organised for his funeral. Each night I went home and broke down in tears before collapsing into bed. I was probably running on auto-pilot but my emotions were still so raw and real that when Louis' tiny white coffin was delivered to VSK I almost reeled at the sight of it.

I got a message to Simon that he should leave anything he wanted to place inside the coffin to go with Louis. It broke my heart for Simon when I saw he'd put Mr Strong in bed with Louis, along with letters and pictures drawn by his little cousins.

With tears in my eyes, I gently picked Louis up and tucked him in for the very last time. Alongside him went Mr Strong and the pieces of paper from Simon's nieces and nephews, and I tucked the softest of his cuddly toys, a floppy red dog, into his arms. Finally I placed a card I'd written in paying tribute to my beautiful son and kissed him on the forehead one last time before placing the lid on his coffin.

"Sleep well, little one," I said.

32. A Mother Without Children

The day of Louis' funeral dawned in perfect sunshine. I'd requested that everyone dress in summer colours to celebrate a courageous little boy who had shone so brightly in all of our lives.

Simon's two sisters pointedly wore black and together read a sweet poem from their family called 'Our Keepsake'.

I wished I had the courage to stand up and read my own tribute but I knew I wouldn't be able to get the words out without falling apart so Jules did the honour of reading it on my behalf.

Louis, my precious son
My little baby Boo
I really cannot fathom life
Now I have it without you
When you came they told me
You may not last the day
But little did I yet know your strength
And instead you chose to stay
By your bed for 128 days
I learnt from all you had to give
The struggle of my tiny boy

Who steadfastly chose to live
Since that moment, you have shown
Such tenacity, strength and will
Your bravery has filled my heart with love
Your memory will fill it still
For 14 months, a beautiful life
Though I knew you fought to survive
I could never really have been prepared
For that moment you chose to die
But, I thank you my darling
For each moment we shared
And the boundless love you gave
For sudden, it is said,
The worst turns the best to the brave

You were dealt a cruel hand my love
With a body not built to last
But I hope that I can honour you
Going forth from our short past
I hope that you are safe from harm
And dancing with the stars
Know that Mummy loves you so
And will keep you in her heart
Thank you for the privilege
Of choosing me for your mum
I could not have ever asked for
A more beautiful or perfect son
Sleep well my precious little one
I love you with all that I am
I plan to live in your tribute
Until I can hold you again

Mum was braver than me, reading a passage from Khalil Gibran and my pride spilled over as a slideshow of Louis' life showed off his milestones and achievements and the image I held most dear – his ever-present smile – while the Dixie Chicks sang him their lullaby 'Godspeed'.

Then finally, the time came to let him go. As Rod Stewart belted out 'Forever Young' I clutched Mum's hand and gathered all my strength to walk tall and proudly out of the chapel. And when I turned to leave I was overcome by a vision of a room overflowing with people in a rainbow sea of colours, which would carry me through the darkness of the ensuing days.

I walked toward the doors seeing faces I never imagined would be at Louis' funeral. As well as friends of mine, their families were there for us too along with many of the people who had cared for Louis at the various stages of his life. His devastated angels – Barb, Gaye and Ash – were ashen faced, Dr Andrew Watkins was there from the Mercy, all of Louis' favourite nurses from RCH, as well as his therapists and the people who'd supported us at home, people from SIDS & Kids and VSK, even his orthotist was there. Hundreds of people hugged me as they filed out of the chapel and it filled my heart to bursting to see how many lives my little boy had touched. I knew he'd always be remembered and that he hadn't lived in vain.

It was more than anybody could hope for even in a long life fully lived. Not only to be remembered but to be so very loved.

Louis' funeral felt like my last rites as a mother. There was nothing else to do now, he didn't need me anymore, no matter how much I needed him.

I wanted out but not in a dead sort of way, because I wouldn't have been much of a mother if I'd wanted to die. That wouldn't do my boys justice at all. No, I just wanted to hop off at a place that wasn't so sad for a while. But that's the problem with the grief train, there's no getting off. I'd already ridden it before and knew the one that carried bereaved parents ran express, destination unknown.

I'd read the book on grief, learnt it back to front, but that didn't make my devastation any easier to bear. There were no shortcuts and there was no easy way out. The train would eventually stop somewhere between life as I'd known it and life as it would be. And though grief was such a familiar foe, this time it begged the question of what to do with all the maternal love burning inside me. And where I could channel it so as not to become bitter.

Nick showed up at Louis' funeral bearing chocolates. The chocolates recalled a charity trivia night I'd gone to a couple of years earlier with Jules. It had been a lively affair in the club room of a bowling green packed to the rafters with the familiar faces of old friends and unfamiliar friends of theirs. At the time I'd been back from London almost a year and beginning to get some groove back. Nick had cheekily pitched a chocolate at me across the room by way of introduction and we'd had a brief conversation.

Our paths didn't cross again until a familiar tragedy struck. Jules told me that Nick and his wife's daughter was stillborn and I was moved to send them a card of condolence.

Louis' funeral was less than a year after his daughter's death and Nick told me he'd wanted to come to return my gesture of kindness but when he planted a farewell kiss firmly on my lips as he left Louis' wake later that evening, I wondered whether he had other ideas too.

Knowing what an empty head and busy mind the next day would bring, I drank myself into anaesthetised sleep that night but was roused from a blissfully unaware sedation with the beep of a text message. It was from Simon, who'd probably drunk too much at his own separate wake for Louis, and said that he wished we were together.

I'd hugged Simon outside the funeral home in the throng of the tearful, departing crowd and thanked him, from my heart, for being such a great dad. He'd returned my hug and thanked me for giving Louis to him. His words had struck me with the awful realisation that I was the only other person in the world who could truly know his pain. And I cried at the cruel irony that he would now and forever truly understand the agony of my grief. Still, there'd been a full stop in our hug and we'd both known it was a very final farewell. A thousand miserable thoughts crashed in as I cried into my pillow, but I forced myself back into the haven of darkness and the protective veil of sleep until the inevitable morning light woke me to face the unavoidable new day. I lay perfectly still, willing sleep to return again, exhausted by the thought of starting the descent into grief, but there was nothing for it other than to get up, have breakfast and hold on.

I'd never aspired to be a stay-at-home mum until the boys had come along and I wouldn't have been anywhere else than right by their sides. Now there was nowhere I needed to be. I'd read somewhere that the search for meaning requires the building of a new life structure and putting it into practice. Life would go on, but I felt too tired to deal with putting mine back together. So I started running and didn't stop for a year.

First I ran to the seaside to stay with Jules, who was living at the coastal sanctuary she and Karl had bought to raise their family when Karl had been well and their future seemed bright. She'd extended an open invitation to me to stay with her for as long as I liked and I took up her offer.

We were lying on the beach in the sun one day, chatting about life and death and how the bloody hell we'd found ourselves where we were, when I was startled by Nick saying, "Hi Jules, hi Means, what a beautiful day," causing me to wonder whether Jules had conspired to bring her two wounded friends together.

Whatever the case, Nick took me by the hand that day and we fell into each other, with our broken hearts. We shared an aching need for comfort and closeness and somewhere to put our homeless emotion.

We bunkered down in Nick's little beach shack, and retreated into grief for our separate losses and individual pain. As the waves of grief crashed down, we took shelter in each other and took consolation from the perpetual motion and magnitude of the sea. It was a pared-back life for the two of us, with his surfboard taking us to where the best waves would be, and Nick's faithful old kelpie, Indie, a compliant and loving companion; plus an endless box of beer to cheer us on.

On weekends Nick and I would play happy families with his three-year-old son, who was a sweet and sensitive little boy full of confused sadness for the little sister who'd never appeared and for his family sliced in two. He let me into his childhood with the purest of innocence and spending time with him nourished imaginings of my sons as they might have been, imbuing them with life and wonder and fits of irrepressible giggles and running and jumping and pillow fights and tantrums.

Finding an outlet for our overflowing emotion, Nick and I thought we were 'in love' and so we did what people in love do, talking about our futures, including our views on marriage and having more babies. I dreadfully, achingly, pressingly wanted another baby as soon as possible before my time ran out, but Nick absolutely and unequivocally did not. However, by then he felt like my life-raft so I clung onto him anyway as we comforted each other through all the milestones our children should have had but wouldn't and those they shouldn't have had but did. We visited graveyards and lit candles at our children's shrines when birthday cakes should have been the order of the day. We camped under the stars on Christmas Eve with Jules to feel closer to our kids, promising them Santa would find them anywhere.

My mum held me close throughout this time, wrapping me up in nourishing, patient love and supplying only what I asked for, when I asked for it, quiet and unassuming, never once offering hollow advice about the necessity of moving on from what felt like perennial, unshifting pain.

I put on a good show but my mum could see the truth. "You have sad eyes, darling," she would say. I knew her loss and pain were also profound – two grandsons and a daughter formerly of happy heart.

Our New Year ticked over with a Mexican fiesta where we donned sombreros and ate a feast of paella with friends. Though I forced myself to show half-hearted faux jollity, the first anniversary of Louis' death loomed large for me, bringing a fresh bout of melancholy and futility that threatened to write off another year.

Marlon's first anniversary had been by far the worst so far. Every anniversary since his death had been more marked by their painful anticipation than by the day itself, when I'd come to cherish indulging in rituals of remembrance. Louis' first anniversary, the swift passing of a year, was accompanied by the now deafening tick of my biological clock.

"Let's just go somewhere," I begged Nick on New Year's Day. "Let's just drive. We can shoot across to South Australia and come home along the coast," I continued, feeling overwhelmed by the urge to run from my memories and seek solace and distraction in a different place. The wilderness of South Australia's Coorong beckoned for me and we threw together a few camping essentials, two of our three trusty companions, and headed due west. Eight hours later in Adelaide we raised a glass to Louis and it felt good to be somewhere else.

We ambled down the Fleurieu Peninsula and south-east towards the mouth of the Murray River and the Coorong, a desolate, wild and windswept dead sea from my childhood. "Do you remember *Storm Boy*?" I asked Nick. "Those giant, endless sand dunes and sense of nowhere? The Coorong is exactly how it feels in the film." Of every place I'd travelled to around the world only the Coorong had imbued in me such a sense of something else, other people, other times, otherworldliness. It was as close to a spiritual feeling as I'd ever been.

Without another soul to be seen across unending miles of sand and pink salt lakes, Nick and I drove a four-wheel drive over the pyramid dunes and along the water's edge, sliding and slicing through sinking sand and dicing with a disastrous bog that might strand us for days without rescue. A shipwreck jutting from the waves spoke of treacherous, uncharted waters. It was almost a tempting thought to go missing and re-emerge as someone else.

But our children would still be dead. That could never change and I'd come to find the change within – to revisit the child I'd been in those happy-go-lucky days and piece together the parts of me that were still intact.

Towering dunes of shifting sand called out an irresistible challenge. We set up camp at the base of the highest dune we could see, and pushed up into the gusting wind whipping off the ocean carrying a bottle of wine and two plastic goblets. We raced each other to the top and collapsed into the cooling sands of sunset, dumbstruck by the view of a vast circle of no-man's land, feeling like we were looking down from the top of a prehistoric world.

I felt minute and insignificant and intensely, exhilaratingly alive. We tiptoed over ancient shell middens and wondered at the ancient history of these Aboriginal lands. I stood upon the sacred ground and thanked our Indigenous people because, looking out across the vast and glorious emptiness, I understood their gift. There amongst the resonating Indigenous spirits of survival, I knew I was ready to refill my own emptiness with goodness. I drew my renewal from the untamed void of nature until I was ready to go home.

PART V

33. Mother Knows Best

It was liberating to choose life again. It felt true to the person I'd always hoped to be and it honoured the memory of my sons. Slowly I found I could laugh in a way that was hearty and real and I began to re-engage with the world, though I still felt like I was going through the motions of a life that was incomplete without the prospect of motherhood on the horizon for me. Still, I was determined to make the best of the life I had, a privilege my sons didn't have.

As new buds of life finally began to appear in me, Mum planted a seed of her own. "You could still try IVF, Aminah. You'll regret it if you don't try," she said sagely, knowing me better than myself. "And I'll do anything I can to help if it's what you really want."

"I'm too old now, Mum, IVF is too expensive, it doesn't work for women my age. It's just too hard," I protested.

I felt too worn out and battered by experience to really fathom another pregnancy and I simply didn't know if I had that much left in the way of emotional reserves. I'd thought briefly about adoption but only briefly, having learnt how long, arduous and uncertain the process was in Australia, and being single would likely have ruled me out anyway.

Mum was the person I'd inherited my stubborn streak from and she gently pressed her point with, "None of that matters if it's what you really want."

To deny the seed Mum had planted from growing roots would have been to ignore the pain behind my eyes, where motherhood lived on through the ever-present memory of my boys, who had both put up such dogged fights to defy the odds of their births. Mum was right. It would be futile to try to live well and become whole again if I didn't at least equal their determination. Despite the fatal flaw in my DNA, it had never been in my makeup to give up and I desperately didn't want to live with regret. Gradually, it felt more like a necessity than a choice to give motherhood one more try.

As it turned out, during Louis' short life the IVF laws in Victoria had been changed to reflect the modern shape of families. And at just about the time I'd been bidding my unbearable farewell to Louis, new legislation was passed allowing single women to use donor sperm to have a baby. The synchronicity of the timing felt like the final nudge I needed to take my last chance.

As the new seed of hope took root, I lay awake each night trying to imagine a healthy baby in my arms – but without a partner to have a baby with it was impossible to conjure a face. Romance was dead. I couldn't just have sex and, boom, have a baby nine months later the good old-fashioned way. I knew I wasn't the hottest prospect as a mate with my disastrous reproductive history, so a sperm donor represented my last real hope of motherhood.

A scene in a bar played out in my head. "Hi, I'm Aminah, nice to meet you. Do you mind if we skip the formalities? You see, I'm 42 and really desperate to have a baby, but I'm a carrier of this horrific genetic condition. Actually it's a really long story and I don't have much time, so would you mind if I tell you the rest in the cab on the way?"

"Oh, I meant to the IVF clinic, not my place, sorry, did I forget to mention that? Well, now that we're here, let's have a baby. What do you say?"

And though I knew using a sperm donor wouldn't provide me with the picture-perfect family I'd hoped for I had a successful blueprint for single motherhood in my mum, who stood right beside me where she'd always been, offering encouragement, support and a soft landing should I fail.

I had nothing more to lose. It was now or never.

"Mum, you're right," I said one day. "I would never forgive myself if I didn't give having a baby one last try."

Between Mum and a precious collection of supportive friends I was surrounded by people who wanted to see me happy, to see me succeed and to see me become a mother again, if that's what I truly wanted. And each of them knew in my heart of hearts that was all I truly wanted. They had carried me through the worst of times and shared in my tragedies and triumphs, and they'd all be there to help me raise a baby. Now, all I needed was some sperm.

I should be so lucky.

I'd selected a fertility specialist on the referral of a friend who worked in IVF. Happily, Fleur was my kind of doctor, a rare straight shooter in a world of maybes who didn't use any of the baffling medical jargon and got straight to the point, telling me my chance of having a baby was a long shot.

"Aminah, at 42, you should really consider donor eggs," she said straight off the bat, no ifs no buts. "Using donor eggs would provide your greatest chance of success."

She might as well have kicked me in the guts, but I respected her honesty immediately. I needed to know that my chances were slim then anything else would be a bonus.

"No," I batted it back to her, "I'm not infertile. I've been pregnant six times. I've had two children. I just need a healthy one."

Working up the resolve to try IVF using donor sperm was one thing but if I used a donor egg my child wouldn't be related to me either and now I didn't want to completely deprive my child of a sense of identity, harking back to my own need to know where I'd come from and who my father was. So I determined it would be my own eggs or bust.

With that conversation out of the way, Fleur and I got down to business. She knew my story and acknowledged it with kindness but in IVF world they were just the facts of my poor obstetric history. Never mind genetics, age was the biggest factor standing between me and motherhood and it didn't much matter how many unsuccessful pregnancies I'd had or babies I'd birthed before.

I was there to have a baby, so that day I joined the bizarre world of IVF, with all of its statistics, drugs, blood tests, specific dates and times, probes, scans, follicle sizes and egg numbers, egg pickups, fertilisation rates and embryo transfers. All but the candlelit dinner.

Fleur thought she could possibly get me pregnant again using my own eggs but ultimately fertility specialists are not in the business of making promises and IVF is a business like any other for making money.

When I walked out of Fleur's office and into the IVF clinic I would become patient number 32787, just another brick in the wall between childlessness and parenthood. The next stop was the Patient Liaison Administrator's office, better known as the cash point. Show me the money or do not pass go, and leave the way you came without a baby.

I walked out of my first IVF appointment grieving afresh for my beautiful boys and the family I might never have and the absence of a partner to hold my hand. Nick was still in my life sporadically and had promised to 'support' me in my decision to try donor IVF but his words didn't make me any less alone sitting in that foyer waiting to try to make a baby with a stranger's sperm.

Never mind being childless, being man-less meant I needed counselling before I could view the donor line-up and make my choice. The counsellor explained how my child would probably want to know who Mr Anonymous was or even want to meet him one day because humans are curious like that. She added that the law had been changed to allow all donor conceived offspring to know the identity of their donor when they reached eighteen.

I reassured her that I knew the curiosity drill pretty well and felt equipped to deal with it, sharing snippets of my life with her, including where I'd come from and how I'd come to be having this unlikely conversation. "It's fine," I said, "there'll be no secrets hidden in the cupboard of any child of mine. They're all nice problems to have if it means I have a healthy child."

Each of the potential pitfalls and awkward conversations she suggested might arise rang familiar and true, but it didn't put me off. If anything it galvanised my resolve and the counsellor decided I was a suitable candidate for the job of sole parent.

The next thing I had to do was go through the 'catalogue' of donors, which quickly dispelled any ideas I might have had of a Hollywood scripted designer daddy gallery. There would be no headshots of handsome, masculine, virile young faces accompanied by impressive resumes of superior SAT scores and Ivy League achievement. "Here are three donor profiles," Sarah said, handing me an A4 envelope. "If you have any questions, don't hesitate to call me."

And that was that. I took my leave from the clinic with a mysterious plain white envelope in hand. Stealing a peek inside it at the tram stop, I was stunned to find that the potential father of my child came in the form of just three pieces of paper. Apparently there had been a dearth of donor sperm since anonymity had been abolished and it remained illegal to import sperm into Victoria, so I was fortunate to have received even three nameless, faceless men to choose from.

A surreptitious flick through the pages as the tram rattled towards home left me bemused at how I was supposed to choose a donor from the stark contents of those three pieces of paper. Reaching home, I made a cup of tea, sat myself down on the couch and pulled out the profiles one by one. There was no photo, just the most basic of vital statistics including the donor's year of birth, height, build, hair and eye colour, vocation, hobbies and interests.

I scanned each for clues, but I wasn't even sure what I was looking for. At first glimpse only one stood out. He said he was happy and had four beautiful, healthy children already. The words 'happy and healthy' sang out to me from the page as the two things that had most eluded me.

The second donor had already sired a donor baby who'd been born with extra fingers and toes. It didn't matter a dot what else he might have going for him, or that an appendix said there was no evidence that polydactyly was hereditary, it was a risk I wasn't prepared to take.

The third donor, I read, was single and had no children of his own. He hasn't been tested, I thought dispassionately, and went back to number one. Healthy and happy bounced off the page again because, when it came down to it, these two things were really all that mattered. I didn't worry about what my child might look like or even what they would grow up to be, just as long as they were healthy and we could both be happy; that was more than I dared hope for. So donor one, also known as 'SR', came out on top. Looking once more over SR's profile I dubbed him Mr Happy. A man of few words, he'd given scant other hints that might bring him to life apart from him being a cattle farmer who coached local football. I satisfied myself with the hope that he was a salt-of-the-earth, honest Aussie bloke who wanted to help others have kids who were as happy as him and as healthy as his own children. In the half-page reserved for a note to any potential offspring, he'd written: *'I hope you are happy and healthy. Have a great life.'*

I couldn't have put it better myself.

That was enough for me and my choice was made. In the absence of Mr Right, Mr Happy would have to do. I called the clinic, locked him in and booked a date with destiny.

Nick and I continued to bumble along together in increasingly peculiar and hapless dysfunction. I was trying to have a baby with anonymous sperm, and although it felt slightly creepy to show him the profile of my chosen donor I felt obliged to because to all other intents and purposes he was still my boyfriend, though I was starting to pull away from him. Nick agreed that Mr Happy seemed like a good option.

Stabbing myself in the stomach with a needle each morning seemed a sadistic way to conceive a child. The drugs made me crazy and the waiting drove me mad. Nick was around but I started to wish he'd go away because I'd never felt more alone. Sitting in the waiting room at the hospital where my eggs would be harvested, I'd rather have been anywhere than there. I hated hospitals, which provoked miserable memories and a consuming fear of loss. I could think of nothing positive sitting there all by myself.

I managed to produce six eggs, which was a decent number for my age. Three were fertilised by direct injection of a single sperm into their nuclei (ICSI), then hatched and grown for a couple of days in a Petrie dish to see if they were fit for purpose before two were transferred to my womb. With Fleur's advice I'd decided to make pregnancy the aim, implanting the embryos two at a time. She slipped them deep inside me and froze the third one – just in case.

I left the transfer certain I was pregnant and wishing away the interminable two weeks I'd have to wait until the blood test confirmed a positive result. The question was, would it be one or both of the tiny embryos that would tuck in for the ride? The days stretched out interminably. During the first week I felt as pregnant as I had with the boys, convinced that all the niggles and twinges were my embryos burrowing their way into my uterine wall, but by the second week my mind was wreaking havoc with itself, convinced that every pain would bring evidence of failure. I started scouring online forums on the internet for other two-week waiters who'd experienced the same peculiar little discomforts or tugging or pinching or prodding pains similar to the ones that were plaguing me day and night, derailing my certainty of pregnancy. I was desperate for reassurance that the symptoms I was feeling meant I was definitely pregnant.

As time dawdled by I distracted myself by learning to speak in the coded tongue of the childless. Never mind a bit of dirty talk in the bedroom, it was all gory TMI (too much information) of CM (cervical mucus) and hormone levels, sperm counts, egg numbers and fertilisation rates, then the dilemma of whether to transfer one embie (embryo) or two and whether it was a freshie (newly fertilised embryo) or a frostie (thawed from the freezer). I tried to resist POAS (peeing on a stick) because HPTs (home pregnancy tests) weren't accurate enough so it was better to wait for the BT (blood test) to reveal a longed for BFP (big fat positive) or a disastrous BFN (big fat negative) to put you back at Day 1 and square one.

I turned online for support when cycle one brought a miserable BFN, with another failed cycle following close behind. It felt cruelly ironic that, having conceived so easily naturally, IVF was not going to work. I found some great women online who truly understood the struggle and provided boundless support and encouragement despite all fighting their own painful personal battles. Many of them were childless too and had suffered more losses between them than I could count. Some were same sex couples or single women needing a donor like myself; some had husbands with poor 'swimmers' or had malfunctioning ovaries or wombs that let them down; others had conceived a child easily the first time around only to be bitterly disappointed not to be able to conceive a sibling. The catalogue of fertility problems shocked even me but the universal call uniting us was the primal scream of motherhood, spurring each of us to keep putting our bodies, hearts and minds on the fine line between hope and science.

I had two frozen embryos left over from my second cycle but when I failed to get pregnant with them I wondered if I had the strength to go on. I felt desperately disappointed and defeated all at once. I'd just about lost all hope, and was certainly losing the will to keep putting my body through the wringer and my mind on the edge of sanity. I wanted off the rollercoaster and said to Fleur, "I'm not sure this is going to work and while I hate to concede defeat I'm not convinced I can face another one."

"Look, it's a bit of a numbers game," she said. "I still think I can get you pregnant but I understand it's not easy so of course it's up to you."

Despite my mental and physical exhaustion I took heart from Fleur's confidence that she could help me get pregnant and decided to give it one more shot before I was done.

I ended up with more eggs than ever before from my last ever egg collection, with seven precious eggs that became six 'good-looking' embryos ready for transfer. Two days later I walked out of the clinic after the transfer of two more embryos, thinking, *Whatever… I'm just going to get on with my life this time rather than sit around fearfully counting the days only to be shattered by another Big Fat Nothing.*

I kept up my exercise routine that week, going for a run almost every day and getting into the festive pre-Christmas spirit of socialising and shopping for presents. Keeping busy and trying to be normal kept me far more relaxed than I'd been before, but as the second week reached its mid-point, I felt the same familiar rumblings and tugging in my abdomen that had signalled my previous embryos' doom.

On Friday afternoon I had the regulation blood test at the IVF clinic. Even when you'd already started a period they insisted on confirming your HCG hormone levels were at zero before commencing another cycle.

That evening I'd been invited to a Christmas party for an ad agency headed up by an old advertising buddy from London. And though I wasn't really in the mood for merriment, knowing my period was about to start, I agreed to go with my work colleague Traci.

"Do you want a champagne?" asked Traci after we'd arrived, gesturing to the free bar, oblivious to my attempts to get pregnant again.

"Sure," I said carelessly, wanting to numb the pain of another Christmas laden with false jollity and emptiness.

The champagne went down beautifully, immediately making me feel lightheaded and happier. By my third champagne I'd washed away most of my lingering sadness and was thinking how much I'd missed enjoying a drink with friends and making new acquaintances. The evening slipped away in comfortably numb revelry as one glass followed another. I'd lost count of just how many I'd drunk by the time I wobbled home and slipped instantly into a blissfully oblivious sleep.

34. Flying Solo

I slept 'til eleven the next morning and woke up with a pounding head. Staggering to the toilet, I fully expected my period would have come so I was surprised to see it hadn't. The implications of this hit at the same time as a surge of memories of the previous night's champagne consumption flooded in.

"Shit, shit, shit, shit, shit, shit," I repeated to my makeup-smudged face in the mirror.

The phone rang while I was still in the bathroom, but stopped ringing just as I got to it. The blocked number of the missed call identified it as being from the IVF clinic, so I made a cup of tea before calling back to get the bad news, only to get an answering machine.

When the nurse called back and asked if I was sitting down, my heart felt like it stopped beating, before starting again at triple the pace as my mind raced at the thought of the five, six, seven, or even eight glasses of champagne I'd downed in miserable defeat the night before.

"It's positive, Aminah! Congratulations, you're pregnant!" the nurse said brightly.

I immediately burst into tears, telling the nurse about how much champagne I'd drunk the night before.

"Aminah, if I had a dollar for every time I've heard that I probably wouldn't have to work anymore," she replied. "It's okay, it's still very early. Mind you, that should be your last drink for the next eight months," she added. "Now, you need to come in for another blood test tomorrow. Relax and enjoy the good news, we'll see you then."

I hung up and tried to take it all in. "I'm pregnant!" I said aloud before doing a little jig in my bedroom. I needed to tell somebody, so I called Mum. "Are you sitting down?" I asked, mimicking the nurse.

Mum's delight was tempered only by a slight hint of trepidation. Like me she probably wondered if the news was too good to be true.

My own joy at finally being pregnant was soon overwhelmed by all my pent-up fear flooding back. I'd been so focused on getting pregnant and then on trying not to focus on getting pregnant after three failures, I hadn't stopped to think about what would happen if I actually got pregnant. Being by myself without anybody to share my worrying thoughts with made me feel isolated and panicky instead of elated and joyful. I didn't want to burden Mum, who had gotten me this far. The rest was up to me.

Very few friends knew I'd been doing IVF. Apart from telling a couple of my closest friends in confidence I'd stayed very low-key, circumspect and vague with the details. I'd sworn even Mum to secrecy to limit the potential audience for further disappointment. And though I wished I could yell it from the rooftops superstition compounded the fear. I had such a long way to go.

I'd opted out of pre-implantation genetic diagnosis or sex selection. Because of my age, getting pregnant had been the first priority. But now that I was pregnant the spectre of myotubular myopathy reared its ugly head again. Memories and dread zigzagged through my mind, criss-crossing with stories of all the lost boys I knew and the mum in Ireland who'd lost three boys to MTM. The threat of its recurrence made jagged edges of my thoughts shredding my natural propensity to think positively. It would be two more months before

I could find out if it was a boy or a girl. There were so many hurdles ahead that the only way I could hope to jump them was one at a time, assuming that one of them might tumble or trip me over at any moment and obstruct the finish line.

I tried vainly to distract myself from the little life growing inside me but it was futile, especially once I'd heard the galloping little heartbeat, pacing out at speed like horses on the track.

Obstetrically speaking I thought I'd seen it all until I went to have my CVS test and clapped eyes on the breathtaking size of the needle about to be used to extract a little piece of the baby's DNA from my womb. Mandy, the woman doing the CVS, was renowned in her field and had a wonderfully encouraging bedside manner but I wondered if she was being ironic when she asked me to relax as she guided the giant spike through my stomach wall.

I held my breath and tried to visualise a lovely place and feel warm sun on my skin as tears slid down my face. Meanwhile, Mandy and the nurse made conversation and asked me about myself in an attempt to distract me. As I recalled extracts from my life, I saw a glimpse of recognition between Mandy and the nurse that conveyed their understanding this was my very last hope.

When the time came to say goodbye Mandy patted me gently and said, "I really hope it's a little girl for you, Aminah." There was such poignant meaning in her voice that I sensed intuitively she could tell even at just 12 weeks' gestation that my baby was a little girl.

I received a call soon after with the best news imaginable. I was pregnant with a baby girl and she was as healthy as could be foretold. I called my mum immediately to share the news.

I decided I'd name my daughter Leila in memory of my dad – a small final salute of recognition that he too had been a parent living without his child. There would be a Leila Hart in the world after all and though he would never know her, she would carry a name he chose along with his surname and I would encourage her to wear it with pride.

The bright light of optimism was quickly dimmed by anxiety and dread. An anterior placenta cushioned Leila's movements, protecting me from the kick in the guts I so dearly wished to feel. I figured it would be just my luck she could be an even rarer breed than the boys: genetics had a name for them, they were called manifesting carriers – girls who suffered milder symptoms of a sex-linked genetic condition otherwise reserved exclusively for boys. I envisaged her being born floppy as nightmares seeped into my dreams.

I couldn't bring myself to tell Nick I was pregnant, thinking I'd jinx my little girl. And when our relationship took an unforgivable turn for the worse I pushed him away, feeling a protective need to distance my baby and myself from the negative energy brewing between us.

I kept mainly to myself, telling only a few of my closest friends who I trusted and needed to help me through the second half of the pregnancy. I didn't want too many people calling me to ask how I was doing because I felt like a nervous wreck and couldn't have looked a friend in the eye and honestly told them I was fine. Instead I tried to hide, making up excuses when I turned down invitations to get-togethers.

At 29 weeks while dog-sitting I fell awkwardly down my front steps as I let the dog out into the misty, pre-dawn haze, landing heavily on my ankle, which cracked noisily under my pregnant weight. Not a soul was around to come to my aid so I sat for a cold-bottomed moment on the concrete until Leila squirmed in protest. I tried to heave myself upright but my ankle wasn't taking an ounce, so I clambered back down to my knees to crawl back to my bed where I lay until morning with a packet of frozen peas to numb the pain.

When the relentless throbbing of my ankle got the better of me I called Mum, who took me to the Emergency Department. A doctor confirmed the evidence of the crack, saying, "It's a spiral fracture of the anterior blah blah near the blah blah joint."

I'd started to switch off, but my ears pricked back up when he said I'd need surgery to knit my ankle back together again. "Huh?" I said, alarmed. "Surgery?"

"Don't worry," said the doctor as he rushed out of the room, "I'll refer you to an ankle and foot specialist who fixes ankles all the time."

Mr Edwards, the 'foot-man', confirmed what Dr Emergency had said, that I'd need surgery and some heavy metal to meld my ankle back together.

"Do you monitor the baby while I'm under?" I challenged him stubbornly.

"No, we don't," he replied as if it were a ludicrously unnecessary idea, "but anaesthetic is very safe and there is no real risk to your baby."

"No risk," I protested, "so, how will I feel if she's moving or not?"

"You won't, but it is very safe," he repeated

"What if I get an infection?" I asked weakly, desperate to find an out. "I just can't go through it, I can't have surgery, I won't," I said with finality.

He looked shocked at such a rebuttal. I doubted many patients came to him for treatment and then refused to let him fix them.

"I could never live with myself if something went wrong with my baby when I was unconscious," I said, explaining about my sons.

Mr Edwards changed tack immediately, softening his approach and calling up an altogether more compassionate bedside manner. He agreed to adopt a conservative approach, saying, "We'll take another x-ray to make sure the bones haven't moved and then put you in a cast."

I hobbled out of the surgeon's rooms a couple of hours later with bright red fibreglass encasing my lower leg. I must have made quite a sight lurching about on crutches with my six months' pregnant belly. Back home it was soon clear that living alone on crutches for the last trimester of my pregnancy was going to be impossible. I had no choice but to move back home to Mum's and let her care for me.

There was such downward pressure when I tried to propel myself around on crutches that I worried Leila might well slip out and I was reduced to crawling to the bathroom on all fours to answer the incessant calls of nature that accompany the last weeks of pregnancy. My social life became virtually non-existent apart from my few cherished friends in the know who insisted on getting me out of the house, including for my birthday.

One day my oldest friend Emma came to take me out for a belated birthday lunch and we laughed that I couldn't even blame alcohol for my mishap as she heaved me out of her sporty convertible and steadied me onto my crutches for the short shuffle into the restaurant.

Over yum cha I lamented my incapacity and rapidly rounding face. "I'm enormous and so bored," I wailed.

"Well, means, you could try giving up that daily tub of chocolate mousse!" she replied, laughing.

"But it's my only friend, Em," I moaned, half laughing at myself. "You're right, though, I should eat less of that mousse."

My obstetrician couldn't have agreed more. "You've gained quite a lot of weight in a short space of time," he cautioned as I hopped literally and heavily onto his scales, hoping not to break them with my mass.

Sheepishly I confessed my chocolate mousse addiction.

"You started off so well, Aminah, with exercise and healthy eating, but you'll need a glucose tolerance test now," he replied, his face serious.

His words had the desired effect as my mind flashed back.

"It's fairly routine," Stephen reassured me, "but you've gained a lot of weight quickly so we need to check what the reason might be."

"Other than the chocolate mousse you don't think there's

something wrong, do you?" I asked remembering previous glucose tests and then panicked as I thought of polyhydramnios and committed to giving up the mousse.

"Try not to worry," he replied. "She looks happy in there, we're nearly there now. I'm going to book you in for a caesar on the fourteenth of August."

35. To Have and to Hold

A cry.

It's the sweetest, most natural sound of a newborn baby. But it was a sound I hadn't heard when my boys were born. Finally here it was and here Leila was with a lung full of air, letting out a hearty cry.

"Here she is," Stephen said softly as he placed little Leila, her face all pink and squashed and swollen from a forceps delivery, snugly onto my chest.

I shed a silent tear as I gazed in amazement at my daughter, registering her every detail. "Hello, my little darling, here you are."

Mum couldn't hide her own tears when I looked at her and cried, "She's finally here." Tears of relief blended with tears of sadness that I'd missed getting to hold Marlon or Louis at their births. They seeped together and flowed until finally they were replaced by absolute, triumphant joy.

Much to my surprise I spotted a ring of fine white fluff encircling Leila's head. "Could she really be blonde?" I wondered. Marlon and Louis had been unmistakably dark-haired and dark-eyed, declaring their West Indian heritage from the first. I'd assumed my gene pool would predominate again, despite knowing Leila's donor was blonde. And her name meant dark beauty which I'd imagined would suit her perfectly.

"I think this baby is blonde!" I said to Mum.

"Really? What colour are her eyes?" she asked.

I couldn't really make them out in the glare of the theatre lights as the delivery team took Leila out of my arms to be 'processed' and Stephen stitched me back together.

Leila let out another cry as she was wrested from her cosy nest on my chest and it was then that I noticed something ever so subtly awry in her cry. Imperceptible to a less vigilant ear, months of hyper-alertness slipped a trace of dread under my elation. "She sounds a little bit husky," I said to nobody in particular.

Stephen had enlisted a paediatrician to be present at the delivery so there was a specialist somewhere in the room but I couldn't discuss Leila's cry with him until Stephen finished sewing me up. Leila continued to cry and the huskiness was undeniable, jump-starting my worst fears.

My mind raced straight to muscle weakness. Panic rose as I again imagined her to be a manifesting carrier of myotubular myopathy. My rational mind knew it was very unlikely because I knew the science, but with the long odds I'd managed to pull out of the hat I could only imagine the worst. I tried to stop myself from freaking out completely right there on the operating table by reminding myself that she'd felt robust and wriggled about in my arms and her initial cry had been emphatic enough to suggest good lung capacity.

"She may just have a slightly floppy vocal cord," the paediatrician said innocently in response to my question.

Wrong word. Despite being aware of my history, he had no idea how frightening the term floppy was for me to hear. Clearly reading the worry spreading across my face, he added, "There's no muscle problem. Her breathing is a little stressed but babies born by caesarean often have a bit of trouble clearing all the fluid from their lungs.

How about we take her to the Special Care Nursery, just for observation while you're in recovery, Aminah, what do you think?"

Worry turned to panic rising up out of my chest, sticking in my throat and rendering me speechless.

"Aminah, there's really nothing to worry about, she's a big healthy baby," he reassured me. "We can just monitor her better there until her breathing settles down, and then she can join you in your room as soon as you're out of recovery."

"Yes, okay, whatever she needs," I said, trying to steady my voice as the idea of being separated from my daughter brought tears back to the surface. I sent Mum with her as they wheeled Leila away to the Special Care Nursery.

Alone in recovery, I anxiously tried to distract myself by pondering on the fact that I had a new baby who was able to let out a gutsy cry at birth, that and Leila's blonde hair. Black women don't usually have blonde babies, I mused. Then my mind started to race off irrationally. What if they put the wrong embryo back in, what if she's not really mine and the real mother wants her back? Then again, I told myself, Mum's side of the family had German genes, Banchie had been blonde, and my aunt Jane and cousin Kate were blonde. Still, I'd fully expected that Leila would look like me and the ridiculous idea that she might not be mine undermined the notion that life could actually be finally turning around. "Stop spoiling it for yourself, Aminah," I reprimanded myself, closing my eyes and trying to meditate.

Discharge from recovery was finally signed off with a return visit from Stephen. "Aminah, Leila will be fine, she's a beautiful healthy baby," that gem of a man said. "Get some rest while you can."

"Thank you, Stephen – for everything," I said tearfully.

As the orderly pushed my gurney up to Leila's incubator, I struggled to get a clear view of her through the perspex but I could see the blurred outline of her naked torso and neck being supported by a nurse as she sucked voraciously on a bottle. My unadulterated relief at seeing her suck and swallow so vigorously was slightly tempered by dismay that she was receiving her first milk from a nurse rather than her mum. "I'd hoped to breastfeed her," I said to the nurse, failing to keep the hint of regret from my voice.

"She's a hungry little girl. She couldn't wait for her mum. But don't worry, this won't affect her ability to breastfeed, we just had to get something into her tummy. She's a good little eater," the nurse replied kindly with the perceptive experience of someone used to dealing with anxious mothers. "She's been perfect. As soon as you're back in your room, the doctors will send her up."

"Thank you," I said, smiling at her and asking Mum if she'd stay with Leila and accompany her back to me when she was discharged from the nursery. I didn't want her out of our sight.

Back in my room, alone for the first time, I let the enormity of all that had happened sink in. "I have a daughter, I'm a mum again," I said out loud.

Leila, who'd been just under a bonny 10 pounds (4.5 kg) at birth, took to breastfeeding like a little champion. Voracious and vigorous in her suck she seemed sleepily satisfied after each feed. Receiving full marks from the midwives for my ability to bathe and feed her and feeling pretty confident in myself with the relatively straight-forward task of caring for a healthy baby, I was soon ready to take her home.

The paediatrician repeatedly refuted my concerns about Leila's raspy cry and insisted that it didn't require further investigation before we left the hospital. He discharged her with a promise to take a look down her throat if the huskiness persisted by the time of her six-week check-up. I had no option but to believe him and so, with a clean bill of health, we headed for home.

We arrived home to find it inundated with flowers and balloons and countless gifts for Leila along with messages of congratulations and support from friends – and friends of friends – in the furthest flung corners of the globe. People I'd never met who'd heard the story of Marlon and Louis wanted to express their happiness at Leila's arrival and welcome her into the world.

It was overwhelming to realise how widely my little girl's arrival had resonated, along with the memory of her brothers. This was how it was supposed to be, I thought. I couldn't help but shed a tear for the boys as I gazed adoringly down at their little sister lying comfortably oblivious in my arms.

"It's quite a big story you've arrived in, little girl," I whispered. It was time to start a new chapter for the happy ending. I kissed her forehead and allowed the warm heaviness of her body in my arms to set my enduring melancholy free.

It wasn't exactly fun, but the sleep deprivation of three-hourly feeds through the night and nobody to talk to but a newborn and myself was a doddle compared to NICU. Indulgently, I allowed myself to stay in my dressing gown when visitors weren't dropping by to lavish yet more gifts on Leila and anoint her with their love.

"She's going to be so bloody spoilt," I joked to my dear friend Sarah one day. The two of us had shared many an hour on the couch comforting and encouraging each other through reproductive journeys of loss and despair. Along with my mum, Sarah had encouraged me to never give up on motherhood.

Despite still being on her own quest to have a baby Sarah was selflessly sincere in her delight at Leila's arrival, replying, "And she'll totally deserve it, Means. Don't even worry about it."

"You're right but it's lucky she'll never remember all of these gorgeous clothes and toys because there's no way I'm going to be able to keep her in this sort of lifestyle," I laughed. "And when am I ever going to find the time to write two hundred thank you cards, for goodness sake?"

There was no time to think about not having a partner, such was the revolving door of visitors and endless cycle of feeding and settling. Somehow it suited me perfectly to nest and nestle with my little blonde bundle whose eyes looked like they were going to remain distinctly blue. Leila's husky voice still niggled at the back of my mind but I joked with friends that she might sing the blues in order to push worrying thoughts aside and enjoy the chaotic bliss of a disorganised, messy, sleepless, hazy life with a newborn.

To me Leila seemed the ideal baby, though I was sure all mums thought the same.

36. Rare and Precious

On her first visit to see Leila, the maternal and child health nurse surprised me by saying she'd lost too much weight.

"I thought she was eating brilliantly," I said, dismayed that perhaps my milk was not enough for her.

"Ten percent weight loss is to be expected, but Leila has lost a lot more than that," the nurse replied before suggesting I express my milk into bottles to monitor exactly how much milk Leila was getting.

Leila's weight continued to stutter pathetically and she was soon diagnosed with 'failure to thrive', which sounded like a sick joke to me. Failure to thrive was what I'd witnessed during eight months in various neonatal units, not something I'd envisioned for my big beautiful girl.

Meanwhile, I'd become more and more anxious about Leila's huskiness and wondered if it was responsible for her failure to thrive. As well as being able to hear it when she cried, her breathing had become noisy during the night. And while I knew it was normal for babies to snuffle in their sleep, I was disconcerted enough to tell the nurse, who suggested I call the paediatrician.

When I explained my concerns to the paediatrician's receptionist and asked if I could move our appointment forward there were no earlier dates available, so all she could do was put us on a cancellation list.

I hoped I was just being neurotic but I'd been far more relaxed with Leila than I'd envisaged and something just didn't feel quite right.

One day Mum and David visited and took turns giving Leila cuddles. David commented on her noisy breathing and Mum agreed that she didn't sound quite right.

That night Leila was tired but still eating reasonably and had no other symptoms of illness so I pushed my fears aside once more and tucked her into her cot alongside my bed. Unable to fall asleep I lay awake, listening to her breathing. The night is always an amplifier but something definitely wasn't right and I wished, for the first time since her birth, there was someone beside me to reassure me in the dark and eerie quiet.

Still unable to sleep late into the night, I gently picked Leila up out of her cot and nursed her into my chest to feel the rise and fall of her breathing. The rasping seemed worse up close and my panic began to intensify. I shone the light of my mobile phone onto her neck and scanned it down to her chest. She was sleeping peacefully but there was an unmistakable recession as she breathed in and the air rasped down her throat.

Despite my rising panic I forced myself to invoke a respiratory checklist. Good colour, rosy pink in her cheeks, check. Pink lips, no blue tinges, check. Her breathing rate normal, check. She's okay, I told myself, I'll just sit here holding her until the morning and call the doctor first thing.

From 8am on I called the paediatrician's office every five minutes despite knowing they opened at nine, hoping he might be in the office early and happen to answer the call. Leila had fed again and slept peacefully in my arms through the night. When she woke

I switched into practical nursing mode and videoed her breathing, which made me feel calmer.

When I finally got through to the paediatrician's receptionist my words tumbled out a little fast. "My daughter is raspy when she's breathing. The doctor said when she was born that she might have a vocal cord issue but she's gotten worse and I really need the doctor to see her today if at all possible, *please*."

"Sorry, he's fully booked today after he gets back from theatre," she replied.

Frustrated and hoping she might be a nurse, I asked if she would listen to Leila's breathing over the phone.

Because there was no way she could squeeze us in, and she wouldn't be able to get the doctor to call me until he arrived after theatre, she suggested I take Leila to a hospital if I was especially worried.

With that my mind was made up, so I bundled Leila into the car and headed for the Royal Children's Hospital, pulling up illegally right at the door of the new hospital. A controlled composure came over me as I reached the safety of Emergency because I knew we'd be in good hands.

The language that would speed our triage tumbled straight out of my memory as I spoke to the receptionist. "My daughter is in respiratory distress, she has intercostal recession and stridor, her respiratory rate is okay but she's deteriorated through the night, and she's only 20 days old," I said as calmly as I could, pointing at Leila's throat and adding, "Look, you can see for yourself."

"If I can just have your Medicare card," the receptionist said, picking up the phone, "someone will be out to take you through immediately."

A nurse appeared straight away and beckoned for me to follow her, bypassing the triage cubicles and nurses' station and going directly to a treatment room. Within moments Leila was attached to all-too-familiar monitors, her little body stripped naked and covered in sticky patches to hold the wires in place while I relayed the story of Leila's huskiness to the doctor.

"Do you come from a medical background?" he asked. "You speak like one of us."

"No, I've just spent an unfortunate amount of time in hospitals," I replied.

"She's definitely having trouble with her breathing, so you were right to bring her in," he said. "I've called the ENT specialist to come down and have a look at what's going on in there."

"This is a bronchoscope," the ENT specialist explained once he'd arrived and introduced himself. "If you could just hold onto her I'm going to pass it down into Leila's throat to have a bit of a look. It will be a little bit uncomfortable for her but it won't hurt."

It still amazed me how I could almost detach myself when a medical procedure had to be performed on my children. Out of necessity I'd had to get over my instinctive impulse to protect them from pain, but I was living my worst nightmare seeing Leila in such a state.

"There's a significant cyst down there," the ENT declared as he extracted the bronchoscope. "It's obviously been growing and causing her breathing to become obstructed."

"Can you fix it?" I asked hopefully, wishing he could do it there and then.

"I'll discuss it with the consultant," he said before disappearing.

Hours seemed to have passed by the time the consultant, Rob Berkowitz arrived, introduced himself and said, apologetically, "I'll have to take a look myself. A congenital laryngeal cyst is very rare," he added, guiding his scope down Leila's throat.

"I only do rare," I replied dryly, holding Leila as gently as I could while she squirmed in discomfort.

I wondered whether everything that happened to me had to be quite so unusual, especially when it came to my children. 'Rare' hardly instilled me with confidence but I knew if there were doctors anywhere that would know what to do, the Royal Children's

Hospital was the place; they specialised in rare and precious children like my own.

"We can remove the cyst," said Rob after a while, "but it will take a bit of planning. We'll have to admit her to PICU in the meantime to get her ready for surgery."

"She's only three weeks old. Can she go to the NICU rather than PICU?" I pleaded. It felt unbelievable to be virtually begging to go back to the NICU, a place I'd hoped never to see again as long as I lived, but better the devil I knew.

The morning stretched into afternoon and we were still stuck in the Emergency Department waiting as the wheels of hospital admission slowly turned.

I called Mum to reassure her that we were okay, saying, "Don't bother coming in. There's no point. We're just sitting in Emergency and it could be hours until they find her a bed in the NICU. You know how it is. I'll call you again once we've been admitted."

Leila slept for most of the day, warmed by the overhead lights, while I gazed around at the machinery and medical paraphernalia, establishing the position of the oxygen supply and suction machine out of sheer habit. I was resigned to a long and tedious process but immensely relieved the problem had been found and there was a plan to make her better. She might not sing the blues after all.

Finally we went upstairs to the fifth floor, where I immediately recognised Rod Hunt as the director of the NICU from Louis' days in the old RCH building. A glimmer of recognition crossed his face when he saw me but I doubted he'd remember Louis from the thousands of babies he must have seen since then.

Once Leila was settled into a cot with a nurse all to herself, Rod came in to welcome us and, sure enough, he remembered Louis and knew who I was. It was incredibly touching to think Louis had made such an impact.

I was jolted out of reminiscing suddenly when Leila's oxygen saturation level dropped and all hell broke loose. Without warning, her condition had suddenly become dangerously tenuous as she started gasping for every breath.

The doctors had wanted to insert her ventilator tube in the controlled environment of theatre to make sure it went in the right place in her crowded airway. They had then intended to do an MRI to ensure Leila's cyst was encapsulated before operating but now there was no time to wait.

Standing by my side, the consultant, Anastasia, called the theatre to see what the hold-up was. While we waited for theatre to call back, she checked Leila's inspiration of air with her stethoscope every minute or two. Frustrated at the delay, she called the theatre again. "This baby can't wait," she said grimly to the person down the line.

Dread flooded my every thought and permeated my every pore making me shiver with cold. I gazed out to the darkened sky beyond the windows and for the first time ever I thought I couldn't take any more. *If I lose Leila I'm going to jump off the Westgate Bridge,* I decided. I can't do it again, I don't have anything left. But underneath the ice cold fear I knew I just had to hold on and trust that Leila would pull through somehow.

"We won't let anything happen to Leila," came Anastasia's voice. "We're just trying to do this in a controlled environment, but if we need to we can do an emergency tracheotomy here. It's okay," she added, pulling me back from despair.

Finally they arrived to take her into theatre, where Rob had decided he'd take the cyst out there and then.

As they wheeled Leila away it was all I could do to stay in the chair rather than run down the hallway after them. To busy myself and keep thoughts of disaster at bay I started expressing milk from my sore and engorged breasts, which were rock hard from a day without release. In the NICU, expressing milk had often been the only thing to distract me and make me feel like a useful mum while the life of my child hung in the balance. It felt barely comprehensible to think I was in the same dire position again.

Two hours later the call came that the surgery was complete, the rapidly growing cyst had been excised and Leila was doing well. My relief was indescribable but I couldn't fully believe she was okay until I saw her for myself. In the meantime the assistant surgeon stopped by the NICU to show me a photo of the horrendous huge hole in Leila's larynx that could so easily have ended her life.

Unlike her brothers before her, I was assured Leila would make a full recovery and when she was finally wheeled back into the NICU I cradled her in her cot and said a thousand silent thank-yous.

When the nurse for the next shift showed up I recognised her instantly but couldn't quite place where from. "Have you always worked here?" I asked.

"No, I used to work at the Mercy. I remember you, you're Louis' mum," she replied. "I'm Megan."

Already bubbling over with emotion from the day's taxing events I was incredibly touched that she too remembered my son and I told her how much it meant to me.

"I could never forget such a beautiful little boy. I remember all of you, your mum too. I used to live just around the corner from her," she replied.

We chatted for a while and she told me she'd had a baby boy who was nearly two.

"Oh, you have a baby, that's wonderful," I exclaimed.

"Yes," she said. "And I called him Louis."

37. Like Mother Unlike Daughter

Almost exactly a month after Leila's birth we headed home from hospital for the second time. There was no fanfare this time but with Leila's total recovery from her surgery it felt like our brand new day, and as I turned the key in the front door I resolved to once again be the relaxed and easy-going mum I'd been before the emergency. I wanted to be able to fully recline into motherhood and think about the future now that my greatest wish had finally come true and I was a mother with a completely healthy baby in my arms.

Having come so close to losing Leila, I decided that the time was right to start writing the story of our unconventional little family, of how we'd come to be mother and daughter. The donor counsellor had said creating a storybook to read to a child was a good way to embed their origins into their family folklore. I loved the idea of reading Leila the story of her and her brothers, which I decided I'd illustrate with photos of her and the boys.

When the time came around to plan the story I wasn't sure what I'd write about her donor. I pulled the three pieces of paper about Mr Happy out of the file of history I'd collated tracing Leila's conception and birth. As I wondered what 'SR' stood for on the donor profile page I vaguely recalled the donor nurse saying, "Once you've had your baby you can find out the donor's first name."

I called the clinic to ask and, just like that, Mr Happy had a name. "Scott," the donor nurse said after looking up his file.

"Thanks," I laughed, before adding, "I guess that's what the 'SR' stands for then?"

"Congratulations on the birth of your daughter, Aminah. I'm sure she'll bring you so much joy, and probably worry in equal measure," she replied, also laughing.

"You've got no idea," I said, hanging up the phone.

"Scott," I repeated to Leila, thinking, *That's the name of the man who helped me make you. He's a farmer and a footy coach, the rest is up to you.*

I told Mum about my plans to write Leila's story for her, mentioning in passing that I'd found out the donor's name was Scott. Mum and I had already agreed that honesty would be our policy for Leila and we would answer her questions as best we could as they arose, just as Mum had always done for me.

Perhaps that same honesty policy was what prompted Mum to admit a while later that she'd been doing some quiet detective work into Scott's identity.

"What?" I snapped at her.

Though I was as intrigued as Mum by Leila's fair features I wasn't yet ready to delve deeper and didn't think there was any rush to find out more. I was just enjoying finally being a mum without complications and had decided I'd be guided by Leila's questions when she started to ask about why she didn't have a dad. I thought there was no rush now our future looked much brighter.

While I'd started weaving a simple story to tell Leila about how she'd come into the world, Mum had been busy sleuthing around the internet looking for Scott, the Simmental cattle breeder who coached country football. "What were you hoping to find?" I asked her, exasperated.

"Well," she replied, "I reckon this guy on the Simmental Breeders Association website might be him. It's only got the initial S, but it's the only 'S' in Victoria, S. Andersen. He lives down near Phillip Island."

"Oh yeah, that'll be him for sure then," I said sarcastically. "Just leave it, Mum. We'll find out more information one day. That's what the Voluntary Register is for if Leila wants to know or she can find out for herself when she turns 18."

"Aren't you a bit curious though? Do you want these details I found?" she insisted, revealing her stubborn streak again.

"I am, but obviously not as curious as you, Mum," I said, rolling my eyes skyward. "At least we'll have these details in case of emergency," I added, thinking it was a huge leap to assume the man she'd found was Leila's donor. Still, I filed the information away and hoped that would be the end of it.

Of course I knew my mother better than that. Mum had always been a great speculator and she loved nothing more than a good puzzle with cryptic clues. I was similar to her in many ways, especially when it came to curiosity and persistence. Just as I hadn't been satisfied with finding my father's incomplete details at the Registry of Births, Deaths and Marriages, I suspected Mum wouldn't be satisfied until she'd discovered whether the cattle breeder with the initial 'S' and Leila's donor, 'Scott', were one and the same man. And with Google at her fingertips, I was powerless to stop her.

Wednesdays had become 'Nennie' and 'Daisy' day and seeing Leila's excitement as we pulled up at my mother's house each week and watching the bond that was developing between them reminded me of my closeness to my own grandparents, who'd provided such a complete and loving sense of family for me.

Nick had also wandered back into my life after he'd heard I'd had a baby and we'd reconnected to the point that Leila and I were spending most weekends with him and his son down the coast. The two of them couldn't have been sweeter or more affectionate with her and we provided each other slices of family life that sufficed for the real thing. I was confident that Leila was getting a good balance of male and female influence. She was a contented and happy little girl, easy-going and always with a ready smile.

Dropping her off one Wednesday, Mum beckoned me in. "Have a look at this, Aminah, I reckon this has to be Leila's dad," she said, pointing to her laptop screen triumphantly. "I reckon Leila looks just like him. It must be him, his name's Scott Andersen," she added, struggling to contain herself as she showed me a captioned photo of a blond man presenting a trophy to a younger guy.

"Muuum," I groaned, peering at the photo despite myself. "Where did you find that?" I asked, shocked at Leila's resemblance to the man in the photo but refusing to make up my mind. It was a strange sensation to be looking at my daughter's possible donor and it didn't feel quite right to be snooping into his life online. "I don't know, Mum, I just don't know," I said, afraid she'd kicked the hornet's nest.

"It's photos from the footy club closest to where he lives," she said, excitedly.

I wished she'd just leave it alone but the train had clearly left the station and I worried that she'd be driving down to tap him on the shoulder if I didn't intervene.

"Why don't you just go down there and check him out, Aminah?" she teased. "Or go to a footy match and have a look?"

"Because you can't just do that, Mum," I said firmly. "He's a donor, I can't just turn up on his doorstep unannounced. Bloody hell, what do you want me to do? Just rock up and say, 'Hi, I think you're my daughter's sperm donor.' You can't just do that!"

But Mum had well and truly let the cat out of the bag now and though I was mildly irritated by her persistence I had to laugh at her tenacity. I probably would have done exactly the same as her if I'd started the investigation myself. Now, neither of us would rest until all the pieces of the puzzle fitted together.

Scott had ticked a box on his profile confirming he was happy to be contacted by the parents of any donor children before they reached 18 so I'd known from the outset contact was an option if and when Leila became curious and started asking questions.

For me, that had happened when other kids had started to ask about my father and tease me for looking different to anyone else in my family. "You're adopted," they'd taunt me as if it was an offence to be adopted, and it hurt my fragile ego when I was seven or eight. The irony of Leila's very different appearance to me, which was the direct reverse of mum and me, was not lost on me now, and I suspected it would only be a matter of time before she asked about her father.

Every tiny milestone in Leila's development was a glorious reminder that she was alive and healthy. Every achievement the boys would never have made beyond infancy was cause for cele-bration. I wasn't doing it tough at all as a single mother – I relished every minute of mothering her and it helped that she was such a placid and happy baby. Together with Mum we took unmitigated delight in Leila and smothered her with love. I aspired to be the mother I'd had and to raise a child as resilient and determined as myself. Mum had given me everything and I'd never have had Leila without her encouragement and support. Leila was a testa-ment to my mother's tenacity, and now her finding Scott was the inevitable flipside.

"Okay, Mum," I conceded, "I'll make an application to the Volun-tary Register." The Voluntary Register was established to facilitate exchange of information between donors and recipients before the child turned 18 and became legally entitled to find out the identity of their donor automatically. So before Mum drove down the coast and collared the poor man herself, I sent off an application asking whether he'd be prepared to release his details and help make Leila's storybook complete.

The Voluntary Register staff said they would contact Scott to gain permission before releasing his identifying details. I'd just had the requisite counselling session to ensure I was of sound mind when the registrar got back to me to say Mr Happy's details could be fully disclosed. Shortly after that I received the document that verified my mother's credentials as a private investigator.

Scott Andersen was indeed Leila's donor and he was happy to be contacted any time. I put his details in Leila's file and congratulated Mum on her fine detective work. Meanwhile I was in the process of organising our first around-the-world adventure to introduce Leila to the rest of the important people in my life.

My dear friend Jonathan whom I'd chosen as the perfect 'god-father' for Leila had, in typically extravagant style, gifted us a trip to visit him in America. Jonathan had been a steadfast friend for over a decade by then, after we'd met during our London advertising days. I was instantly charmed by him when he joined the HHCL family just as I was taking my sabbatical, a bubbly glass overflowing with effervescence and contagious enthusiasm for life, people, advertising and Whitney Houston, not always in that order. We'd hit it off immediately and, upon my return, he'd scooped me up into his posse of party people and a social whirl of hedonistic fun, frivolity and enduring friendship.

A black man with a sort of cafe latte mixture background like myself, Jonathan is of Nigerian and English parentage. He and his four brothers had been raised on a northern England council estate by his gutsy single Jewish mum, Sue, on limited funds. Much like mine, his mother's nurturing, encouraging love had helped him to chase his dreams and live life on whatever terms he chose. When he'd come out as gay she wondered why it had taken so long. "As if I didn't know," she liked to say. She delighted in his ambition and he shared the spoils of his success generously with his beloved mum and friends. He'd bolted from the Leeds council estate with a diploma in his hand and a wrecking ball to smash every glass ceiling, window and wall that might stand in his way and he did it with charm, a contagious sense of fun and a flair for business and fashion in equal measure, always immaculately turned out.

He'd celebrated exuberantly the unexpected news of Leila's arrival, lavishing us with gifts both impractical and characteristically overgenerous. An iPad so that he could 'meet' his goddaughter and a note insisting she eat her every meal from the finest of Tiffany's bone china and the silver spoon he'd sent. Never mind a baby's propensity to turn plates into food-bearing Frisbees.

I couldn't wait to introduce Leila to Jonathan, who had always had a thing for blondes. I was excited she'd get to experience in person the exuberance of her godfather. And after the US we were travelling on to London to meet the rest of her family, so it would be a truly emotional journey.

I decided to drop Scott a line before we left. Having asked for his details I thought it rude not to make contact. I drafted and deleted an email many times over, vacillating over what to write. I had no idea how much or how little he'd want to know about Leila so I just tried to express my thanks.

Hi Scott,

I recently made an application to obtain your details so thank you for agreeing to share them with us.

I thought you might like to see photos of the beautiful daughter that you have helped create. Her name is Leila (pronounced like Layla) and she was born last August so is now six months old. I noted your birth date and Leila was due very close to your birthday last year on the 23rd but arrived on the 14th.

She is an absolutely gorgeous baby in every way. Happy, content, smiling and laughing all the time. She even wakes up smiling.

I suspect that she has received the best of both of us as you mentioned that you have a happy and easy-going disposition, as do I. She has your blonde hair and blue eyes I think, as I am dark-haired, brown eyed although there is blonde/blue on my mum's side of the family also. She also seems to have inherited very olive skin from me, so good protection from our harsh sun. She is long which is not surprising as you and I are both tall and she has long legs. Wherever we go, she charms people with her ready smile and receives endless compliments for being such a lovely baby. I tend to agree.

All in all she is an absolute delight and I feel incredibly lucky to have her. Thanks barely seems enough to say to you but grateful and thankful is what our family is.

The plan is to be honest and open with Leila always and so it is great to be able to tell her who you are as she grows and becomes inquisitive as children do.

I attach some recent photos of Leila but please let me know if you would like to see more or earlier ones or know anything more about her.

This email address has been set up solely to make contact with you and will be kept only for that purpose and remain confidential.

Thank you again Scott. What you have done is incredibly selfless and generous to say the least.

With kindest regards
Aminah (Leila's mum)

It felt odd to be sharing such details about my daughter with a complete stranger. Fed up with my own procrastination, I eventually hit 'send' despite my reservations.

Scott responded immediately with a courteous email in which he commented on Leila's beauty, introduced his family and said that seeing Leila made his donation feel worthwhile and, in fact, seeing her had made my day. It was a lovely reply that made me glad I'd been so open.

I thanked him again and invited him to check in any time if he wanted to know more about her or her progress, before telling him we were going overseas for a holiday. I thought we would leave it at that but another email arrived, apologising for the brevity of his previous email and exclaiming how overwhelmed he'd been by her pictures before asking a host of questions about her and me and my plans to give her siblings. He and Mum would get on well, I thought, pair of bloody stickybeaks.

I felt bad for overwhelming him and then worried that perhaps I'd said too much after all, so I apologised and answered each of his questions as best I could. I wasn't sure whether to mention that I was a single mum, afraid he might not approve, but he asked when I wanted to introduce Leila to him so I thought I'd save the finer points till then. Our departure date was nearing so I suggested we take time while we were away to think about how a meeting might work for everybody involved and asked whether he'd had any previous experience, but he was flying blind too.

I dropped Scott the odd photo update of Leila's big adventure while we were away and he responded with snippets about himself and further questions about us. The formality of his first email quickly disappeared and his self-proclaimed easy-going style came through as we corresponded and revealed more of ourselves.

Meanwhile Leila charmed everyone from the moment we embarked on the first plane, smiling sweetly at anyone who paid her attention. Even I couldn't have hoped for a more peaceful journey as Leila proceeded to sleep for 12 of the 15 hours we were in-flight and babble and coo at anyone who'd listen during the time in between. As we disembarked at LAX Leila was unanimously declared 'the most well-behaved baby ever to take to the air' by co-passengers and flight attendants alike. In Atlanta, where I was regularly mistaken for Leila's nanny, she was given a celebrity welcome by her 'uncles'

Jonathan and his partner Mirco as well as Jonathan's parents, who all lavished her with affection and kept her constantly in their arms and entertained. Jonathan surprised us with the arrival of some other dear friends from London and each day we spent together was a celebration of friendship and Leila's presence in our lives. Meanwhile, the guest of honour smiled and gurgled her appreciation at all her new admirers and I couldn't have felt prouder of her.

Arriving back in London I felt more resistant to my sadder memories than I'd feared and excited to see everyone again and introduce Leila, especially to Ayesha and Kaynahn. Both of them were clearly besotted with her at first sight and we spent many hours at that first meeting catching up on each other's lives as we hadn't seen each other since well before I'd had Louis, and wondering at Leila's fair features and happy disposition.

I'd invited my London family and friends to celebrate my birthday with a picnic on Hampstead Heath and I braced myself for the journey back to my former hometown. I was thrilled that everyone made the effort to come and the sun appeared making for a glorious London day on the Heath. Jake came along with Ria and Sam and their two kids, and Zak was there too. All of them seemed sincerely delighted to be sharing such a happy occasion and showed great affection for Leila. But I could tell it wasn't an easy day for Jake. Apart from the slight uneasiness in our initial greeting, he kept a 'safe' distance from me, preferring to play cricket with the kids for most of the day. A couple of times when I glanced in his direction, I caught his eye and noticed a familiar look of melancholy but we both looked away quickly, turning our attention to other people. We didn't have a proper conversation that day but I was very grateful to him for coming to see me and meet Leila. Ironically he was leaving for the Cannes advertising festival a couple of days later.

Somehow our lack of conversation left me wanting to know how he was truly faring. I made a plan to meet up with Ria again the following week, just the two of us, and resolved to ask about Jake's wellbeing then. Ria and I decided to meet for lunch in the Freemason's Arms pub across the road from Marlon's bench. But first it was time for me to commune with Marlon and introduce him to his baby sister.

I meandered wistfully past South Hill Park Gardens, the street where Jake and I used to live and the café that Marlon had visited, memories of my life there coming back as I retraced the nostalgic and still painful steps towards Marlon's playground.

When Leila and I eventually arrived at Marlon's bench and sat down a sprinkle of rain misted down aptly as we took cover under the big old oak tree that sheltered his memorial. The shiny newness of the wooden seat had long since faded, weathered and worn with the passing of time. It fitted better into its natural surroundings now, assimilated like the memories I'd filed away. Sitting there, I snuggled Leila into my lap and let the happy tears merge with the sad as I told her the story of the brothers she'd once had.

38. No Place Like Home

The journey to London had been a sentimental one but I was carrying a new wholeness within myself. I felt I'd finally come full circle to complete the journey I'd begun almost two decades earlier with the search for my father. For a wistful moment I'd felt like Dorothy as the plane touched down in Melbourne, and I recalled her waking up safely in her bed after her hazardous odyssey along the Yellow Brick Road to Oz and her ultimate realisation that all she needed was right there at home with her family.

I snatched our bags from the carousel and hurried out to the two-minute pick-up into Mum's warm embrace.

"You look good," she said, smiling lovingly, her voice full of relief. "You look happy."

"I am," I said, returning her smile, "and don't worry I'm not planning to move back to London. There really is no place like home."

When Mum delivered us home it was time to get back to the reality that bit down as I opened my mail. "How much do I owe you?" I asked Mum, who'd been paying my bills in absentia.

"Don't worry, darling," she said rolling her eyes, "just add it to the tab."

While we were in London, Scott had asked when we were coming back. I'd thought little about the meeting with him planned for after our return, but contemplating it as we winged our way back to Australia, I felt a greater sense of peace about Leila meeting her biological father. I felt I owed her a less tumultuous journey of discovery than my own had been. And it was within my power to grant her that or at least push the door ajar so she could walk through it whenever she was ready.

In all of our correspondence Scott had seemed friendly, curious and kind. He was eager to know more about both Leila and me without ever being intrusive or assuming. He delighted in Leila's development and, while not effusive by any means, had conveyed his excitement each time I'd shared one of Leila's milestone or captured a memorable moment in her life. He was keen to meet her, though not in a pushy way, so by the time we'd settled back in I was comfortable that the time was right.

I had to assume he had her best interests at heart and if it were to be a one-off meeting, I figured Leila wouldn't remember it anyway.

I wrote a brief email to Scott and we made an arrangement to visit his place just after Leila turned one.

Meanwhile, life swung seamlessly back into a routine but there was one big question buzzing incessantly in my ear and I was running out of time to give it an answer. With my 44th birthday just behind me, my time to give Leila a sibling was very nearly past.

I still had six frozen embryos from the stimulated cycles of IVF but I wasn't sure I could manage with two children on my own. Raising Leila by myself was one thing because I had the template and the support, but everybody I spoke to said that two children would be a game changer and I wasn't sure if I could do it. But I also longed to complete my modified family and give Leila the sense of belonging I feared she'd miss without any siblings or cousins in Australia. Her sole cousin Kaynahn lived on the other side of the world and was already grown up and I worried, having had her aged 43, she might one day end up alone in the world.

I thought about the embryos in the freezer, waiting to make a grab for life; the alternative was unthinkable and I couldn't just throw them away. All of the effort and emotion I had put into making them and the yearning for a family of my own made the decision for me; I'd roll the dice again.

It might bring a new level of chaos to our cosy little home, along with a life of sleep deprivation and exhaustion. Overseas trips would be out for the next decade at least and a private school education might not come without scholarships, but on balance they were all small prices to pay. And, most importantly, Leila would get a playmate, a sidekick and an ally for life, even if they fought like siblings.

Of course, Mum was the first and only person I told and I swore her to secrecy once more. "Don't worry about it until it happens, Aminah," she said, as philosophical as ever. "Women do it every day. If it happens you'll deal with it like you always do and I'll be here to help. I'm not planning on going anywhere, darling."

I laughed and said she'd better bloody not.

Leila's first birthday was joyous, although it went straight over the birthday girl's head. Yet to take her first steps, she crawled around the party wondering what all the fuss was about but quite liking the balloons and the cute moody faces my aunt Jane had iced onto cupcakes formed into a figure 1. There were blondes, brunettes and redheads, happy faces, sad and mad. The five-year-old daughter of friends picked up a blonde girl cupcake with a scowl on its face and declared it to be Leila to everyone's amusement.

The following Sunday rolled around after a weekend spent with Nick down the coast looking at a house to buy. Mum had decided (or I'd persuaded her with my persistent nagging) that we should buy a beach house to spend our summer holidays in and as a base for Leila and me without tramlines and pollution at our door.

And now I was steering my car across the Mornington Peninsula for the long drive around Westernport Bay to Phillip Island to meet Scott. As the crow flies we could have been there in half the time but going this way gave me 90 minutes to gather my jumbled thoughts. While the way Scott and I had organised this visit was greatly preferable to Mum's idea of just turning up on his doorstep, I felt sick in the stomach with nerves and anticipation. What might I say to this stranger when I knocked on the door of his house holding his biological daughter, my daughter, in my arms?

There was a subtle tremor in my clammy hands on the steering wheel. I was unaccustomed to feeling so nervous and I wasn't sure how to calm myself down. I usually went into new situations blindly, hoping for the best, figuring out how to deal with things as they happened. This had been no different and I was wishing I'd thought it through more.

What if I didn't like him? I wondered. *What if we had nothing to say to each other? What if he liked Leila but didn't like me? What if he turned out to be a weirdo? Maybe donating sperm was only for oddballs and egomaniacs hoping to spread their seed. Surely he couldn't be just the normal, laid-back guy from his emails.* My mind was racing wildly out of control so I turned up the stereo to block out the nonsensical noise inside my head. Then I wondered if a neutral meeting place might have been more sensible. *What if Leila screamed at the sight of Scott? What if she vomited or did a stinky poo?* I pulled into the last petrol station before we reached his house and changed Leila's nappy to calm myself down. After that I bought a drink and sat in the car for a bit to pull myself together.

As I parked outside a blue house on a hill, I wondered whether Scott could see us through any of the windows. There was no turning back now, nothing for it but to go forward. *I'll treat it like an interview,* I thought as I unbuckled Leila from her car seat.

I strode towards the door with the most confident stride I could muster in case anybody was watching and knocked loudly on the door.

Scott greeted us with an easy smile and welcomed us inside. Leila's resemblance to him was absolutely uncanny and there was no mistaking he was her donor. Having never heard his voice before, I'd been expecting a much gruffer kind of farmer and it was a relief to hear a slight waver in his voice too.

I was caught slightly off guard when Scott gestured towards the stairs and said, "Come and meet Belle," having not anticipated meeting any of his children. A flurry of questions went through my mind. *Who did Belle think we were? What did she know about Leila? Did she know they were related?* Suddenly I felt jittery again but I forced myself to shut up, follow Scott's lead and try to relax.

"Belle, this is Aminah and Leila," Scott said casually to his pretty blonde daughter as we reached the top of the stairs. I couldn't gauge what she knew so I just said, "Hi Belle," as casually as I could. "Hi," she replied shyly, looking down at the floor and grabbing hold of her dad's arm as if for protection.

"Is Caroline not here?" I asked, surprised to find it was just the four of us upstairs. I'd expected to meet Scott's partner and had hoped another woman might make conversation easier.

"She's taken her girls up to Magnetic Island," he replied.

"Lucky them, Magnetic Island is beautiful, tropical. We camped up there when I was a kid," I said. "I'm not enjoying being back in this cold weather after spending the summer overseas. Even though London summers aren't as hot as ours it was quite warm and America was hot and humid. I'd never been to the south before," I rambled nervously.

"Yeah, I've heard the weather's pretty crappy over in London," he laughed, unfazed by my waffle. "I've never been myself, haven't travelled much. Sounds like you had a good time. Thanks for the photos, Leila looked like she had fun too."

"It was great to introduce her to her godfather in the States and her family in London, as well as all my friends over there," I prattled on. "There's so much love for this little girl, she really had no idea," I added, then stopped myself, because he had no idea either. I hadn't yet told him about Marlon and Louis.

"Have you been farming today?" I asked to change the subject.

"Yeah, actually we've got a couple of lambs in the garage. Belle, let's show Leila your lambs."

Belle smiled and nodded timidly and they led us back down the stairs and into the garage to see two tiny little lambs. I wondered if Scott had planned this as he offered us a bottle of milk to feed one of the lambs, which seemed like a stroke of genius to deflect attention from us adults and draw our focus onto the kids. Leila looked bemused, unsure of what to make of the lambs and more taken with Belle showing her how to feed them.

Once the lambs' bottles were empty Scott offered me a cup of tea and led us back upstairs, saying, "Belle's got some toys out for Leila to play with and some for her to keep, haven't you, Belle?" and motioning for me to put Leila down on the floor with Belle and an array of soft toys while we took a seat at the kitchen table.

"Belle, that's so sweet of you, thank you," I said as I plopped Leila down beside her and let them get acquainted.

We relaxed a bit as we drank our tea but Scott didn't seem much of a talker so off I went again, waffling on. He showed a genuine interest, asking questions that unfurled my whole story, and also shared some of his own in return. I managed not to get emotional when he acknowledged my boys and conveyed his regret. "I'm really sorry you lost your boys, Aminah, and that you had to go through all that. It must've been tough."

It was rare, in my experience with strangers, men in particular, to find them able to articulate empathy in plain and simple English, so I was grateful to Scott for doing so. I loved talking about Marlon and Louis without having to feel bad for the listener when they heard how the story ended. A lot of people didn't know what to say, so they'd either try to get away from me as quickly as possible or, worse, say nothing at all. Most bereaved parents want nothing more than acknowledgement of their child and the significance of their loss, not sympathy or pity or awkwardness or avoidance. Parents who've lost children know their loss makes others uncomfortable. Yet this laconic Aussie farmer had managed to say so simply what so many others failed to without meaning-less platitudes and without making me feel like a pitiful victim stuck in a wretched life.

"Why didn't you have any kids with Nick?" he asked shyly.

I explained how Nick and his ex-wife had also lost a baby and he didn't want to have kids with me so I'd done it alone.

"Are you going to have any more then?" asked Scott, laughing slightly at his own directness, which I sensed didn't come naturally to him.

"I'd like to. I'm trying," I said and explained the six embryos I had left over from earlier rounds of IVF. I told him how I'd already transferred two that unfortunately hadn't stuck, adding, "I'm trying again this month, so keep your fingers crossed."

"That's great, Aminah," he said with a smile and I knew he was sincere.

After offering me a second cup of tea he stood up, flicked on the kettle and said, "I think Jye's here somewhere, probably still in bed after a big night, I'll go and find him."

I was watching Belle and Leila playing happily on the floor when Scott reappeared followed by a long-haired hippyish-looking guy with a goatee and his dad's ready smile. 'Hi,' he said, and hugged me before casting his eyes down to the kids and saying, "Hi Belle, hi Leila," and dropping down to the floor beside them.

Sitting next to Leila the similarity struck me instantly between Jye's and Leila's blue eyes, leaving no question of them being related. I was impressed by how at ease and natural and relaxed he was with

HOW I MET YOUR FATHER

Leila and Belle. Not many 18-year-old guys had such interest in babies in my experience.

We stayed a little longer and I snapped a couple of photos of Leila with Belle and Jye before the time felt right to leave. Scott scooped Leila up and carried her down the stairs for me.

As I waved goodbye, not knowing whether we'd see any of them again, I kicked myself for not getting a picture of Leila's first meeting with her biological father.

Once they'd disappeared from my rear-view mirror I turned to Leila in her car seat and said, "Did you have fun, bubba? What lovely people they are. It was very sweet of Belle to give you some of her toys. Belle, can you say 'Belle' darling? Belle, Belle, Belle," I chanted as we turned back onto the highway and headed for home. After flicking the radio on, I turned to Leila again, saying, "What about Jye?" But her eyes were already closed.

Well what a whole lot of worry about nothing that was, I thought to myself, laughing at my near panic attack just two hours earlier. Scott couldn't have been a more easy-going guy. Straight up and down I thought, yep, salt of the earth.

I definitely had some new characters to add to Leila's storybook and I could tell her a little bit more about who Scott was. *You're a lucky little girl,* I thought happily. *You definitely got your mellow personality from Scott.*

I had a lovely feeling about Belle and Jye too. Belle was very nurturing and I reckoned if Leila were ever in trouble Jye was the type of person who would come to her rescue. He seemed like the sort of guy who'd do anything for anyone.

That evening I dropped Scott another email:

Hi Scott

Really enjoyed meeting you, Belle and Jai (spelling?) today. They were so lovely with Leila and especially great to see a hungover 18-year-old being so sweet and attentive!

Thanks for being so open and welcoming.

It just occurred to me that the text I sent with the photo might not have gotten through with your old-school phone so here it is again.

Please feel free to ask anytime if you'd like to see Leila as I said.

Thanks again.

Aminah

Ten minutes later a reply came from him:

Hi, never got it earlier but my phone just started working again! I thought it was great, feel really happy about today. Jye was telling Luke and Bailey about Leila tonight. Yeah will organise with Caroline and look forward to catching up. I have a real pep in my step. Thank you Aminah!

And that's where we left it while I went off to try and have another baby.

39. Peas in a Pod

The morning after meeting Scott I caught the tram into East Melbourne to see my fertility specialist for a scan. After that I'd go to the IVF clinic to have blood taken to determine when my body would be ready to receive another two frozen embryos.

Something had subtly changed in my mind, and I felt a slight release of the pressure I'd put myself under to give Leila a sibling. If it didn't work out at least now I knew there were other people in the world who she could look up if I was not around and I took great comfort from that.

A couple of days later an email popped up from Scott with a photo of a baby boy he'd received a couple of years earlier along with a note of thanks from another grateful mother. The little boy's eyes struck me instantly – they were similar to Leila's eyes, Scott's eyes. I replied to Scott joking that when Leila grew older every time she brought a boy home I'd be checking out his eyes like a crazy woman! Another couple of weeks passed and I'd had two embryos implanted when Scott emailed again, this time with a 'family audit' from the IVF clinic. Our visit had apparently piqued his curiosity about how many other children might be out there. The answer shocked him as much as it did me. There were six listed families including Leila, with the correlating gender and years of birth of six other donor children.

"Holy Moly," he'd written signing off with a kiss.

Holy shit, I thought summed it up better. I'd never imagined learning about other children from the same donor this early in Leila's life and I felt slightly disconcerted. I'd expected to leave finding out about other potential donor 'siblings' up to Leila when she was old enough to truly understand donor conception and seek them out herself if she chose to.

I thought how ironic it was that Leila had 'brothers and sisters' everywhere while I was struggling through the dreaded two-week wait between embryo transfer and pregnancy blood test trying to resist the urge to POAS. Of all the IVF cycles I'd had, the only positive pregnancy test had come when I hadn't done a home pregnancy test before the obligatory blood test and that positive was Leila, so I was holding out against temptation.

All of the babies in the family audit were born between 2009 and 2012 so I emailed Scott back joking that there were at least five blue-eyed boys I had to be on the lookout for. I also thanked him again for giving me Leila as I felt more grateful than ever for his gift. Having seen his pride in his own kids and his delight in Leila, I wanted to convey to him just how much he'd changed the lives of those six families for the better. I remembered him saying that when he was younger he'd wanted ten kids so I joked to him that he'd bettered his wish by one. I thought how if all babies turned out like Leila I'd have wanted ten of them too.

"I'm very happy you contacted me and so happy to have met Leila. It's given my life a real boost. I've even shown my best mates the video of her with 'Chippy' (the toy chipmunk). I really want you to give her a sibling. Thanks so much," he wrote.

★

The weeks rolled by in a blur after I found out the two embryos had failed to stick and I braced myself for a final attempt with the only remaining embryo.

The IVF clinic called before my scheduled appointment to say my last embryo hadn't survived thawing. The devastating disappointment I felt when I heard this surprised even me. I called my mum with the news, and I could tell she was sad as well and, as always, sympathetic and encouraging.

I cried and cried and cried and then I cried some more. I would forever be a mother of three, with only one surviving child. And though I knew I was lucky to have even one healthy child, that didn't stop the grief of loss from surging back.

I hugged Leila a little tighter as I tucked her into bed that evening, and thanked the universe I had her there to hold. Flicking back through my diary later that night in a reflective review of the year I wondered why humans are never satisfied. Then Scott's words popped into my head: "I really want you to give her a sibling, it's exciting." He hadn't pried further into whether I was pregnant or not, but I thought I'd let him know my attempts to have another child were over and Leila would have no siblings.

A reply quickly pinged in and took me completely by surprise with an offer of help and a promise that it could still be possible for me to have another child. The chances of sleep vanished as I deliberated over what he meant.

In the days after my final cancelled cycle the time ebbed slowly away dragging me into its undercurrent as life got back to normal. Leila sucked up the minutes of each day with her appetite for discovery, happily distracting me from myself. My master's degree was coming to an end with ten thousand words of thoroughly researched reason demanding every moment of my attention when I wasn't with Leila, but I was happiest just enjoying my time with her as a mum. Knowing she would be my last child, I didn't want to miss a second.

September swept out the worst of winter's chill and brought brighter, sunnier days. When an SMS suggestion to catch up arrived from Scott I realised over a month had passed since our first meeting. He suggested a catch-up later that week but said he couldn't venture far from the farm. "I've actually got some valuable calves due. They're artificial insemination calves which is kinda coincidental," he joked, making me laugh out loud.

We agreed to meet for lunch in Tooradin, a tiny, one-horse, blink-and-you-miss-it town midway between Melbourne and San Remo. Though perched at the end of a scenic inlet from Westernport Bay, it doesn't have much else to write home about. Swinging my car off the highway towards the waterfront, I found a playground for Leila and set up a blanket on the foreshore for our picnic lunch. It was a glorious spring day, perfect for avoiding responsibility and dissertations, so I wasn't in the slightest bit fussed if Scott was late due to calving problems at the farm.

Scott appeared minutes after I arrived looking fresh and clean, and not at all as if he'd been pulling calves out of their mothers, apart from a tell-tale graze across his forehead where he'd copped a cow-kick in the head. Our rapport was easy by then and our nerves had vanished completely. And I needn't have worried about Leila, who immediately crawled over to him and plopped herself snugly into his lap. He smiled broadly, clearly chuffed that she'd gone to him so readily.

Scott and Leila's resemblance was so astonishing I had to force myself not to stare. They looked like two peas in a pod and there was no mistaking their relationship. Scott's intuitive desire to cuddle Leila and be affectionate was so natural that I had to look away so as not to give away the emotion in my face.

A white Labrador came past and I pointed it out to Leila. "Tell Scott what a doggy says, bubba," prompting her to bark, which in turn made us laugh. A slightly awkward moment followed when, feeling a little ridiculous, I asked Scott what he wanted Leila to call him and he said, "I think it'd be kinda nice if she called me 'Dad'."

"Oh, okay," I said and I looked for another distraction to cover my surprise. "Leila, look at the birdie," I said, pointing to a seagull scrounging nearby. "What does a birdie say, Leila?"

"Woo woo," she said barking again.

Scott was hesitant in asking what I was thinking about trying again but I explained again that now with all the embryos gone I was out of options.

"I said I'm happy to help you if I can," he prompted.

"Yeah, I wasn't sure exactly what you meant?"

"Like the cows," he laughed, "artificial insemination, a turkey baster."

I replied that I'd thought that was a joke amongst the lesbian community.

"Well, I dunno," said Scott, "but I was going out with this woman a few years ago who was friends with a gay couple and that's what they did. I don't know if it was a turkey baster, but it worked. They had a baby."

I got the giggles. "You'd really do that?" I asked.

"Yeah, Aminah, if you really want another baby. Like I said, I'm happy to help. We don't have to do it now," he joked. "But think about it anyway."

I drove away that day gobsmacked, my head spinning. Scott wanted to be Leila's dad and was offering to help me have another baby. Surely it was all too good to be true. I thought about the reality of Scott becoming Leila's dad, what it might mean for her and what it might mean for me. It had taken me a long time to get around to the idea of becoming a single mother by choice and now her biological father was offering to be her dad. Leila wasn't lacking for males in her life, but Scott was actually her father and I wasn't sure it was even up to me to deny her that when it was me who'd set the wheels in motion for them to meet.

Nick was very good with Leila and there was no denying how fond he was of her. There was a beautiful reciprocity in being able to dote on each other's children. We were into a slightly awkward habitual groove of spending most of our weekends together, but I had steadfastly refused to have sex with him and could sense his growing frustration. He'd declared his enduring feelings more than once, and though I cared for him as a friend it was different to our early days when I'd clung to him as my last hope.

Occasionally my absolute refusal to be drawn back into a romantic relationship with Nick sparked a flicker of anger in him, but our friendship had found a new equanimity which was a great deal less volatile. Jules had suggested I should end the friendship so we could both move on, but I was worried that would leave him feeling rejected and I didn't want to be that mean. Jules was right in one way though, I was being selfish. Nick was living as if he was my boyfriend and was providing a family environment for us while I insisted on separate bedrooms. Something was bound to give.

I took Scott up on his offer to make a baby by 'AI'. I researched artificial insemination and discovered that a regular ten-millilitre syringe from the chemist would suffice and we agreed to meet up again soon, after his calves were all born. He truly was a breeder, of cattle and beautiful kids.

40. Love After All

Despite Jules' warning that Nick would never be satisfied with a platonic friendship, we'd been cruising along as weekend buddies for over a year. He seemed to have accepted my insistence that friendship was all that was on offer and, apart from the odd facetious dig about a man not being a camel, he'd resisted attempts at seduction.

Meanwhile I had found a beach house for Mum and me to buy, a little red cedar cottage that looked unloved and had sat unsold for weeks. I called on Nick's building expertise and he confirmed it wouldn't fall down so I signed on the dotted line.

I'd helped Nick paint his house around the corner when he'd bought it, so when I started giving our new holiday house a fresh coat of paint he returned the favour. He also taught me how to paint a good seamless wall, saying, "Always roll the roller from top to bottom without stopping."

As we painted away one Saturday afternoon whistling along to the music, I sensed a slight agitation in Nick's mood. His voice was edgy and pressured and it was clear something was on his mind. I chatted away about nothing in particular and glanced over my shoulder to see two walls painted only down to their halfway point.

Something was definitely up. Apropos of nothing, but as if he'd read my mind, he launched into a diatribe about unrequited love.

I couldn't lie, if anything I'd been feeling a need to move on, to get out and go on dates again and have a little romance for myself, so I told him nothing had changed for me.

The colour rose in his face and his brow furrowed in anger as he leapt off the ladder he'd been on and disappeared out the door. There was no point in trying to reason with him, so I went back to my painting. He called an hour later and apologised but I knew we were done. I'd kept my own desires on hold in the name of friend-ship so I resolved to put myself back out there once more and see if I could find a new fella.

Dating as a single mum was a whole new world but any desper-ation I'd felt before I'd had Leila was gone and I hoped I'd meet someone grown up, possibly with kids of his own. Never mind the twist that I might be trying to conceive a baby using Scott's sperm, I believed the two things could run concurrently though both were fraught with pitfalls and uncertainty. Hilarious sitcom-like scenes played out in my head of me meeting a new guy and dating for a while only to discover I was pregnant – via a syringe – and having to tell him that I hadn't been unfaithful except with a piece of plastic, albeit loaded with another man's sperm. I laughed at my own plotline – it was definitely time to put a little fun back into my life.

Leila was a happy and healthy one-year-old and she now had a dad who she saw every Tuesday. I had finally completed my master's and started a professional placement. Life felt much sunnier though there was still one thing missing. A hundred and one personal devel-opment books said you could manifest your heart's desire, and while I believed it was unmitigated nonsense I'd mentioned it to the universe anyway.

One night I rallied the troops for a girls' night out. A few glasses of Riesling later, I stumbled into the path of a proverbial tall, dark stranger who caught me by the arm.

After I'd steadied myself he introduced himself. Registering his good looks, I laughed and said, "You caught me just in time." A little bit tipsy and with nothing to lose, I offered to buy him a drink some time and gave him my number.

Three days passed without a phone call but then he texted, saying, "Let's meet for that drink, are you free tomorrow night?"

It's hard to read between the lines of text messages, but he'd seemed nice enough so I threw caution to the wind and agreed to meet him at my local so I could beat a hasty retreat if needed. But he was the consummate gentleman and I liked him immediately. After the second date two days later I suspected he liked me too, but a shadow crept into our conversation when he talked about his ex-wife and all the women he'd dated since his messy and unsolicited divorce, and I sensed a hint of bitterness.

As the next weekend approached I was disappointed he hadn't called, so I headed down to the holiday house to continue painting. It had become more of a chore than a challenge without help, so I amped up the volume on the speakers to let music fill the void and grafted away, oblivious to the messages pinging through on my phone. The light had faded by the time I saw I'd missed three messages from Tim asking what I was doing. My heart did a happy flip in anticipation of another date.

The following Tuesday Leila and I had our weekly lunch with Scott. Still busy with calving, he'd asked us to come closer to him and we'd agreed to meet at a tiny village off the highway called Loch, but I'd overshot the turnoff and ended up at Bass.

I pulled over and called Scott to apologise. "It'll take you too long to get back here," he laughed. "Keep going to Kilcunda and I'll meet you at the pub."

The view from the Kilcunda Ocean View Hotel aka the 'Killy pub' is breathtaking, stretching out across Bass Straight with the pounding waves rolling into the rugged dune-fringed beach.

"Why didn't you bring me here before?" I asked him, smiling. "It's such a beautiful place." Catching up with Scott was like seeing an old friend by now. Leila sat on his knee, the bond between them stronger than ever. And though I'd worried Leila might prefer him with his big family, her expansive capacity for love left plenty for both of us and I was happy for her to have such a lovely bloke for her dad. He was so tender with her and he'd become just as smitten by her sweet-natured lovability as me.

I mentioned to Scott that I'd started dating again and told him I'd met someone and even revealed my insecurities in my curiosity to get a man's point of view. "I like him," I said, "but I think he might be a bit of a player."

"He sounds like an arsehole," Scott said emphatically, "if he's slept with all those women"

"Oh. Yeah. Maybe. I suppose," I said, unsure what to make of his response. "Hey," I added, changing tack, "you know how I said yes to doing the artificial insemination? Well, I've changed my mind. I mean, I'm so grateful that you were prepared to do it and I hope I won't live to regret it but I think I'm happy to just have Leila. I just don't want to push my luck."

"Yeah, no worries, Aminah, that's fine," Scott replied, as easy-going as you like. "You're probably right and you can always change your mind later." I'd feared he might be offended but it didn't faze him at all and we carried on as normal. However, the vehemence of his comment about Tim got me wondering whether there'd been a subtle protectiveness in his response.

I sent Scott my by-now customary text when we got home to let him know when we'd arrived safely.

I apologised to him that he'd have to put up with me as well each time he saw Leila, at least for now. He replied that he was fine with it, that he enjoyed my company anyway and that it helped that I looked like an international model. There it was. The beer we'd drunk had made him bolder and there was a cheeky flirtation coming through.

I showed the message to Mum, who said, "Well, he probably thinks you're gorgeous, darling," and cut to the chase by asking, "Do you like him?"

"I don't know, Mum," I shrieked, flushing with embarrassment. "I've never thought about him like that," though I wondered at my own protestation.

Em's birthday always announced the start of summer and it was a particularly hot November so she'd gathered a group of friends to a Richmond pub to celebrate. Everyone was in merry spirits and the drinks were going down fast when my phone vibrated. Looking down I saw it was a call from Scott, which was unheard of on a weekend. I dashed across the beer garden to a quiet spot.

"Caroline's just attacked me," he said, sounding alarmed. "She thinks we're having an affair."

"What?" I yelled over the noise. "That's ridiculous, why on earth would she think that?" I said. "Well, is there anything I can do? Are you okay?"

"It's fine. Listen, Aminah, don't worry. It's over. I just wanted to let you know in case she calls you or anything like that, she's pretty irrational."

"Oh. Okay. I hope it's all okay," I replied, then hung up the phone, shell-shocked.

Bloody hell, I thought as I walked back to the group, wondering what had made Caroline think we were having an affair. He'd mentioned she'd been erratic and angry as their relationship faltered and I didn't much fancy being dragged into it – or being blamed, for that matter. I knew she'd had a serious altercation with one of Scott's sons, so I was relieved she wasn't going to be in Leila's life after all.

★

A weekend of good times followed and I heard nothing more about Scott's drama. The following Tuesday he'd invited us to his place for lunch because his oldest son, Luke, and younger son, Bailey, wanted to meet Leila after Jye had told them about her.

As I knocked on the front door I felt a resurgence of nerves at the idea of being on display, but again my fears proved unfounded. Luke and Bailey had the same easy-going style as Scott and had a similar relaxed ease with Leila as Jye had shown months before. I grabbed a fabulous photo of the four Andersen men lined up side by side with Leila in Scott's arms and there was no question she was an Andersen too.

With all of Scott's boys so easily accepting of Leila, Scott decided the time was right to tell Belle that Leila was her little sister. I left that gathering knowing I had a confession to make too.

Meanwhile, Mandy had arrived home from London for a flying visit before Christmas and was due to fly back the next day and I needed to share my secret with someone and knew it would be safe in London with her. "Mate," I said feigning a serious tone after we'd met up and exchanged the standard gossip and laughs, "I think I'm in trouble."

"Oh, Means," she said, her face turning solemn, "what's happened?"

I crumpled into laughter and groaned, "Oh mate, I think I've got a crush on Leila's dad," and we both collapsed into hysteria.

The uproarious laughter that followed threatened to steal our bladder control. "Darls, mate," she said in her best ocker, "you're hilarious. That is hilarious."

"Mands, you're not helping," I protested. "It's not good, this is not good."

"Mate, it's great, you're going to hook up with Leila's dad. You're going to shag him," she hooted.

"I will not!" I shouted over her laughter. "I mean, I wouldn't dare, I can't wreck things for Leila."

"Yeah, mate, I know, but you'll shag him," she repeated and we both peeled over with laughter again.

We'd never held anything back in our friendship, exchanging the most graphic of details, usually accompanied by uncontrollable laughter, rallying each other through the worst of times.

Mandy was delighted at the thought that Leila's mum and dad might get together, and she didn't share any of my concerns that it could all go very wrong.

"But, mate, it's bad, it's a terrible idea," I said. "He doesn't even know I have a crush on him and he probably doesn't even feel the same way."

"Rubbish, darl, of course he does, he's male after all."

I flicked up the photo of Scott with Leila on my phone and showed it to her fully aware of her penchant for blondes.

"Mate, you better shag him because if you don't, I will," she said, and on that hysterical note we parted company with a hug after a good belly laugh as usual.

"Please don't tell anyone, darl," I pleaded.

"Sure, mate," she smiled with a wink, "stop worrying and have some fun."

The next time I saw Scott, I decided to play it straight. I told him about my conversation with Mandy and he told me about one he'd had with Luke after we'd left the week before, when Luke had told his dad that he was so 'gone', meaning his dad fancied me too.

"Was he right?" I asked directly, feeling nervous about his response. But I needn't have worried because he gave me a shy smile and said, "I've got a bit of a crush on you too."

"Okay, so what do we do now?" I asked feeling like I was fifteen again, but resisting the temptation to state the obvious. "Leila is my priority and I don't want to ruin what you and she have," I said and then went on to share my doubts and reservations with him honestly, though the words that came out of my mouth were contradicted by what was going on inside my head as I imagined him getting up and grabbing me with what Mandy had described as his Popeye arms, and throwing me onto the couch.

If it hadn't felt so confused I would have taken action myself but as it was we had to be adults about it and think through what I'd said. Leila was the most important person in the picture and I was sincere in not wanting to stuff it up for her. Scott agreed we should tread carefully but he expressed less concern that we would ruin it all, saying their relationship was firmly entrenched. I knew I'd never take her away from him now, their relationship was my responsibility but in a way it had become none of my business and I was simply their facilitator.

The festive season was upon us and my dates had petered out. The opportunity for a casual relationship had made me extricate myself before I got hurt.

Belle had told Scott she was delighted by the news that she had a little sister and Scott wanted Leila to meet all her cousins at Christmas when the Andersen family got together. He said Christmas would be unusual with all three of his siblings at home with their spouses and kids in tow for the first time in years. He'd told them all about Leila and now he wanted to show her off. He asked if it would be greedy to want to see us twice in one week knowing we'd be heading up the Murray River to Bundalong after Christmas for our annual holiday. "Come down on Friday," he said.

It turned out that on Friday he was coming from the farm at Inverloch and we were coming from the city when I spotted him in his car where we'd simultaneously reached the merge in the highway to find the traffic had stopped dead. There shouldn't have been a traffic jam that early before the holiday rush, so it was obvious there'd been an accident.

Frustrated at the delay and worrying that Leila would wake up hungry at any moment, I picked up my phone and called him. When he answered I said, "Hi, look to your right, we're opposite you. Let's turn around and go to the pub, otherwise Leila will get hungry and I've got no food in the car to give her. Shall we go to 'Killy' pub and I can feed her there?"

"No, let's go to the Bass pub," he replied, motioning back the other way, so we turned our cars across the median strip and headed for the nearest pub.

One beer turned into two then three then four as the road remained closed and the pub soon filled up with people who couldn't get home for dinner. The publican would be pleased with the unexpected windfall of the night, one person's misfortune, another person's gain I thought as the queue grew to four deep at the bar, and hoped the car accident hadn't been fatal.

"I might call Mike and John to come and meet us for a meal," Scott said as it became obvious we wouldn't be getting to his place in a hurry.

Scott's brother Mike and best mate John and his family soon joined us for dinner and we made a night of being stranded, but as the evening moved past Leila's bedtime she started to get restless.

The impromptu party atmosphere in the pub had got the better of me by then and I was well over the limit, so Scott suggested we all spend the night at John's, saying he was sure Andrea wouldn't mind driving my car back to their place.

By the time we got back to John and Andrea's Leila had fallen asleep in the car and though I'd thought I'd be able to transfer her seamlessly to her travel cot, she had other ideas, with her second wind kicking in. I tried to comfort, coax and coerce her back to sleep to absolutely no avail and, despite having raised seven kids between them, Scott, John and Andrea also had no luck. Leila bounced about in her cot keeping us entertained but I knew I'd be the one to suffer the next day when her mood reflected the lateness of her bedtime. Scott had never seen Leila in any other state than her smiling sweetness and light and I wasn't sure he'd be quite so fond of a sleep-deprived version of Chucky the Doll.

"We'll have to turn out the lights," I said and nobody argued the toss. We'd all drunk our fill by then anyway so everyone was happy to call it a night. I hadn't thought about our sleeping arrangements until John disappeared down the hall and returned with a double mattress which he tossed down on the floor with some bedding before bidding us good night, flicking off the lights and closing the door.

My efforts to tuck Leila in were futile; even in the dark she was too overtired. "I'll rub her back," Scott said, "that used to put all my kids to sleep."

Dubious, I let him take over, and stripped off my jeans in the dark before I settled under the doona. Then, all of sudden, I got a bout of nerves. Luckily Scott's back rub worked a charm as Leila's breathing evened out leaving us in the darkened silence of the farmhouse.

Scott slid into the bed beside me and, ever the consummate gentleman, was careful to stay on his side, but his body's heat reached out across the space between us and I felt its pull. We lay in nervous silence for a while and I thought he was about to roll over and go to sleep so, thinking of Mandy saying to stuff it and seize the day, I grabbed the initiative. "So what are you going to do, Mr Andersen?" I said suggestively into the dark.

"What d'ya mean?" he asked with the nervous waver I hadn't heard in his voice since our first meeting back in August.

"Well, I think you should kiss me," I said.

My words hung heavily in the air as I reached out to touch him and make my point hoping he couldn't hear the thudding of my heart. Scott wrapped me in his Popeye arms, pulled me close and kissed me and our nerves instantly melted away to nothingness as we got lost in the moment.

Afterwards as we lay in the dark, ready to drift off to sleep, Scott whispered into my ear, "I want you to come to the Andersens' Christmas as my partner, Aminah, I want us to be together. I want us to be a family."

★

HOW I MET YOUR FATHER